PATRIARCH DANIEL

Rebuilding Orthodoxy in Romania

T0334768

St Vladimir's Seminary Press

ORTHODOX CHRISTIAN PROFILES SERIES

Number 10

The Orthodox Christian Profiles Series acquaints the reader on an intimate level with Orthodox figures that have shaped the direction of the Orthodox Church in areas of mission, ascetical and liturgical theology, scholarly and pastoral endeavors, and various other professional disciplines. The people featured in the series are mostly our contemporaries and most remain active in shaping the life of the Church today. A few will have fallen asleep in the Lord, but their influence remains strong and worthy of historical record. The mission of this series is to introduce inspirational Orthodox Christian leaders in various ministries and callings that build up the Body of Christ.

Chad Hatfield
Series Editor

Patriarch Daniel

Rebuilding Orthodoxy in Romania

ST VLADIMIR'S SEMINARY PRESS
YONKERS, NY 10707
2021

Library of Congress Control Number: 2021930989

This publication was made possible through the generous support of Father Mihai and Preoteasa Anamaria Faur, and Bede Cope, Esq.

ISBN 978–0-88141–685–5 (print)
ISBN 978–0-88141–686–2 (Kindle)

PRINTED IN THE UNITED STATES OF AMERICA

Table of Contents

Introduction

At the Thrice-Holy Hymn in the hierarchical Divine Liturgy, the presiding hierarch, standing in the holy doors facing west and holding the *trikirion* and *dikirion*, says, "Lord, Lord: Look down from heaven and behold, and visit this vine, and perfect that which your right hand has planted." In His Beatitude Daniel's tenure as the patriarch of the Romanian Orthodox Church, this liturgical phrase finds its persona. With confidence in the mercy of our God, one finds in this Orthodox Patriarch a man determined to work with the Master of the vineyard in the rebuilding and perfection of that portion of the vineyard of souls given over to his pastoral care.

The task of rebuilding the physical aspects of the post-Communist Romanian Church would be daunting in itself, but combined with the rebuilding of the interior life of Romanian Christians, the task has been gargantuan. God, in his goodness, raised up the leader needed to perfect the trampled vineyard once again. This servant leader is Patriarch Daniel. One of Romania's scholars and theologians, he has brought a vision, or strategic plan, that has guided the rebuilding of the patriarchate at every level. Nothing has been overlooked.

The goal of this book is to introduce this dynamic "father of a nation" to the English-speaking world. The accomplishments of his ongoing patriarchal ministry are so extensive that this book can give only a small sample of his leadership. This is done through chapters addressing such contemporary issues as unity in the Orthodox world. One area of particular interest to His Beatitude is the spiritual life. His counsel on the unity between theology and the spiritual life of the Church reflects his own interior life and many years of experience as a priest and scholar. He knows the danger of separating the study of theology from ascetical life. The two must go hand in hand. Separation can lead to theology becoming a pure intellectual exercise, while the ascetical life can become a kind of false pietistic religion of its own.

His address on the great Romanian theologian Fr Dumitru Stăniloae as a teacher of prayer is a prime example of the deep treasury of Romanian spirituality. Various other homilies and addresses introduce the reader to recently glorified Romanian saints such as Jacob, Silas, Paisius, and Nathan of Putna, Joseph the Merciful of Moldavia, and George the Pilgrim. One chapter introduces us to Neagoe Basarab as an example of politics being enlightened by faith.

The consecration of St Andrew Cathedral in 2018 by His Beatitude Patriarch Daniel and His All Holiness Patriarch Bartholomew is an external sign of the tenacity and determination of Patriarch Daniel to restore a national center for Orthodox worship that also serves as an example of the ministries of the Church. Within the compound there will be a hospital; a retreat house for providing hospitality to clergy, clergy families, and lay guests; a conference center hosting various cultural and religious events; and a refectory that provides meals for those in need.

This book contains addresses to younger generations who were born after the collapse of the Communist regime. The new challenges of secularism and poor catechesis are due to the many years of the Communist Yoke. Patriarch Daniel's encouragement and teaching to these younger generations is, however, clearly universal and can be heard and applied in almost any global setting.

As with any high-profile national figure, this patriarch does instill a sense of national pride. However, he does so by underscoring the foundations that Orthodoxy has provided for every aspect of Romanian culture and life. His reflections on the well-known sculptor and artist, Constantin Brâncuși, who was a subdeacon in the Orthodox Church, demonstrates how well His Beatitude knows his subject and how to relate cultural pride back to the humility of the contribution of the Church. This foundation stood firm even in the days of persecution during the last century.

An interview given through Romanian public television on December 24, 2017, revised by the journalist Andrew Victor Dochia in January 2018, gives us a clear insight into the personality of this modern patriarch. Readers will find in this interview the voice of a pastor, teacher, diplomat, and apologist for the faith. He does not shy from correcting that which needs correction, and he sets a vision that is always looking forward to the future. His confidence is contagious.

Finally, this work concludes with an extensive biography. Once again, this is included as so many in the English-speaking Orthodox world do not know Patriarch Daniel, who leads the second most populous Orthodox patriarchate in the world. His legacy, which is not yet completed, is one that should encourage all of us to be good and faithful servants making whatever sacrifices are needed with joy.

I want to thank His Beatitude Patriarch Daniel for his blessing to undertake this project to produce this introductory work through the Profiles Series of St Vladimir's Seminary Press. I am indebted to Madalina Daciana Reznic who labored mightily in translating an abundance of materials from Romanian into English. I would also be remiss if I did not acknowledge the skills and assistance given to me by Alexandru M. Popovici, who is currently the academic and recruitment advisor for St Vladimir's Orthodox Theological Seminary. His own tenacity helped me to complete this publication. This book, as with all SVS Press publications, reflects the teamwork that comes from the great sense of collegiality shared by the many hands and eyes that bring our books into print.

The Very Rev. Dr Chad Hatfield
President and Professor of Pastoral Theology, SVOTS
Editor, Profiles Series, SVS Press

PART I

The Unity between Theology and Spirituality in the Life of the Church[1]

The unity between theology and spirituality is based on the unity between God the Word and God the Holy Spirit in their relation to the world, but also on the fact that man, created in the image of God, is a theological and Spirit-bearing being, capable of dialogue and communion with God.

Since the revelation of God—which culminated in Jesus Christ, the God-Man—is preserved and bears fruit in the Church, the unity between theology and spirituality is an essential dimension of the life of the Church.

[1]This chapter and the following one, "Spiritual Life and Theology in Contemporary Orthodoxy," are excerpts (pp. 201–211 and pp. 288–300, respectively) from the doctoral dissertation "Theology and Spirituality: Their Relationship with the Contemporary World" of His Beatitude Patriarch Daniel of the Romanian Orthodox Church, prepared under the supervision of the Rev. Dr Dumitru Stăniloae and defended on October 30, 1980, at the Institute of Orthodox Theology in Bucharest. The present version was published in the volume *Theology and Spirituality* in 2010, as a pious homage to the memory of Fr Dumitru Stăniloae, who was aptly named " 'Demetrius the Theologian,' confessor of the true faith during the hardship of communism and interpreter of the monastic *Philokalia*, from whom I have learned fervent passion for the dogma of the Holy Trinity, constant admiration for the theology of the holy fathers, and intellectual honesty in the writing of theological studies." Patriarch Daniel of Romania, *Teologie și Spiritualitate* [Theology and spirituality] (Bucharest: Basilica, 2010), 8.—Trans.

Spirituality and Theology as the Experience and Understanding of the Revelation of God, Who Gives Himself to the World

God's revelation is not a sum of truths or principles, but is first of all the action and the powerful living word of a personal Being, who created the world so that he might give himself to it, and who enters into communion with man, beckons man, and responds to man. Revelation is made through nature (creation) and person (history). It involves or implies a divine-human interpersonal relationship. In Christ, God reveals not only a teaching but the divine life itself expressed in the humanity assumed by the Son. Thus, God does not reveal a sum of truths that can be detached from the Living Person and deemed to have intrinsic value. The whole revelation concerns the God-Man relationship and invites one to experience communion with God. Even when God reveals himself as overwhelming glory, as omnipotence, this revelation is made so that we can recognize our partner in eternal dialogue, in whose life we are called to partake. If God reveals the mysteries of history and eschatology, of eternal life, this happens neither to satisfy a simple curiosity, nor to provide an understanding in itself, but to offer knowledge about people's union with God; and when revelation refers to nature (or creation in general), it refers to its fundamental and ultimate significance: the relationship with God the Creator, the Holy One, the Savior.

In particular, the faith of the people of Israel and the faith of the Church begin from an experience of God, who intervenes in history and comes into contact with one person or a multitude of people at the same time.

That is why the Christian theological act that relies on revelation is not simply a systemization of the revelation data found in the holy Scriptures (although this is necessary) but is especially an understanding of a way of life proposed to people and a response to this summons, given in the concrete context of the Church's historical reality.

To theologize means, above all, to adapt human understanding to the divine thinking about people and the world; it means making a transition from the experience of self and the world as autonomic realities to a radically new experience of self and the world: an experience undergone in the light of revelation and in living communion with God. [It is] a new experience but lived without evading the concrete reality of the Church in the world.

The adaptation of our understanding to revelation or, more precisely, to the thinking of God expressed in his word and works, is always a transformation, a conversion, a *metanoia* (change of one's thinking and living). It is precisely this metanoia, personal or collective, that marks the very starting point of Christian spiritual life and theology.

We must note, however, that receiving the revelation is not blind obedience, which would invalidate our reason upon facing a certain amount of revealed truths, but a trustful openness to a Person or to the Supreme Persons—the Holy Trinity—given to us and a *pascha* (passover, transmutation) of our understanding as it meets the divine-human thinking of the eternally living Christ. In this sense, one can say that there is a "crucifixion" of the old Adam's thinking in us, locked in closed autonomy yet eager for infinite communion; nonetheless, this "crucifixion" aims at a fulfillment on another level, where Truth is identical to Love.

Naturally, we receive the gospel through faith in the sense of a personal adherence to the invitation that proposes the Way, the Truth, and the Life (cf. Jn 14.7)—in other words, the divine sense of reality perceived from within the communion of temporal and eternal love of people and God.

But as the word of the gospel of Christ infuses us with its indwelling significance and warmth (cf. Jn 14.23)—meaning that it becomes an existential, experienciable, assimilable truth because it is an assimilator of our lives—adherence to the gospel is revealed and increasingly realized as an attachment to the Person of Christ, as a self-offering to God, whose loving presence becomes the center, source, and support of our life. His love gives a whole new meaning to life and reality, which is that our true existence is rooted and fulfilled in and with God.

For this reason, martyrs and saints—in other words, the converts and friends of God—confess Christ to their death. Yet they do it not for the beauty of his teaching, but for the truth and reality of his living Person, from whom they can no longer separate because he has become the Life of their life (cf. Rom 8.35).

In this sense, there is an inner connection and reciprocity between personal communion with Christ and a deeper understanding of his words in revelation. The more we feel his personal, loving presence, the more we hearken to his word and meet him in the fulfillment of his commandments. The more intimate we are with him, the more deeply we understand the "intimacy" or the depth of his words in every epoch. The more we understand the meaning of his words, the more we attach ourselves to him and grow stronger through him. The more we live according to his will expressed in the commandment of love for God and our neighbor, the better we know him, gaining the knowledge given by communion and our working together with him (cf. Col 3.3–4; 1 Pet 8–9).

Thus, we simultaneously experience a change of our own person (conversion to Christ becomes permanent in communion with Christ) and a deeper and more exhaustive understanding of his revelation expressed in the holy Scriptures and holy Tradition. Consequently, in our being there occurs a restoration and a continuous fulfillment of the original "gnoseological" state: that of the theophilic (God-loving) and theological (God-professing) being.

That is why the primary premise of theology is not to comment philologically on the holy Scriptures but to see and feel people and creation differently: to see through the eyes of Christ, to think according to Christ; to become integrated into the life of Christ—yet not with the purpose of losing oneself as a unique, unrepeatable individual, but to find in him the fullness of one's own life.

This inmost unity between spiritual life and theology, as transformed knowledge, is embodied in the wonderful words of the Apostle Paul, who says, "We have the mind of Christ" (1 Cor 2.16). Such a mindset, specific to those renewed in Christ, gives birth to a new expression, a theological-spiritual expression, the understanding of which requires an adequate life: participation in the life of Christ in the Holy Spirit (cf. 1 Cor 2.13–14). This new, permanent experience of self and the world, in which the horizon of a closed or opaque immanence is overcome and a new horizon opens (cf. Ps 35.9) is, in a way, a liberating rupture which involves, on multiple levels, "the labor of a new birth" (cf. Gal 4.19). The labors of spiritual birth, as a "linguistic problem," are manifested in the difficulty of harmonizing natural knowledge with spiritual knowledge, which is lived in the reality of personal and ecclesial faith as well as in the tension from seeing the Gospels as mere human writing or perceiving in them the divine expressed in human words.

In other words, theological knowledge involves a transformation or sanctification of our thinking in the Holy Spirit. Witnesses of the faith deeply experienced in the life of the Church have always been aware of this. The mere acceptance of the idea that God exists does not express the living faith that engages the whole person. Faith is not just a simple intellectual adherence, because feeling the personal and working presence of God in one's own life, in the Church, and in the world is a fact accomplished within a trained relationship that is lived as communion sustained by the Holy Spirit.

St Silouan the Athonite says that however learned people may be, it is impossible for them to know the Lord as long as they do not live by his commandments, because we truly know the Lord not through science but through the Holy Spirit. Many philosophers and scientists have come to believe that God exists, but they never knew him. . . . To believe that God exists is one thing, but to know God is something else. . . . By intelligence only it is possible to know what is earthly, but only partially, whereas the knowledge of God and of heavenly beings comes only from the Holy Spirit. In the Holy Spirit we recognize the Lord, and the Holy Spirit fills man completely: his soul, mind, and body. That is how we arrive to know God in heaven and on earth.[2]

---

[2]Cf. Archimandrite Sophrony, *Starets Silouane, Moine du Mont-Athos: Vie – Doctrine – Ecrits* [Starets Silouan, monk of Mount Athos: Life, doctrine, writings], trans. from the

Spiritual life is a theological place precisely because in it there occurs the "metamorphosis," the renewing and adapting of our thinking to the divine-human thinking of Christ, to revelation. In the spiritual life, our reason does not only seek to find but opens and gives itself over in communion. Here, God is not an "object" of neutral or "objective" investigation, but the One who helps us realize this knowledge: "God," says St Maximus, "is not an object of knowledge that the soul could reconstruct through logical chaining, but it (the soul) recognizes him beyond any logic and reflection in a simple and unspoken union. Only God, who dwells in those who are worthy of this unspoken grace, knows how this union is forged."[3]

From this communion of love with God, faith-conviction in its true form is born, because the energies of the Holy Spirit shape within us the organ of feeling the personal presence of God in the Church and in our lives; they rouse or awaken from atrophy the "eyes of faith" so that the faculties of our being recapture their theophoric (God-bearing) ability and, in a broad sense, activate each believer as a theological, or theocentric, being.

This truth is expressed in the Orthodox faith through the statement that the Holy Spirit is the charismatic source of knowledge: "The Holy Spirit provided all things; he gushed forth prophecy, he taught wisdom to the illiterate; he showed forth the fishermen as theologians" (Stichera of Pentecost).

Theology is based on God's revelation lived in the life of the Church, because the same God who revealed himself in history is especially present in the Church. Theology refers to God. But precisely because it refers to God, it also refers to all that he has created because the revelation of God is done in relation to the created world. Therefore,

Russian by Hieromonk Symeon (Paris: Éditions Présence, 1973), 324–325. In English: *St Silouan the Athonite*, revised edn (Yonkers, NY: St Vladimir's Seminary Press, 2021).

[3]*Ambigua* (PG 91:1220BC), quoted in H. U. von Balthasar, *Liturgie cosmique*, 53 [Cf. Maximos the Confessor, *On Difficulties in the Church Fathers: The Ambigua*, ed. and trans. Nicholas Constas, 2 vols., Dumbarton Oaks Medieval Library (Cambridge, MA: Harvard University Press, 2014), 1:372–73.—Ed.].

the concern of theology is not narrowed down to God only; rather, it always considers the relationship between God and the world. Even when referring to God himself, theology is aware that he is in fact the ontological support of the divine economy (work) in the world (God *ad extra*). Since for faith all existence or created reality regards God as its ultimate foundation and meaning, theology is a coherent view of the whole of existence, but without being identical to philosophy—for it stems from revelation and therefore does not consider human reason to be an exclusive criterion for knowledge—and without identifying with the positivist scientific research that studies and describes nature and history in their immediate structure and phenomenology.[4]

Theology's preoccupation is God as the origin and purpose of all existence in relation to him. That is why Christian theology is done through reference to Christ, who is the Alpha and Omega of the whole of created existence (cf. Rev 1.8). Since creation is the gift of God, theology deciphers in it God's "words" waiting to be received—there are multiple ways of their being revealed—and recognized as created light from the uncreated God. Thus, the world and history represent for theology the milieu in which God continually launches new appeals and incites communion and cooperation in raising the creation to a richer participation in the fullness of eternal and infinite divine life.

Reference to Christ in the act of theologizing is also predicated on communion with him. It is not only accumulation or systematization—as methodical as it may be—of revelation data; rather, this reference is made within the "thinking of Christ," with which we are impregnated by living with him in the life of the Church: the holy mysteries, prayer, doxology, service to others, confession of the gospel, missionary work, etc. Eternally based on revelation, theology cannot lack personal and ecclesial Christian experience without risking becoming a science of religion (*Religionswissenschaft*).

---

[4]The theologian W. Pannenberg states that the subject of theology is quite different from that of the sciences. It is not a part of material, measurable, feasible reality (*machbar*). But it is God as the foundation that gives meaning to the whole reality. *Wissenschaftstheorie und Theologie* [Theology and the philosophy of science] (Frankfurt, 1973), 312 and 348.

Since theology must explicate the full faith of the Church—and this faith is expressed not only in strictly catechetical or academic form but also in liturgical, ascetic, and ministering spirituality—theology cannot neglect any of these aspects in which the life of the Church and the fruition of revelation are transparent.

Liturgy, for example, interprets a theological view of the whole of reality and is the source of a new experience of the Church and her relationship with the world, called to become the epiphany or light of the kingdom of God. The real continuity of the Church is expressed in the fact that Christian life is above all an experience of the kingdom of God, which is already given in Christ and whose fulfillment we are awaiting. The experience of the kingdom as intimate life with the Triune God makes spiritual life a *locus theologicus*, a motive and a medium of theologizing.[5]

In the Divine Liturgy, matter opens to spirit; humanity draws together in Christ, foretasting eternal life; the localizing, and thus body-separating, dimension is relativized and subordinated to the law of communion in the Spirit; and eternity enters time, filling it with maximum value and transfiguring it, for "eternity is not something, but Someone, or rather, it is the Trinity's life of love."[6] Although it involves methodical study or didactic and philosophical training, true theology is always born out of the life of the Church that prays, confesses, and serves. Her knowledge culminates in doxology, spiritualization, and service, for she is initiation in the divine-human love. That is why

[5]Cf. Alexander Schmemann, "Prière, liturgie et renouveau" [Prayer, liturgy, and renewal], in the collective work *La theologie du renouveau* [The theology of renewal] 2 (Paris: Éditions du Cerf, 1968), 105–114. The author considers that in the present time "there can be no renewal in any area of Church life or, simply, of the Church herself without a spiritual renewal first. But this is emphatically not a mere pietistic statement, a call for more prayer. It means, above everything else, the overcoming of the tragic divorce between the thought of the Church and the experience of the kingdom of God, which is the only source, guide, and fulfillment of that thought, and the only ultimate motivation of all Christian action" (pp. 113–114).

[6]O. Clément, *Transfigurer le temps* [Transfiguring time] (Neuchâtel and Paris: Delachaux & Niestlé, 1950), 99.

a theology that separates or opposes spirituality and communal and social service ignores precisely the mystery of the divine-human love. Our ministry must always have a salvific purpose; through it, Christ's presence (cf. Col 3.17) must become transparent. The state of prayer, of being face to face with Christ, gives us strength and makes us mystically feel that the face of our neighbor is the face of Christ, who rejoices or suffers in him.

"Social" theology separated from the spiritual experience of the Church risks becoming a fashionable ideology rather than a permanent and consistent ministry. Then again, a spirituality inured to peers or a society beset by problems becomes "docetic" (superficial, without essence) and weakens the life of the Church instead of strengthening it. This sets off a tension or opposition between the supporters of "horizontalism" and the proponents of "verticalism," the latter being particular to the contemporary West. The spirituality of the first tendency is exhausted in activism; as for the second, the theological sense is stifled either by an emotional spiritualism or by one that is intellectual or aesthetic.

From another standpoint, it is worth mentioning that contemporary Western theology has sought too much to make faith credible through all sorts of rational arguments, while faith is a reality that permeates our whole being and therefore does not confine itself to a mere intellectual convincing. This does not mean, however, that in theology the concept has no importance; on the contrary, it is important but considered in relation to spirituality itself, so that "theology is the theoretical consciousness of spirituality as its unmediated expression because it is lived, while being its mediated expression as well because it is conceptually conveyed." There may be a theology that talks about spirituality, "inventing" it, while there is another theology that is permeated by spirituality. The latter is therefore the theoretical consciousness of experienced spirituality.

Ordinarily, as the results of revelation's fruition of the living God present in the Church, theology and spirituality intertwine so intimately that even the distinction between them cannot be absolute but quite relative; and as for their definition, a description in plastic imagery will always complete any definition of a strictly intellectual or conceptual-didactic order.[7]

The life and word of the Church in history, originating in the Holy Spirit's vigil lamp inside the temple of life in Christ and in the heavenly Father's realm of communion with humanity, spirituality and theology, in their deepest dimension, are conversion and doxology; prayer and study; obedience and confession; the word about God's becoming human and man's deification; the search for sinlessness and struggle against sin; concern for history and openness to eternity; prophetic sensitivity and courage for martyrdom; Holy and Great Friday and the dawn of Resurrection; sacrificial love for others and a guard against disease that alienates in many a way; undeterred faith and utter humility; compassion and service for the ailing; divine life "borne in clay vessels" and the conviction that unites us with the resurrected One; the "madness" of the Cross and the ineffable wisdom always described in insufficient words; service to people and praise to God; the liturgy that unites heaven and earth; the word that frees and heals; the word that awakens and nourishes; the word of the divine Word; the life of the Life of the Most Holy Trinity.

[7]Cf. Iliescu, "Reflecţii despre teologie şi spiritualitate" [Reflections on theology and spirituality] (MS), in the personal letters of January 28, 1978, and April 4, 1978, addressed to the author [of the present work].

Spiritual Life and Theology in Contemporary Orthodoxy: A Short Presentation[1]

The spirituality and preoccupations of theology in the Orthodox Church are better known, so we will focus only on some aspects of the existing situation that characterizes Orthodoxy.

In the Orthodox Church, there is no current crisis of substance and hermeneutics such as the one encountered in Western Christianity.

[1]S. Bulgakoff, *L'Orthodoxie* [Orthodoxy] (Paris: Librairie Félix Alcan, 1933 and 1959); P. Evdokimov, *L'Orthodoxie* [Orthodoxy] (Neuchâtel and Paris: Delachaux & Niestlé, 1965); J. Meyendorff, *L'Église orthodoxe hier et aujourd'hui* (Paris: Éditions du Seuil, 1960 and 1969), in English as *The Orthodox Church: Its Past and Its Role in the World Today* (Crestwood, NY: St Vladimir's Seminary Press, 1981); O. Clément, *L'Église orthodoxe* [The Orthodox Church] (Paris: Presses Universitaires de France, 1961); Timothy Ware, *L'Orthodoxie, L'Église des sept Conciles* [Orthodoxy, the Church of the Seven Councils] (Paris: Desclée de Brouwer, 1968), English original, now in its third revised edition: *The Orthodox Church, An Introduction to Eastern Christianity* (London: Penguin Books, 2015); N. Zernov, *Eastern Christendom* (London: Weidenfeld & Nicolson, 1961); E. Timiades, *Lebendige Orthodoxie* [Living Orthodoxy] (Nürnberg/Eichstätt: Johann Michael Sailer Verlag, 1966); P. Bratsiotis, *Die orthodoxe Kirche in griechischer Sicht* [The Orthodox Church in the Greek view], 2 vols. (Stuttgart, 1959 and 1960); M. A. Costa de Beaurégard, "Père Ion Bria, Théologue de Foucauld" [Father Ion Bria, theologian of Foucauld], *L'Orthodoxie, Hier-Demain* [Orthodoxy, yesterday-today] (Paris, 1979); V. Lossky, *Essai sur la théologie mystique de l'Église d'Orient* (Paris: Aubier, 1944 and 1977), in English as *The Mystical Theology of the Eastern Church* (Crestwood, NY: St Vladimir's Seminary Press, 1976 and reprints); Rev. Dr D. Stăniloae, *Teologia Dogmatică Ortodoxă* [Orthodox dogmatic theology], 3 vols. (Bucharest: Editura Institutului Biblic şi de Misiune, 1978); J. Popovich, *Dogmatica Bisericii Ortodoxe* [in Serbian] (Belgrade, 1970); N. Nissiotis, *Die Théologie der Ostkirche im ökumenischer Dialog* [The theology of the Eastern Church in ecumenical dialogue] (Stuttgart, 1960); *De la théologie orthodoxe roumaine dès origines à nos jours* [On Romanian theology from its origins to the present day] (collective work) (Bucharest: Editura Institutului Biblic şi de Misiune 1974); Rev. Prof. C. Galeriu, "Teologia ortodoxă română contemporană: Coordonate şi sinteză," *Ortodoxia* 3–4 (1978).

The demythologizing proposed by R. Bultmann, the theology of the "death of God," and the "secularization program" of some Protestant theologians are foreign to Orthodox theological reflection. Moreover, neither the crisis of authority and structures nor the tension between theology and the magisterium encountered in the Roman Catholic Church have an equivalent in Orthodoxy. Priests do not leave their parishes, and monks do not renounce their vows even though monastic life is not as thriving everywhere as it was in different epochs of Church history.

Likewise, sacerdotal vocation is generally high, and the liturgical life is more intense than in many Western Churches. And even if the participation in divine services is not the same everywhere, the sacred sense is better preserved, and there is no massive militancy for a "secularization of the liturgy."

Yet, this does not mean that Orthodoxy should do nothing, and that its theology and spiritual life are not sometimes confronted with the problems of the contemporary world, with the modern person's mentality. And this is all the more so since it is no longer possible to speak today of Orthodoxy as a homogeneous geographic space because, despite a profound unity and similarities, there are many differences from one local church to another, not to mention the new situation created by the Orthodox diaspora present in various cultures, whose confessional ethos is different from the traditional Orthodox one.

Renewal efforts are required in Orthodoxy as well, in terms of both theology and spirituality, something which goes with the character of a living church. Such efforts already exist, but the manner of conceptualizing renewal in the Orthodox Church is very often different from the one in Western Christianity. And this difference finds its explanation in a complexity of objective reasons, not only of a cultural nature but also concerning the way of living and understanding the very mystery of Christianity. Alas, the centuries of separation between the West and the Christian East have deepened the differences, often turning them into a doctrinal and spiritual opposition.

In the following pages, we will focus on some of the main features that we believe define the current situation of Orthodoxy in general:

1. Patristic and philokalic renewal
2. Fidelity to Tradition and efforts to deepen the great themes of the Christian faith according to the exigency of our time
3. Sensitivity to the problems of the contemporary world
4. Ecumenical dialogue, understood as an effort to restore visible Christian unity

1. *The patristic and philokalic renewal* is reflected in the translation of the work of the Church's holy fathers and great confessors as well as in studies or commentaries on these works, undertaken in order to highlight better their timeliness and their depth of thought and the Christian experience throughout the centuries—during very different historical circumstances—of great theologians and spiritual men: martyrs, shepherds, teachers, ascetics, servants, parents and children, witnesses and saints of the Church of Christ. In other words, patristic renewal is not just a simple cultural phenomenon; not only does it correspond to a need for information, but it also imposes itself as a necessity for the Church's own life, as a sensitization and rejuvenation of her consciousness expressed together with Tradition as living memory in the Holy Spirit.

The Orthodox theology of the twentieth century rediscovers the value of Palamite theology, closely related to the spiritual life or grace, of uniting the human person with God.

After the Romanian theologian Dumitru Stăniloae published the book *The Life and Work of St Gregory Palamas* (1938), various other studies about the same great theologian of the fourteenth century began to be published in the West. In 1950 Cyprian Kern published *An Anthropology of St Gregory Palamas*, in Russian, in Paris.[2] A considerable contribution to a fairer understanding of St Gregory Palamas' theology in the West was brought forth by Fr John Meyendorff, who published *A Study of Gregory Palamas* in Paris in 1959, followed by

[2]Paris: Éditions du Seuil, 1959.

another book, *St Gregory Palamas and Orthodox Spirituality*.[3] He also offered a critical edition of *Defense of the Holy Hesychasts*[4] written by St Gregory Palamas.

In Greece, the works of the holy fathers and other spiritual men are constantly being published, but in particular we note that, of late, the Patriarchal Institute for Patristic Studies in Thessaloniki and Vlatadon Monastery are of particular importance. Professor P. Christu's studies on St Gregory Palamas' work deserve all the attention.[5]

Regarding patristic literature, of great importance is the effort to translate about one hundred volumes of the Greek and Latin fathers' most representative work into Romanian, at the initiative of Patriarch Justin Moisescu, who showed great interest for the holy fathers in his personal published works.[6]

Studies on the holy fathers or Byzantine theology were also written by Orthodox theologians such as G. Florovsky,[7] I. G. Coman, Basil Krivochéine,[8] Justin Popovich,[9] and Meyendorff[10] (as well as many

[3]Paris: Éditions du Seuil, 1959; in English as *A Study of Gregory Palamas* (Crestwood, NY: St Vladimir's Seminary Press, 1998) and *St Gregory Palamas and Orthodo Spiriatuality* (Crestwood, NY: St Vladimir's Seminary Press, 1974).

[4]Saint Grégoire Palamas, Défense des Saints hésychastes [Defense of the hesychast saints], introduction, texte critique, traduction et notes par J. Meyendorff (Leuven: Spicilegium sacrum lovaniense, 1959).

[5]See Ch. Yannaras, "La théologie en Grece aujourd'hui" [Theology in Greece today], *Istina* 2 (1971): 145–146.

[6]Dr Iustin Moisescu, *Evagrie din Pont: Viața, scrierile și învățătura* [Evagrius of Pontus: Life, writings, and teachings] [in Greek] (Athens, 1937); Dr Justin Moisescu, *Sfânta Scriptură și interpretarea ei în epoca Sfântului Ioan Hrisostom* [Holy Scripture and its interpretation in the time of St John Chrysostom] (Bucharest, 1942).

[7]*Părinții răsăriteni din secolul al IV-lea* [The Eastern fathers of the fourth century] [in Russian] (Paris, 1933); *Părinții bizantini din secolele V–VIII* [The Byzantine fathers of the fifth to eighth centuries] [in Russian] (Paris, 1933).

[8]B. Krivochéine published *Catéchèses* [Catecheses], by St Symeon the New Theologian, as vols. 96, 104, 113 of *Sources Chrétiennes* [Paris: Les Éditions du Cerf, 1963–1965].

[9]J. Popovich, "Théorie de la connaissance et connaissance de Dieu chez St. Isaac le Syrien" [Theory of knowledge and knowledge of God in St Isaac the Syrian], *Contacts* 69 (1970): 32–53 and no. 70 (1970): 119–147.

[10]*Le Christ dans la théologie byzantine* [Christ in Byzantine theology] (Paris: Éditions du Cerf, 1969), and in English: *Christ in Eastern Christian Thought* (Crestwoood, NY: St

Romanian theologians from younger generations: Stephen Alexe, C. Voicu, Cornițescu, and others).[11]

The philokalic renewal experienced its greatest moment in our time in the Romanian Orthodox Church with Fr Dumitru Stăniloae's translation of the *Philokalia*[12]: the theological notes and the explanations accompanying the volumes of the Romanian *Philokalia* are of special importance precisely because they allow the faithful and young theologians alike to discern the theology that structures ascetic Orthodox spirituality. Translations of the *Philokalia* have been begun in French (in Paris) and in English (in London) as well.

2. Fidelity to Tradition and the Effort to Deepen the Great Themes of Christian Faith According to the Exigency of Our Time.

a) The fidelity of the Orthodox theologians to Tradition is expressed by the profound understanding they have of its meaning, *as Tradition is not simply an external authority but the Church's life itself.* Several studies on the Orthodox understanding of Tradition were written by theologians such as D. Stăniloae,[13] G. Florovsky,[14] V. Lossky,[15] and others.

Vladimir's Seminary Press, 1975); *Initiation à la théologie byzantine* (Paris: Éditions du Cerf, 1975), and in English: *Byzantine Theology: Historical Trends and Doctrinal Themes* (New York: Fordham University Press, 1979).

[11]Ş. Alexe, "Sf. Niceta de Remesiana și ecumenicitate patristică din secolele IV și V" [St Nicetas of Remesiana and patristic ecumenism in the fourth and fifth centuries], *Studii Teologice* [Theological studies] 1960, nos. 7–8; C. Voicu, *Teologia muncii la Sfântul Ioan Gură de Aur și actualitatea ei* [The theology of work in St John Chrysostom and its timeliness] (Sibiu, 1975); T. Serviciu, *Doctrina hristologică a Sf. Chiril al Alexandriei* [The Christological doctrine of St Cyril of Alexandria] (Timișoara, 1972); C. Cornițescu, *Umanismul după Sf. Ioan Hrisostom* [Humanism after St John Chrysostom] [in Greek] (Athens, 1969); cf. *De la théologie orthodoxe roumaine* [On Romanian Orthodox theology] (Bucharest: Editura Institutului Biblic și de Misiune), 169–194.

[12]Philokalia, trans. from Greek, vol. 1 (1947), vol. 2 (1947), vol. 3 (1948), vol. 4 (1948), vol. 5 (1976), vol. 6 (1977), vol. 7 (1978), vol. 8 (1979).

[13]See *Teologia Dogmatică Ortodoxă* [Orthodox dogmatic theology], vol. 1, 49–71.

[14]G. Florovsky, "Le Corps du Christ vivant: Une interprétation orthodoxe de l'Église" [The Body of the living Christ: An Orthodox interpretation of the Church], in *La Sainte Église universelle* [The holy universal Church] (Neuchâtel: Delachaux & Niestlé, 1948), 9–57; *Bible, Church, Tradition: An Eastern Orthodox View* (Belmont, MA: Nordland, 1972).

[15]V. Lossky, *A l'image et à la ressemblance de Dieu* (Paris: Editions Aubier-Montaigne,

b) *Theological Orthodox gnoseology* (knowledge) was especially brought to the fore by the works of theologians V. Lossky,[16] Nikos Nissiotis,[17] Paul Evdokimov,[18] D. Stăniloae,[19] C. Yannaras,[20] Justin Popovich,[21] O. Clément,[22] Anthony Plămădeală,[23] Nicholas Chițescu,[24] I. Bria,[25] and A. Schmemann.[26]

c) The interest of Orthodox theology for *anthropology* manifests itself in the process of deepening the patristic theology of the human person as a being created in the image of God. As Nikos Nissiotis remarks, "Orthodox anthropology is not that of man, but that of God's humanity, and man's theology is no longer his hymn about God, but his deification (*theosis*) through God."[27]

1967), in English as *In the Image and Likeness of God* (Crestwood, NY: St Vladimir's Seminary Press, 1985).

[16]*Essai sur la théologie mystique de l'Église d'Orient*, in English as *The Mystical Theology of the Eastern Church* (Crestwood, NY: St Vladimir's Seminary Press, 1975 and reprints); *La vision de Dieu* (Neuchâtel: Delachaux & Niestlé, 1962), in English as *The Vision of God* (Crestwood, NY: St Vladimir's Seminary Press, repr. 2013).; "Foi et théologie" [Faith and theology], *Contacts* 35–36 (1961): 163–176.

[17]*Prolegomene la gnoseologia teologică* [Introduction to theological gnoseology] [in Greek] (Athens, 1965); *Filosofia religiei și teologia filosofică* [Philosophy of religion and philosophical theology] [in Greek] (Athens, 1965); "La théologie en tant que science et en tant que doxologie" [Theology as science and doxology], *Irenikon* 33 (1960): 291–310.

[18]*La connaissance de Dieu selon la tradition orientale* [The knowledge of God according to the Eastern tradition] (Lyon, 1967).

[19]*Teologia Dogmatică Ortodoxă* [Orthodox dogmatic theology], vol. 1, 92–110.

[20]*De l'absence et de l'inconnaissance de Dieu* [On the absence and unknowability of God] (Paris, 1971).

[21]Popovich, "Théorie de la connaissance [Theory of knowledge]."

[22]"Situation de la parole théologique selon la tradition orthodoxe [Situation of the theological word according to the Orthodox tradition]" (foreword to C. Yannaras's book *De l'absence et de l'inconnaissance de Dieu* [On the absence and unknowability of God], 9–39); "L'homme comme lieu théologique" [Man as theological place], *Contacts* 68 (1969): 290–305.

[23]"Rugăciune și cunoaștere în învățătura ortodoxă" [Prayer and knowledge in Orthodox teaching], *Studii Teologice* 1958, no. 3–4, 216–224.

[24]"Dogmă și viață creștină" [Dogma and the Christian life], *Studii Teologice* 1954, no. 1, 39–64.

[25]"Spiritul teologiei ortodoxe" [The spirit of Orthodox theology], *Ortodoxia* 2 (1972): 177–194.

[26]"Liturgy and Theology," *The Greek Orthodox Theological Review* 17 (1972): 86–100.

[27]N. Nissiotis, "Vers une théologie existentielle" [Towards an existential theology],

Vladimir Lossky, addressing the mystery of the human person in relation to that of the divine Persons, defines the human person as "the irreducibility of man to his nature." [28]

Another theologian, Christos Yannaras, insists on the ontology of the person.[29]

But it seems that the most substantial contemporary Orthodox theological study of the human person, both in his or her relationship with God and the world, belongs to Fr Dumitru Stăniloae, who synthesized and deepened the patristic theology concerning the human person's mystery in his or her unique connection with God and creation.[30]

Some Orthodox theologians place Orthodox anthropology in confrontation with different philosophical trends of our time.[31]

d) Within the present Orthodox ecclesiology, the so-called *ecclesiology of communion* or *eucharistic ecclesiology* has been emphasized—especially by some Western Orthodox theologians—which highlights the sacramental plenitude of each local church. Among the Orthodox theologians who insisted upon the importance of eucharistic ecclesiology are the following: N. Afanassief,[32] N. Koulomzine,[33] J. Meyendorff,[34] A. Schmemann,[35] and J. Zizioulas.[36]

Contacts 33 (1961): 39–51, at 42.

[28]Lossky, *A l'image*, 11.

[29]C. Yannaras, "Personne et communion" [Person and communion], *Contacts* 84 (1973): 310–316, at 310–312; *Persoană și eros: Eseu teologic de ontologie* [Person and eros: A theological essay on ontology] [in Greek] (Athens, 1976), 376.

[30]*Teologia Dogmatică Ortodoxă* [Orthodox dogmatic theology], vol. 1, 345–427.

[31]J. Popovich, *Omul și Dumnezeul-Om* [Man and the God-Man] [in Greek] (Athens, 1969); N. Nissiotis, "Existenţialismul contemporan" [in French], *Contacts* 81 (1973): 21–53; P. Nellas, *Zōon theoumenon* [Divinized animal] (Athens, 1979), 316.

[32]*L'Église du Saint-Esprit* [The Church of the Holy Spirit] (Paris: Éditions du Cerf, 1975), "L'Église de Dieu dans le Christ" [The Church of God in Christ], *La Pensée Orthodoxe* [Orthodox thought] 2, no. 13 (1968): 1–38.

[33]N. Koulomzine, J. Meyendorff, A. Schmemann, et al., *La primauté de Pierre dans l'Église orthodoxe* (Neuchâtel and Paris: Delachaux & Niestlé, 1960), in English as *The Primacy of Peter in the Orthodox Church* (Crestwood, NY: St Vladimir's Seminary Press, 1992).

[34]See Note 33.

[35]See Note 33.

[36]*Unitatea Bisericii în dumnezeiasca Euharistie și episcop in primele trei veacuri* [The

Although eucharistic ecclesiology underscores an important note of Orthodox ecclesiology in general, the latter cannot be reduced to a single aspect, and, above all, one cannot overlook the universal aspect of Orthodox ecclesiology that reflects the "consubstantiality" of local churches, as they testify to the same Orthodox faith and lead the same spiritual life.[37]

e) In current Orthodox theology, there is also a great interest in the *theological significance of spirituality*. Liturgical theology[38] especially emphasizes the existential aspect of the holy mysteries and their importance for the Christian life;[39] the theological significance of the liturgical feasts;[40] theological studies on icons;[41] the Liturgy as prayer par excellence by the Church;[42] and personal prayer,[43] especially prayer of the heart.[44] All these aspects preoccupy Orthodox theologians of

unity of the Church in the divine Eucharist and the bishop during the first three centuries] [in Greek] (Athens, 1965).

[37]Cf. D. Stăniloae, "Din aspectul sacramental al Bisericii" [On the sacramental aspect of the Church], *Studii Teologice* 9–10 (1976); *Teologia Dogmatică Ortodoxă* [Orthodox dogmatic theology], 2:195ff.

[38]Cf. *De la théologie Orthodoxe roumaine* [On Romanian Orthodox theology] (the part refering to liturgical studies).

[39]Schmemann, *Pour la vie du monde* (Paris: Desclée de Brouwer, 1969), in English as *For the Life of the World* (Yonkers, NY: St Vladimir's Seminary Press, 2018); D. Stăniloae, "Legătura dintre Euharistie și iubirea creștină" [The connection between the Eucharist and Christian love], *Studii Teologice* 1–2 (1975); A. Grigoraș, *Dogmă și cult* [Dogma and worship] (Bucharest, 1977).

[40]C. Andronikof, *Le sens des fêtes* [The meaning of the feasts] (Paris: Éditions du Cerf, 1970).

[41]P. Evdokimov, *L'art de l'Icône: Théologie de la Beaute* [The art of the icon: A theology of beauty] (Paris: Desclée de Brouwer, 1970); L. Ouspensky, *Essai sur la théologie de l'icône dans l'Église orthodoxe* [Essay on the theology of the icon in the Orthodox Church] (Paris: Editions de l'Exarchate Patriarcal Russe en Europe Occidentale, 1960); Rev. Prof. E. Braniște, "Teologia icoanelor" [The theology of icons], *Studii Teologice* 1952, no. 3–4.

[42]P. Evdokimov, *La prière de L'Église d'Orient* [The prayer of the Eastern Church] (Paris-Tournai, 1966).

[43]Bloom, *Prière vivante* [Living prayer] (Paris: Éditions du Cerf, 1972); *Ecole de la prière* (Paris: Éditions du Cerf, 1972).

[44]J. Serr and O. Clément, *La prière du Coeur* [The prayer of the heart] (Paris: Ab. de Bellefontaine, 1977); Chariton de Valamo, *L'art de la prière* (Paris: Ab. de Bellefontaine, 1976), in English as *The Art of Prayer: An Orthodox Anthology*, compiled by Igumen Chariton of

countries with a population that is mostly Orthodox, and especially those in the West (in the diaspora).

Monastic life, Christian asceticism,[45] and spirituality lived in the midst of a secularized world are the object of constant preoccupations.[46]

It bears noting that Orthodox theologians often start from liturgical spirituality and go on to develop a vision of the creation, of the world, and of the contemporary individual, revealing not only the profound meaning of the liturgical vision of reality but also the unity between theology and liturgical life.[47]

3. *The Sensitivity of Orthodox Theology to the Problems of the Contemporary World*

The great socioeconomic, cultural, and technological changes that characterize our civilization induce Christian theology to respond in a new or more profound way to unprecedented situations and problems in the history of humanity. Contemporary Christian theology is particularly interested in issues such as human solidarity, peace, ministry, family, ecology, technological and social evolution, etc.[48]

Valamo, translated by E. Kadloubovsky and E. M. Palmer, with an introdution by Timothy Ware (London: Faber and Faber, 1966).

[45]P. Evdokimov, *Les âges de la vie spirituelle des Pères du desert a nos jours* [Ages of the spiritual life from the desert fathers to our time] (Paris: DDB, 1964); A. Schmemann, *Le Grand Carême: Ascèse et Liturgie dans L'Église orthodoxe* (Paris: Ab. de Bellefontaine, 1977), in English as *Great Lent: Journey to Pascha* (Crestwood, NY: St Vladimir's Seminary Press, 1974 and reprints); B. Krivochéine, "La spiritualité orthodoxe" [Orthodox spirituality], *Messager de l'exarchat du patriarche russe en Europe occidentale* [The messenger of the Exarchate of the Russian Patriarchate in Western Europe] 53 (1966), 14–29.

[46]D. Stăniloae, "La prière dans un monde sécularisé" [Prayer in a secularized world], *Contacts* 103 (1978): 237–250; A. Schmemann, "Le culte divin a l'âge de la sécularisation" [Divine worship in the age of secularization], *Istina* 4 (1973).

[47]For example, I. Zizioulas, "La vision eucharistique du monde et de l'homme contemporain" [The eucharistic vision of the world and of contemporary man], *Contacts* 57 (1967): 83–92.

[48]N. Mladin, *Studii de teologie morală* [Studies in moral theology] (Sibiu, 1969); C. Sârbu, "Solidaritatea umană" [Human solidarity], *Mitropolia Moldovei și Sucevei*, 9–12 (1969); D. Belu, "Ortodoxia și activismul uman" [Orthodoxy and human activism], *Studii Teologice* 1950, no. 1–2; D. Stăniloae, "Învățătura creștină despre muncă" [The Christian

As Savvas Agouridis points out, contemporary Orthodox theology is not only—as a doxological and Paschal adoring stance—a "liturgical" transfiguration of space, as it is accused of being by those who look upon it superficially.[49] It is true that Orthodoxy is neither too "horizontal" nor too "activist," for it simply wants to maintain a balance between the horizontal and the vertical.

If sometimes the social aspect of the Church's mission was less pronounced, the motives were entirely historical, not dogmatic, because in the East as in the West, the path to God leads through our neighbor.

The Orthodox Church maintains an optimistic view of the world, yet this optimism is not an anthropocentric one; rather, it has a theandric or divine-human foundation in Christ.

The social message of love for one's neighbor, of being in his or her service, is inseparable from the soteriological aspect. The Church's service in the world must never be separated from the search for salvation, from the spiritual experience that assumes the integral reality of life and impresses onto this social action the character of participation in God's work for the world.

4. *Ecumenical dialogue*[50] is a preoccupation of most Christian churches today. This dialogue is manifold and is characterized by exchanges

teaching on work], *Studii Teologice* 1953, no. 1–2; I. Zăgrean, "Creștinismul și drepturile fundamentale ale omului" [Christianity and fundamental human rights], *Studii Teologice* 1952, no. 3–4; I. Tudoran, "Credință și tehnică," *Mitropolia Ardealului*, 4–6 (1968); Metropolitan N. Corneanu, "Teologia în slujba vieții" [Theology in the service of life], *Studii Teologice* 1968, no. 5–6; Bishop Anthony Plămădeală, *Biserica slujitoare* [The serving Church] (Bucharest, 1972); N. Nissiotis, "Le sens théologique de la révolution technologique et sociale" [The theological meaning of the technological and social revolution], *Contacts* 59–60 (1967): 232–251; P. Evdokimov, "L'Église et la Société" [The Church and society], *Contacts* 59–60 (1967): 190–231; G. Khodr, "The Church and the World," *St. Vladimir's Theological Quarterly* 13, 1–2 (1969); D. Savramis, "Orthodoxe Soziallehre und innerweltliche Askese" [Orthodox social teaching and inner-worldly asceticism], *Ökumenische Rundschau* [Ecumenical review], Heft 3 (1980): 275–291.

[49]S. Agouridis, "Dieu et Histoire" [God and history], *Contacts* 57 (1967): 69–74, at 69.

[50]Bishop A. Plămădeală, "Ecumenism și relații externe bisericești, 1944–1979" [Ecumenism and external church relations, 1944–1979], *Ortodoxia* (1980); cf. also *Romanian Orthodox Church News*, 1979, no. 3, 7–23; I. Bria, *Aspecte dogmatice ale unirii Bisericilor Creștine* [Dogmatic aspects of the union of Christian churches] (Bucharest, 1968); D.

of visits and mutual knowledge; contacts between representatives of churches at different levels; exchanges of teachers and students; publications and the organization of meetings, colloquia, and theological conferences; prayers for unity; the drawing up of common documents concerning some shared points of faith; collaboration on the practical field of social diakonia; and the effort of having a common attitude to the various problems faced by today's world.

The specific note that Orthodoxy brings to this dialogue is expressed in several ways, out of which we underscore *the interweaving of the dialogue of social diakonia with the permanent and firm emphasis on the necessity of restoring the unity of faith,* because the factor of faith cannot be subordinated to anything else without the risk of losing the identity of the Church or her special character in the ministry done in the name of the gospel.

Concerning the unity between theology and spirituality in the contemporary ecumenical dialogue, Orthodoxy offers a very special synthetic theological-spiritual vision, integrating life and the whole of reality created by God. Through the theology and testimony of its spirituality, Orthodoxy helps Western Christianity rediscover the mystery of the Holy Trinity as the source of the life and meaning of the Church and of Christian existence in general.

Popescu, *Eclesiologia romano-catolică după documentele Conciliului Vatican II și ecourile ei în teologia contemporană* [Roman Catholic ecclesiology according to the documents of the Second Vatican Council and its echoes in contemporary theology] (Bucharest, 1972) and D. Radu, "Comunitatea conciliară, problemă ecumenistă actuală" [The conciliar community, the current ecumenical problem], *Studii Teologice* 1976, no. 5–6; P. David, *Premise ale dialogului anglicano-ortodox, aspectul revelației divine* [Premises of the Anglican-Orthodox dialogue: The aspect of divine revelation] (Bucharest, 1977); I. Ică, "Relațiile între ortodocșii și luteranii din România din secolul al XVI-lea până astăzi" [Relations between Orthodox and Lutherans in Romania from the sixteenth century to the present day], *Mitropolia Ardealului* 1–3 (1980); I. Zăgrean "Pozițiile ecumeniste în teologia ortodoxă din Apus" [Ecumenist positions in Orthodox theology in the West], *Mitropolia Ardealului* 6–7 (1967); *Guideline for Orthodox Christians in Ecumenical Relations* (New York, 1973); D. Abrudan, *Creștinismul și mozaismul în perspectiva dialogului interreligios* [Christianity and the Mosaic religion in the perspective of interreligious dialogue] (Sibiu, 1979); C. Vasiliu, *Relațiile între Biserica Romano-Catolică și Biserica Ortodoxă de la enunțarea Conciliului Vatican II Jan. 1959–December 1970* [Relations between the Roman Catholic Church and the Romanian

The Roman Catholic theologian Yves Congar writes:

What I love in Orthodoxy is the profound and unified meaning it ascribes to tradition. Orthodoxy spontaneously links all the elements of revelation to their center, thus following the genius of the church fathers. If it talks about redemption, it talks about the Trinity; everything comes from here, even the most concrete details of life, and it is always brought to this center, being enlightened by it. And this inseparable Trinitarian center is a sacramental center. The celebration of the mysteries makes Orthodox Christians enter the world of the Trinity. They live intensely from the Holy Spirit. Their sacramental conception of the Church is the same as ours; it unites us intimately with them.[51]

Nevertheless, the Holy Trinity is not only the center of sacramental life but also the source of inspiration for Orthodox Trinitarian ecclesiology, in which universality is structured in communion. But this universality is dependent on the consubstantiality of faith as a support of unity and communion. And the consubstantiality of faith does not stifle in any way the gifts and special character or personality of the local churches that are in communion. Some Western theologians have intuited that at the foundation of this ecclesiological form lies the essential principle of communion, *koinonia*, of non-subordinate participation, this also being the basis for achieving collegiality and synodality in the Church.

Referring to the idea of collegiality that the Second Vatican Council wanted to promote, theologian E. Schillebeeckx affirmed, "By the idea of collegiality, the Church of the West has made an effort to render a vital place to the sublime idea of the East's *koinonia*."[52]

Orthodox Church since the proclamation of the Second Vatican Council, January 1959–December 1975] (Bucharest, 1976).

[51]Yves Congar, "J'aime l'Orthodoxie" [I love Orthodoxy], in *2000 ans de Christianisme* [2000 years of Christianity], vol. 2 (Paris: Aufadi, 1975), 97.

[52]*L'Église du Christ et l'homme d'aujourd'hui selon Vatican II* [The Church of Christ and the man of today according to Vatican II] (Lyon: Le Puy, 1965), 129.

Regarding the necessity of unity between theology and spirituality in ecumenical dialogue, Orthodoxy emphasizes that theology is not only science but also doxology.[53] But theology is doxology only to the extent that spiritual experience becomes a constitutive part of the theological act itself. Upon mentioning that a certain exaggerated scientism in theology bears the risk of a reductionism proper to scientism, which "simultaneously disconsiders empirical experience—which is richer than scientific experience—and wisdom, which is a sign of the human person's thinking and the manifestation of his or her human quality," Protestant theologian G. Siegwalt points out that the Eastern tradition has always insisted on theology as *theosis*, as deification; *lex credendi* (rule of faith) is in fact *lex orandi* (rule of prayer), and communion with God involves communion with one's neighbor. Theology is therefore liturgical and practical, and it encompasses a sapiential knowledge, a wisdom owing to life experience, to faith in love. [54]

If in the above lines we have expressed just a few testimonies about some aspects of the contribution Orthodoxy can bring to ecumenical dialogue, we will now mention the fact that some Orthodox theologians consider the dialogue of Orthodoxy with the West necessary to Orthodoxy itself, in the sense shown by the French Orthodox theologian Olivier Clément. He believes that what Orthodoxy can especially appreciate in Western Christianity is "the Western sense of Christians' ethical and historical responsibility," "the critical spirit and the intellectual rigor of the West. . . ."[55] And elsewhere he also notes, "And what could the West discover in the best that the East has to offer, if not its own roots immersed in quietude?"[56]

---

[53]Cf. N. Nissiotis, "La Théologie en tant que science et en tant que doxologie" [Theology as science and doxology], *Irenikon* 33 (1960).

[54]Cf. "Expérience et Révélation: Remarques de méthodologie théologique" [Experience and Revelation: Notes on theological methodology], *Revue d'Histoire et de Philosophie Religieuses* [Review of religious history and philosophy] 55 (1976): 528 and 534.

[55]O. Clément and S. Rougier, *La révolte de l'esprit* [The revolt of the spirit] (Paris: Stock, 1979), 534.

[56]O. Clément, "Regard orthodoxe sur l'Histoire" [An Orthodox look at history], in *2000 ans de Christianisme* [2000 years of Christianity], 2:37.

The One Church and the Many Churches; Orthodoxy: Its Identity and Its Witness[1]

I. The Meaning of the Adjective *Orthodox*

The Greek word *orthos* means "right" or "just," and *doxa* means both "opinion" and "glory." Consequently, "orthodox" means "right opinion" and "true glory." Having the right or true opinion in the faith therefore implies giving God the right glory or true worship.

In the Early Church, the term "orthodox" was attributed to both doctrine and the Church as a whole in contrast to heresies, which were arbitrary or false opinions.

II. The Conciliar Structure of Orthodoxy and Its Organization Today

Orthodoxy, as a communion of churches linked together by their confession of the same Orthodox faith, consists today of a number of autocephalous and autonomous churches.

An *autocephalous church* is a church which is self-governing and free to take its own decisions concerning the election and consecration of its bishops, ecclesiastical administration, theological education, pastoral and missionary activity, social involvement, ecumenical

[1]Originally published in a slightly different form in Patriarch Daniel, *Confessing the Truth in Love: Orthodox Perceptions of Life, Mission and Unity*, 2nd ed. (Bucharest: Basilica, 2008), 108–130. Reprinted by permission.

relationships with other churches, and relations to the national and civil authorities. Autocephalous churches consider one another to be sister churches.

An *autonomous church* is a local church which enjoys a certain degree of independence but has not yet become autocephalous. For example, the election or consecration of its bishops, or, at least, of its primate (the first among bishops), is subject to the consent of the autocephalous church on which the autonomous church is still reasonably dependent.

However, an autocephalous church is not independent in the sense that sovereign states that can change their governments are, because autocephalous churches ought to confess the same faith and have the same sacramental life. Autocephalous churches individually and collectively are responsible for the same faith which they all confess and by which they live. In Orthodoxy, *koinonia* (communion) implies both the freedom of the local church in its ecclesiastical and pastoral practice, and the duty to maintain the fullness of the faith and sacramental life together with its sister churches.

Therefore, an autocephalous church is a mature church, capable of safeguarding, transmitting, and living the Orthodox faith without influences from the outside; but autocephaly does not give one church the right to exercise its freedom to the detriment of the *koinonia* with the Orthodox Churches as a whole. In Orthodoxy, unity in the faith and sacraments is more important than a juridical unity which is real, but secondary. For this reason, according to the theological and ecclesiastical understanding of its members, Orthodoxy cannot be equated either to the churches which developed as separate institutions after the Reformation or to a universal church with one apostolic see in the center to which all the local churches are subordinate.

The local Orthodox Churches consider themselves to be the fullness of the Catholic or Universal Church in a given place. This is the basis of their equality and their concept of unity as *koinonia*. According to Orthodox understanding, Orthodoxy is not one confessional church among other confessions but the historical continuity of the One, Undivided Church which has always remained unchanged with regard to the content of her faith and of her sacramental and spiritual life. That is so because it is not the historical outcome of an interpretation of the Church's doctrine or order which differs or departs from the catholic understanding of the Church by the apostles, the fathers, and the ecumenical councils. Her basic collegial and conciliar structure on a global scale (which neither excludes the primacy of a local church's bishop nor considers it higher than a collegial or "sisterly" relationship) is a witness to this, despite certain ambiguities owing to particular historical circumstances.

Each Orthodox Church has a synodal structure. The synod, or college of bishops, is presided over by the patriarch or archbishop who is the primate of that particular Church (cf. the thirty-fourth Apostolic Canon).

In an autocephalous Church, the highest episcopal authority on questions of doctrine and discipline is that Church's synod of bishops, whereas in the worldwide Orthodox Church, it is the synod of the entire episcopate, or the ecumenical council.

Ecumenical councils were summoned in the past when it was necessary to clarify a problem, especially pertaining to doctrine, that was seen as a threat to the faith confessed and lived by Orthodoxy, and therefore to the unity of the Church.

A council is not automatically recognized as ecumenical simply because it has convened or declared itself ecumenical.

It is by means of a *reception process* in the body of the Church as a whole that it is recognized as ecumenical. Its definitions of the Church's faith or its decisions ought to correspond to the *Orthodox understanding* of the Church *in her unbroken continuity through the ages* according to which the content of the faith must remain unchanged despite the new definitions required by the different periods of history.

Orthodoxy recognizes the following seven councils as ecumenical: Nicaea (325), Constantinople (381), Ephesus (431), Chalcedon (451),

Constantinople (553), Constantinople (680–1), and Nicaea (787). Since then, a number of regional councils have taken place in the Orthodox Church, and in recent times there have been several Pan-Orthodox conferences: Rhodes (1961, 1963, 1964), Belgrade (1966), and Chambésy (1968, 1976, 1982, 1986). The Orthodox Church plans to hold a Pan-Orthodox council in the future. The preparations continue, albeit slowly.[2]

Within the conciliar system of the Orthodox Church on a global scale, the patriarch of Constantinople enjoys a primacy of honor by reason of coordination (*primus inter pares*—the first among equals), but this does not entitle him to subordinate any of the sister Churches. Before the schism of 1054 between Rome and Constantinople, the Orthodox Churches recognized the primacy of the Church of Rome over the *koinonia* of the Churches in the world. They would be prepared to accept this today also, on the condition that full agreement be reached between Rome and Orthodoxy concerning faith and ecclesiology in its conciliar form, so that monarchical primacy (universal jurisdiction) becomes collegial primacy again.

The autocephalous and autonomous churches which make up Orthodoxy today have been established either on the basis of the four ancient patriarchates (Constantinople, Alexandria, Antioch, and Jerusalem; with Rome being the fifth and located in the West) or on the basis of national states (Russia, Serbia, Romania, etc.).

1. The Four Ancient Patriarchates

A. The *Ecumenical Patriarchate of Constantinople*, with its see in Fanar, Istanbul (Turkey), comprises 3,500,000 members, including the dioceses of the diaspora under its jurisdiction in Western Europe, North and South America, Asia, Australia, New Zealand, and the Far East.[3]

---

[2] The "Holy and Great Council of the Orthodox Church" was held in Kolymvari, Crete, June 19–26, 2016.

[3] The sources of the data on these churches are *Vestitorul Ortodoxiei* [The Herald of Orthodoxy], nos. 143–144 (Bucharest, October 1995), and the *Handbook of Member Churches of the World Council of Churches*, ed. Ans J. van der Bent (Geneva, 1985).

B. The *Greek Orthodox Patriarchate of Alexandria and All Africa*, which has its see in Alexandria (Egypt), has 350,000 members. Its jurisdiction also covers the new African Orthodox churches which are the outcome of the Greek mission in Eastern and Central Africa (Kenya, Uganda, Tanzania, and Zaire).

C. The *Greek Orthodox Patriarchate of Antioch and All the East*, with its see in Damascus (Syria), has 750,000 members. Its jurisdiction covers Syria, Lebanon, Iran, Iraq, the Arabian Peninsula, all the East, and some areas of Turkey, as well as the Arabic-speaking Orthodox faithful living in North and South America, Australia, and New Zealand. Although it is entirely Arabian, the Patriarchate of Antioch includes the word "Greek" in its title as a qualifier to distinguish itself from another Orthodox Patriarchate—namely, the Syrian Orthodox Patriarchate of Antioch and All the East, which also has its see in Damascus.

D. The *Greek Orthodox Patriarchate of Jerusalem*, whose episcopate is Greek, although the majority of its 260,00 members are Arabs. The Orthodox patriarchs of Jerusalem consider themselves the legitimate successors of James, the first bishop of Jerusalem in the time of the apostles. The Patriarchate of Jerusalem is also the main custodian of the Holy Shrines in the Holy Land.

2. Other Autocephalous Churches

A. The *Russian Orthodox Church* (Patriarchate of Russia), with its see in Moscow, has 50,000,000 members. Beyond the former Soviet Union, the jurisdiction of the Moscow Patriarchate covers the autonomous Church of Japan; several exarchates in Central and Western Europe, Central and South America; and parishes and representations in North America, Canada, etc.

B. The *Serbian Orthodox Church* (Patriarchate of Serbia), with its see in Belgrade, has 8,000,000 members. Its jurisdiction also includes the Serbian Orthodox diaspora (in Western Europe, Australia, and America).

C. The *Romanian Orthodox Church* (Patriarchate of Romania), which has its see in Bucharest, comprises 23,000,000 believers.[4] The Romanian Orthodox Church diaspora consists of the two metropolitanates for Western, Central, and Southern Europe; the Archdiocese of the United States of America and Canada;[5] and the parishes of Australia and New Zealand.

D. The *Bulgarian Orthodox Church* (Patriarchate of Bulgaria), with its see in Sofia, has 8,000,000 members in the country and in the diaspora.

E. The (Orthodox) *Church of Cyprus*, presided over by an archbishop whose see is in Nicosia, has 442,000 members.

F. The (Orthodox) *Church of Greece*, presided over by an archbishop whose see is in Athens, comprises 9,025,000 members. Its jurisdiction covers most of the territory of Greece, while the rest (Crete, Mount Athos, etc.) comes under the jurisdiction of the Patriarchate of Constantinople. The Church of Greece has no jurisdiction over the Greek diaspora since this is subject to the jurisdiction of the Patriarchate of Constantinople.

G. The *Polish Orthodox Church*, presided over by the metropolitan of Warsaw and of all Poland, has 1,000,000 members.

H. The *Georgian Orthodox-Apostolic Church*, whose catholicos-patriarch resides in Tbilisi, has 5,000,000 members.

---

[4]According to Institutul Naţional de Statistică (The National Institute of Statistics), Romania's population was 19.4 million as of January 1, 2019, http://www.insse.ro/cms/sites/default/files/com_presa/com_pdf/poprez_ian2019r.pdf.—Trans.

[5]Elevated to the status of Metropolitanate of the United States of America and Canada on October 30, 2016, and headed by His Eminence Nicolae, archbishop of the Romanian Orthodox Archdiocese of the United States of America and the Romanian Orthodox metropolitan of the Americas, with the metropolitan see located in Chicago, Illinois.—Trans.

I. The *Orthodox Church of the Czech Lands and Slovakia*, presided over by the metropolitan of the Czech lands and Slovakia, whose see is in Prague, has 60,000 members.

J. The *Orthodox Church of Albania*, autocephalous since 1937 and reorganized in 1991 by the Ecumenical Patriarchate after the fall of the atheist communist regime of Tirana, has 160,000 members.

K. The *Orthodox Church of America* (OCA),[6] presided over by the metropolitan of all America and Canada, has 1,000,000 members.

3. Autonomous Churches

A. The (Orthodox) *Church of Sinai* is in fact a 900-member monastic community independent in all respects, but whose superior is a bishop consecrated by the Patriarchate of Jerusalem.

B. The *Orthodox Church of Finland*, founded in the eleventh century and dependent on the Russian Orthodox Church until 1917, has been dependent on the Patriarchate of Constantinople since 1923 and has 56,086 members.

C. The *Orthodox Church of Japan*, founded in the nineteenth century by Russian missionaries, is still dependent on the Patriarchate of Moscow, but almost all of its clergy are of Japanese origin. It has 25,000 members, and it became autonomous in 1970.

D. The *Orthodox Church of China* was the outcome of Russian missionary work at the end of the nineteenth century and became autonomous under the jurisdiction of the Moscow Patriarchate in 1957. Today it has 20,000 members.

E. The *Orthodox Church of Estonia*, with its see in Tallinn, has 200,000 members.

---

[6]Not recognized yet by the Ecumenical Patriarchate.

---

4. The Orthodox diaspora

The Orthodox diaspora is a new factor owing, above all, to immigration in modern times.

The Orthodox in diaspora are mainly of Greek or Russian origin, but there are also many Serbians, Romanians, Arabs, Bulgarians, Albanians, and others. In general, the Orthodox in diaspora come under the jurisdiction of the mother Church of the country from which they emigrated, but it sometimes happens that, for various reasons (political or psychological, in particular), they may change jurisdiction. For this reason, for example, the Ecumenical Patriarchate has under its jurisdiction not only Greeks but also Russians, etc., and, as for converts to Orthodoxy, they also choose the jurisdiction which suits them best.

Often, the body of a Church seems to be profoundly marked by historical circumstances. That is the case for the Russian diaspora, which is covered by four different jurisdictions:

a) The *Synod of the Russian Church* in exile (sometimes known as the "White Russians"), with 20 bishops and 300 parishes founded after the Russian Revolution of 1917.

b) The *Patriarchate of Moscow*, with 12 bishops and about 70 parishes.

c) The *Russian Archdiocese of Western Europe*, which is dependent on the Patriarchate of Constantinople ("Paris jurisdiction").

d) The *Orthodox Church in America*, which was granted autocephaly in 1970 by the Patriarchate of Moscow (but this has not been recognized by all the autocephalous churches).

Despite its complex and sometimes embarrassing nature because of jurisdictional overlap, the Orthodox diaspora, especially in the West, plays an important role in general in the encounter between Orthodoxy and Western Christianity (Roman Catholic, Anglican, and Protestant) and in the renewal of contemporary Orthodox theology.

There are *other Churches* in the world which are *called orthodox*, but which do not belong to the family of Orthodox Churches listed above although they are also Eastern Churches. These churches, known as the *Oriental* (Pre-Chalcedonian) Orthodox Churches, to distinguish them from the family of Eastern Orthodox Churches, are the product of the christological controversies of the fourth and fifth centuries. The Nestorian Church broke away at the time of the Council of Ephesus (431). The Churches that did not accept the christological dogmatic formula of Chalcedon (451) that "Christ is one Person in two natures" and adopted the formula stating that Christ is "the one, incarnate nature of the *Logos*" and which are also called Orthodox are the following: the *Syrian Orthodox Church* (Patriarchate of Antioch and of All the East), with the see of its patriarch in Damascus and 142,000 members; the *Malankara Orthodox Syrian Church* (of India), with 1,600,000 members; the *Coptic Orthodox Church*, whose head is called pope and has his official see in Cairo, with 3,900,000 members; the *Ethiopian Orthodox Church*, whose patriarch resides in Addis Ababa, which has 16,000,000 members; the *Armenian Apostolic Church*, whose supreme catholicos has his see in Echmiadzin in the former Soviet country of Armenia, which comprises 4,000,000 members. There are also Armenian Patriarchates in Jerusalem and Constantinople and another Armenian Catholicosate of Cilicia in Lebanon.

In recent times, it has been recognized that many of the factors which contributed to the separation of these Churches from the Church as a whole at Chalcedon were political, ethnic, and cultural. The different definitions of Christology in these two families of Orthodox Churches at the time of the Council of Chalcedon have not affected the content of the faith in Christ, whom both groups confess to be true God and true Man. The obstacles to re-establishing communion between these two families of Orthodox Churches appear to be lessening, or at least they are no longer considered to be essentially related to dogmatic content but more to its definition and to culture. Certainly, more preparation is required on both sides for the previous communion to be restored.

It is a serious matter to get used to separation as if that were a normal thing. The long-established fact of the separation does not justify its abnormality or the counter-witness it provides to the nature and calling of the Church of Christ. The sacramental and liturgical life of these Churches known as "Oriental Orthodox" and their conception of the Church are close to those of the other Orthodox Churches.

III. The Spiritual Life of Orthodoxy

A. Liturgical and Sacramental Life

The Orthodox Church is a liturgical church par excellence. The center of the life of the Orthodox Church is her liturgical life. The heart of liturgical life is the *Divine Liturgy* (the Eucharist).

1. The Divine Liturgy, as its name implies, is simultaneously the work of God and the work of the faithful, or of the Church. *Leitourgia* means "public work," or work in the service of the people, or of the multitudes.

a) But since, according to the Orthodox view, *the main agent at work during the Liturgy is Christ himself* together with the Father and the Holy Spirit, the Liturgy is also called the *Divine* Liturgy. While the faithful chant the Cherubic Hymn, the celebrant priest or bishop prays a long passage which says of Christ, "For you are the *One who both offers* and is offered, the *One who is received* and is distributed."

b) The Divine Liturgy is not merely a remembrance of the acts which Christ performed for us that we may come closer to God and unite with him; *it is also the celebration of the presence of the crucified and risen Christ among his people.* During the Divine Liturgy, the concelebrants greet one another with these words:

> "Christ is in our midst!"
> "He is and ever shall be!"

And before the eucharistic communion, there is the following confession: "I also believe that this is truly *your pure Body* and that this is truly *your precious Blood. . . .* O Son of God, *receive me today as a partaker of your mystical supper."*

c) The cosmic dimension of the Divine Liturgy is expressed in the fact that the Church offers God the bread and the wine which are a *pars pro toto* (a part taken for the whole) for the entire creation: "Your own of your own we offer to you, in all and for all." During the Divine Liturgy, the Church embraces everything in her prayers: the past, the present, and the future; the living and the dead; human activities and nature. Prayer is offered for the brothers and sisters in faith, for the sick and the imprisoned, for friends and enemies, for the abundance of the fruit of the earth, and for the entire world because it is God's world; despite the sin which disfigures it, creation is called to be transfigured and sanctified in communion with God.

d) *The Divine Liturgy, or the continuation of Pentecost in the Church.* God's gift to the Church is his response to the Church's gifts to him. We offer the bread and wine and we receive God himself, the Body and Blood of Christ filled with the Holy Spirit. Without the Holy Spirit, communion with Christ is stripped of ontology. This is why the Orthodox Church gives so much importance to the invocation of the Holy Spirit in her liturgical and sacramental life, and especially in the eucharistic epiclesis: "Send down your Holy Spirit upon us and upon these gifts here offered. And make this bread the precious Body of your Christ. And that which is in this cup the precious Blood of your Christ. Making the change by your Holy Spirit. That these gifts may be to those who partake for the *purification of soul, for the remissions of sins, for the communion of the Holy Spirit, for the fulfillment of the kingdom of Heaven."*

e) The Divine Liturgy is also the *mystery of change, of transfiguration, and of renewal*; it expresses the presence of the kingdom and anticipates its coming fulfillment. This is where the most profound *eschatological dimension* of the life of the Church is manifested.

f) *The Liturgy is the "Weltanschauung" of Orthodoxy.* The Divine Liturgy is the synthesis of all the theological reflection of Orthodoxy and its spiritual experience. The Divine Liturgy constitutes the most profound vision which Orthodoxy has of God as a mystery of love and communion; of humanity as created in the image of God; of creation, the gift of God, called mysteriously to become a sacrament of his presence; and of his love, called to transfiguration and eternal joy in the communion of the holy and life-giving Trinity. Herein is the meeting of time and eternity, of heaven and earth, of God and humankind, of matter and the Spirit of God; here God acts, and humankind responds actively. In the Divine Liturgy dogma and hymnody, words and symbols, action and doxology, the banality of our everyday life and the radical newness of the Spirit of God, the burden of this life and the joy of encountering God—everything converges to celebrate the living God who shares in our life so that we may share in his. This is why nothing can better express the mystery of the Church and her vocation than the Divine Liturgy.

The Orthodox Church has a number of Liturgies:

- *The Liturgy of St John Chrysostom* (this is the Liturgy celebrated almost throughout the whole year on Sundays and other days of the week).

- *The Liturgy of St Basil the Great* (of Caesarea), celebrated ten times a year especially during Great Lent. It is not very different from that of St John Chrysostom.

- *The Liturgy of the Presanctified Gifts*, which is celebrated on Wednesdays and Fridays during Great Lent and the first three days of Holy Week.

- *The Liturgy of St James*, the brother of the Lord, which is celebrated once a year on the feast of St James (October 23), but only in certain places.

In general, the eucharistic elements, the bread and the wine, are brought to church by the faithful together with a diptych (list of the names) of the living and the departed for whom the prayer of the Church as a whole is requested.

The Orthodox priests and the faithful who wish to participate in the Liturgy have to prepare themselves, be reconciled with everyone, be in a state of prayer and fasting, and have confessed their sins. No food is taken before the eucharistic communion because on that day no food or drink is more important than the Body and Blood of Christ. The asceticism of fasting is a preparation for the joy of Holy Communion. We give ourselves completely to God, who also gives himself to us in the mystery of Holy Communion.

After the Liturgy, all the faithful, both those who have communed and those who have not, are invited to share the blessed bread (antidoron), which differs from the consecrated bread but is still an expression of agape.

2. In addition to the sacrament of the Eucharist received during the Divine Liturgy, the Orthodox Church recognizes the following as *mysteries/sacraments* as well: *baptism, chrismation* (confirmation), *forgiveness of sins* (penance, reconciliation), *ordination, marriage* (also called crowning), and the *anointing of the sick* (also called unction).

Through the sacraments, Christ makes himself contemporaneous with us and communicates himself to us through the Holy Spirit. The purpose of each sacrament is that we should participate in the divine-human life of Christ, which implies our salvation and our sanctification. In baptism, we meet the Christ who was baptized in the Jordan, the Christ who died and rose again. In chrismation, there is the Holy Spirit sent by Christ to his apostles. In the mystery of forgiveness, it is Christ who, during his earthly life, forgave and reconciled the sinners who repented, men and women. In ordination, we meet the Christ who sends his apostles out to preach the gospel, to baptize and to lead the baptized along the path of salvation—that is, to communion with the Father, the Son, and the Holy Spirit. In the mystery of marriage, we meet the Christ who shared in the wedding feast at Cana and who transforms the love of the couple into communion with God and a reflection of the love of Christ for his Church, who makes family life into an image of the life of the Trinity. In the sacrament of the anointing of the sick, we meet Christ the healer, the physician of our souls and bodies as he was at the time of his mission and ministry on earth. It is above all (but not only) through the sacraments that Christ is with us until the end of time and sanctifies us through the power of the Holy Spirit.

3. The *prayers and blessings for human activities and for nature* are another aspect of the spiritual life of the Orthodox Church and of her cosmic dimension. Whereas the sacraments pertain only to human beings, the Church calls all activities and the natural environment to sanctification and blesses them. The world is potentially "theological": it is God's world. For this reason, all activities must become liturgy and doxology directed to God. It is the grace and love of God that are invoked on everything.

A book called the *Euchologion* contains the following prayers and blessings: for the laying of the cornerstone of the foundation of a house, for fields and gardens, for the first fruit of the harvest, for the opening of a congress, for vehicles, and for traveling; prayers during times of drought, floods, torrential rain, epidemics, etc.

Orthodoxy sees no opposition between spirit and matter as the Manicheans and the Neo-Platonists do; it makes no radical distinction between sacred and secular but rather between the secularized and that which aspires to sanctification or has been sanctified. All these prayers for the sanctification of nature are based on the profound understanding that Orthodoxy has of the purpose of the incarnation, of God's becoming flesh: God became human so that human beings could share in the life of God; he accepted matter in the form of his own body, so that matter could participate in the life of the Spirit.

4. *The sanctification of time, the present expression of the history of salvation, and the expectation of the kingdom to come, or the feasts in the Orthodox Church.*

The Orthodox Church calendar begins on September 1. The greatest feasts of Orthodoxy relate to the events of salvation brought about by Christ; others relate to saints. The major feasts are connected with Christ and with the Mother of God, or the Virgin Mary.

- The Nativity of Christ (December 25);

- The Circumcision of Christ (January 1);

- The Baptism of Christ/Theophany (January 6);

- The Presentation of our Lord in the Temple (February 2);

- The Entry of our Lord into Jerusalem/Palm Sunday (one week before Pascha);

- Pascha, the Resurrection of our Lord—the greatest feast of the Orthodox Church;

- The Ascension of our Lord Jesus Christ into Heaven (forty days after Pascha);

- Pentecost (relating both to Christ who sends the Holy Spirit and to the Trinity as a whole) (fifty days after Pascha);

- The Transfiguration of our Lord Jesus Christ (August 6);

- The Elevation of the Venerable and Life-Giving Cross (September 14).

The four major feasts in honor of the Mother of God are:

- The Nativity of the Mother of God (September 8);

- The Presentation of the Mother of God in the Temple (November 21);

- The Annunciation of the Mother of God (March 25);

- The Dormition of the Mother of God (August 15).

There are many other feast days honoring the saints. The first Sunday after Pentecost is the Sunday of all Saints, because saintliness is the work of the Holy Spirit in the Church. The veneration of the saints does not take away from the worship and adoration of God, because the saints' holiness reflects God's grace in humankind. The veneration of the saints is the liturgical expression of what theology calls *communio sanctorum* (the communion of saints). The veneration of the saints, like the prayers for the dead, is an expression of a love stronger than death, of the link which exists between the visible and invisible dimensions of the Church.

This factor is also underscored by Orthodox iconography. An icon is primarily a liturgical expression of a confession of faith in the truth of God's incarnation. It belongs to the symbolic language of faith found in the Bible (typology, analogy, symbology, etc.), but at the same time it expresses the radically new fact that God became man in Jesus Christ, and that henceforth he has had a human face. The Old Testament prohibits the making of images for pedagogical reasons, so that Christ, the icon, the image of the invisible God, may be received (Col 1.15).

Before being a means for church instruction or an expression of aesthetic beauty, an icon is primarily a witness to the truth of God's incarnation, of his coming and presence among us. An icon is not an idol. It does not take the place of Christ; it points to Christ. It is not a wall between us and Christ but a window to him. What the Word of God is for the ear, the icon is for the eye. The content of their message is identical. Just as the Word of God is above all an invitation to communion with him, so is the icon a call to an encounter with God in prayer. While the Old Testament heard the Word of God, the New Testament both heard and saw it: "[That which] we have heard, which we have seen with our own eyes, which we have looked upon, and our hands have handled, concerning the Word of life . . . that which we have seen and heard we declare to you, that you also may have fellowship with us; and truly our fellowship is with the Father and with his Son Jesus Christ" (1 Jn 1.1–3).

The veneration of icons was re-established in Orthodoxy by the Seventh Ecumenical Council, the Second Council of Nicaea (787), in the face of the iconoclastic reforms of the eighth and ninth centuries, and it was reaffirmed especially by a council in Constantinople in 843. The veneration of icons is not the adoration which is due to God alone but a respect which moves beyond the icon to the prototype it depicts. The veneration of icons belongs to the same category as the veneration of the cross or of the Gospel book.

Icons belong to the world of the Orthodox faith and Orthodox liturgical life. An icon is different from a mere religious picture, because it is primarily a liturgical object and belongs to the sacred art of the Church. The reality to which an icon refers is always seen in its communion with God and its eschatological transformation. An icon does not portray the transcendent enclosed in a three-dimensional world, but rather the transparency of earthly reality to divine light, history in communion with eternity. This explains the golden or blue background of icons and all their special characteristics.

The sanctification of time, or rather of our life in time, is expressed not only by the annual feasts but also in the rhythm of daily prayer, especially in monasteries. Thus, there are several services: vespers, compline, matins, and the hours (*prime, terce, sext,* and *none*). Because the day is understood as an image of eternity or of the history of salvation as a whole, these services are connected to different periods or moments in this history of salvation. For example, the vespers service represents the period of the Old Testament, while the matins service is the dawn of the Lord's messianic activity (the Divine Liturgy represents its fulfilment). *Prime* is a prayer at the beginning of the day, *terce* commemorates the descent of the Holy Spirit at Pentecost, *sext* recalls the crucifixion of our Lord, and *none* his death on the cross.

B. Fasting and Joy, Asceticism and Prayer

Paradoxically, the Orthodox Church is simultaneously a church of asceticism and a church of joy. Her feasts are jubilant, especially the celebration of Pascha—an explosion of liturgical gladness—but it is true that there are many days of fasting prescribed by the Church.

Almost every major feast is preceded by a period of preparation during which fasting and prayer play an important part.

Orthodox spirituality does not separate the cross from the resurrection or fasting from joy. In Orthodoxy, the cross is not somber but luminous because he who died on the cross triumphed over death. The power of the cross in the form of struggle against selfish, possessive passions and hatred is an anticipation of the resurrection as the joy of communion in God. "Through the cross, joy has come into all the world," says one of the prayers of the Sunday matins service.

Prayer and fasting—as struggle against selfish desires, as dominion of the spiritual over the biological, and as a school of sharing—prepare us for the joy of the Orthodox festal days.

In the Orthodox liturgical year there are four periods of fasting:

- *Great Lent* (which begins seven weeks before Pascha);

- The *Apostles' Fast* (which starts eight days after Pentecost, on a Monday, and ends on June 28, the eve of the feast of Sts Peter and Paul);

- The *Dormition Fast* (August 1–14);

- The *Nativity Fast* (November 15–December 24).

In addition, every *Wednesday* and *Friday* are observed as days of fasting (except between Christmas and Theophany, during the week following the Sunday of the Publican and the Pharisee, during Bright Week (the week following Pascha), and during the week after Pentecost until the Saturday before All Saints Sunday). Wednesday and Friday are fasting days because Christ was betrayed on Wednesday and crucified on Friday. The other days of strict fasting are the *Elevation of the Cross* (September 14), the *Beheading of St John the Baptist* (August 29), and the *Eve of Theophany* (January 5).

During Holy Week fasting is more intense as it accompanies the celebration of the passion of Christ our Redeemer.

Prayer goes together with the activity of the faithful in their everyday life, and it is recommended that, as much as possible, everyone pray without ceasing. Continuous prayer or the *Jesus Prayer* is especially prevalent in Orthodox monasteries but also among some laypeople. The collection of patristic and ascetic writings that provide the most detailed analysis of prayer is the *Philokalia*, an anthology of documents written between the fourth and fourteenth centuries. Presently, the *Philokalia* is being translated into several modern languages in Romania (twelve volumes), Great Britain, France, etc. An interest in the *Philokalia* can also be observed among a number of Western Christians (Roman Catholics, Anglicans, and Protestants).

IV. The Major Concerns of Orthodox Theology Today and the Involvement of the Orthodox in Ecumenism

Orthodox theology is being studied today mainly in Orthodox faculties of theology, in the autocephalous Orthodox Churches and in the diaspora. Almost every autocephalous Church has one or two faculties of theology and several theological journals. The Orthodox theologians of the diaspora are making a substantial contribution to the renewal and deepening of Orthodox theology.

The major concerns of Orthodox theology today can be said to reflect three main lines which are not parallel but quite often merge with one another.

A. The Return to Patristic Sources

At the first congress on Orthodox theology held in Athens in 1936, a number of theologians emphasized that the program for Orthodox theology in the future should also include a clear return to patristic sources to achieve a neo-patristic synthesis which would not be a mere repetition of the fathers but rather a deeper grasp of their spirit. This would purge Orthodox theology of the negative influences of scholasticism and of some trends in the West, where theology was not related to the life of the Church.

This return to patristic sources is most evident in Greece, Romania, Serbia, and other autocephalous Churches, as well as in the diaspora (France, USA, Great Britain). The translations of the fathers done in the West, especially in the collection "Sources Chrétiennes," have recently provided a stimulus for this.

B. The Renewed Study of Theology's Traditional Subjects; Concern for the Social Involvement of the Church and for the Encounter between Faith and Modern Culture

1. *The importance of the mystery of the Trinity* for the life of the Church and for the mystery of the human person in communion has been the subject of contemporary detailed reflection by theologians such as D. Stăniloae, C. Yannaras, K. Ware, D. Popescu, P. Christou, etc.

2. *Pneutomatological Christology* emphasizes the inseparability of the work of Christ and that of the Holy Spirit in the economy of salvation and in the life of the Church (N. Nissiotis, J. Zizioulas, D. Stăniloae, B. Bobrinskoy, etc.).

3. An *ecclesiology of communion* (eucharistic and Trinitarian) has been the major concern of a number of Orthodox theologians in the diaspora: N. Afanassief, A. Schmemann, J. Meyendorff, and especially J. Zizioulas in his book *L'être ecclésial*.

4. The *encounter between faith and modern culture* has caused Orthodox theologians to reflect on subjects such as the following:

- Faith, science, and technology (Nissiotis);

- Christian cosmology and secularizing ideologies: an Orthodox theology of the modern world (D. Stăniloae, O. Clément);

- Christian faith and morality today (C. Yannaras, O. Clément);

- Christian faith and modern art (P. Evdokimov, L. Ouspensky);

- Orthodox mission and culture (I. Bria, etc.);

- The Church and the emancipation of women (P. Evdokimov, E. Behr-Siegel);

- The ministry of the Church in today's world is a subject that concerns most Orthodox theologians at the present time.

C. The Orthodox Contribution to the Ecumenical Movement

The Orthodox Church became involved in the ecumenical movement very early on. In 1920 the Ecumenical Patriarchate of Constantinople wrote a famous encyclical to churches worldwide stating that they should not consider themselves strangers to one another but seek unity. This encyclical also refers to the necessity of establishing a League of Churches (*koinonia*), a suggestion which became a reality later, in 1948, in the form of the World Council of Churches (WCC).

Representatives of autocephalous Orthodox Churches (but not all) attended the conferences and assemblies in Lausanne in 1927 (Faith and Order), Edinburgh in 1937 (Faith and Order), Amsterdam in 1948 (the founding of the WCC), Lund in 1952 (Faith and Order), and Evanston in 1954 (WCC). At the assembly of the WCC in New Delhi in 1961, the Churches from Eastern Europe became members of the WCC.

Many Orthodox Churches are members of the WCC today and are engaged in bilateral and multilateral dialogues (with the Roman Catholic Church, the Anglican Church, the Old Catholic Church, the Reformed Church, and the Lutheran Church). Orthodoxy's main theological and spiritual contribution to the ecumenical movement today consists mainly of the following:

1. The *Orthodox sense of the living God, or of the Holy Trinity,* as the basis for the whole life of the Church, her theology, her spirituality, and her understanding of the vocation of the world and of the nature of Christian unity. The Orthodox insisted that the basis of the WCC should contain a reference not only to Christology but also to the Trinity.

2. *Cosmic and pneumatological Christology*, or the inseparability of the work of Christ from that of the Holy Spirit in the economy of salvation and in the life of the Church. This avoids separating the Church as institution from the Church as communion or "movement-event."

3. The *eucharistic view of Christian unity*, which does not place the spiritual and the social on opposing fronts.

4. The *Orthodox view of the Church and the Orthodox sense of catholicity*, which emphasize both the importance of the local church as the fullness of the Universal Church in a given place and the necessity for each local church to preserve the unity of the faith and of the sacramental life with the other local churches, which are of the same nature and fundamentally equal to one another. This ecclesiology makes it possible to avoid both the subordination of the local churches to a universal juridical center and the fragmentation of the Church into differing denominations.

5. *Liturgical life as the center of the life of the Church* and its importance for the Church's witness.

6. The *Orthodox understanding of mission as "martyria."*

7. The *unity between theology and spirituality* and the apophatic and doxological dimensions of theology.

8. The *importance of symbolic and iconic language* in expressing the faith; the unity between words and images.

9. The *importance of the ascetic and spiritual life* for all the activities of the Church.

On the other hand, in their encounter with Western Christianity, the Orthodox must appreciate and learn from its charismata:

1. The *critical sense and intellectual rigor of the West*;

2. The *Western sense* (slowly brought into balance after its going to the opposite extreme) of the *independence of the Church from the state* and of the universal Church's mobilization to help local churches;

3. The *Western sense of Christians' ethical, social, and historical responsibility*;

4. The *Western concern for mission*;

5. The *dialogue with the modern sciences* (O. Clément).

The encounter between Orthodoxy and the Churches of Africa, Asia, and North and South America, within the framework of both the World Council of Churches and in the diaspora, is a new reality and experience.

Father Dumitru Stăniloae, Teacher of Prayer[1]

F r Dumitru Stăniloae's entire life and work reveal him as a teacher of prayer. He had the great gift of bringing people closer to him, and in that closeness one could understand what could not be grasped in his theology, which, profound as it was, required a spirit of spiral thinking. Unable to follow him any longer when he spoke, at any given moment, one was left only with utter admiration. Father deepened the meaning of his words upon subsequent repetitions, with each bringing additional nuances. Yet, those who could not understand his entire theology in the classroom were able to receive further clarification by visiting him at home sometimes, or by accompanying him to the tramway station or along his commute. He lived in Bucharest at two different locations. His last address in Bucharest was 6 Cernica Street (now Dumitru Stăniloae Street), and I visited him there several times. I would call an hour or two beforehand, and he would say, "Come now," or, "I have somebody here, come later." He had a very modest home, a very small apartment, and when there were too many of us, we could barely find a place to sit. His office was like a monk's cell, crammed with books.

Sometimes, in his clarifications, when he explained things without the written text before his eyes, Father was a different man; his writing style and his oral style were entirely distinct. That is why—someone once said—if he did not put something in writing, he could not say all he had to say. His oral communication was unlike his written word:

[1]Patriarch Daniel, *Ştiinţa Mântuirii* [The science of salvation] (Bucharest: Basilica, 2014), 218–227. Lecture given at the Faculty of Orthodox Theology in Bucharest on February 5, 2003.

perhaps simpler, more accessible. He wrote extensively, but he spoke very little as a preacher. Even when it came to his own writing, he constantly emended and perfected it. When teaching doctoral courses, he would peruse his own sentences, sometimes stopping in the middle of a page. I remember that once, he pored over one such page for six hours, re-reading his own work, adding to it, and clarifying it. He would pause on a phrase and then fix his gaze on the corner of the window as if he were talking to someone else, not looking at us the entire time. Then he would begin to expound on it, further clarifying it. He was much more profound in the clarifications, as is also the case with his explanatory notes on the *Philokalia*. In fact, Fr Stăniloae did not explicate the theology of the holy fathers but deepened it, using appropriate terminology. He had a creative power and an extraordinary inspiration, starting with his own writing, which he constantly exceeded. We learned this as doctoral students in Bucharest, but the patriarchate's printing house personnel knew it even better. When they submitted the galley proofs for corrections, he would create them anew, writing something else. And he would modify even those he had personally corrected previously, one more time before the final draft, always adding a bit extra. He would say, "I'm always dissatisfied with myself."

Father's method of theologizing was also very interesting. As I mentioned before, when he did not write or have the written text in front of him, he would answer questions more simply. That is why I liked to visit him at his home. When he spoke to us directly, he tried to be more catechetical, more comprehensible. He shared with us his views on the life of the Church, on Romanian theology, on the theology of other Churches, on other confessions. In everything he said, there was theologizing, but done in a more familiar, more intelligible, way. It was a sort of mystical theology, but more of the discipleship kind, that made you feel you were not only a student but a spiritual son as well. I have made these few remarks so that the spiritual atmosphere of the years during which I was meeting with him in Bucharest can be better understood.

His wife, Preoteasa[2] Mary, was a special woman. Perhaps, besides the prayer of Fr Stăniloae, her prayer mattered the most, for she truly was a woman of profound reverence. She was very pious and spent her life fasting, helped Father, and handled all the administrative problems of their household, so that he could dedicate himself to writing. Fr Stăniloae would wake up at four o'clock in the morning and would write until nine o'clock. After that, he would welcome visitors. It was impressive to see how a man who wrote so extensively could receive as many visits as he did there in his small abode on Cernica Street, at number six.

I have mentioned this because during the rite of Proskomedia, every time I pray for Fr Dumitru Stăniloae, I also pray for Preoteasa Mary. I believe this essential detail should be known because both in the life of the priest and in the life of the teacher and the theologian, it is very important whether the family helps him or not, whether his is a family of reverence or not, whether his wife is prayerful or not. In the case of Fr Stăniloae, he himself used to say, "My wife prays more than I do." And she would reply, "Well, Dumitru says so, but he prays even while he's writing." There was a very profound spiritual communion between them, strengthened by prayer.

The testimonies that I put forth about Fr Stăniloae as a man of prayer relate only to a few moments in his life. The first is about his calling to the priesthood. Once, when he came to Strasbourg to help me with my doctoral dissertation, he made a very special confession to me about how God called him to become a priest, or a theologian. Fr Stăniloae first enrolled at the Faculty of Theology at the University of Chernivtsi in 1922, and after a year, in 1923, he enrolled at the Faculty of Letters in Bucharest. During vacation, he went home, and his mother told him, "Dumitru, I dreamed something special about you." He asked, "What was it?" to which she replied, "I had a dream in which someone told me, 'Make priestly vestments and gift them to the Church on Dumitru's behalf.' So," his mother added, "I understood

[2]The Romanian title of honor used to refer to a priest's wife.—Trans.

that to mean that you should become a priest." "I do not know if that is what it means," was his answer.

He went back to college and began to realize that the school was very poor spiritually. So, in the following year, he returned to the Faculty of Theology in Chernivtsi, from which he graduated in 1927. In 1928 he defended his doctoral dissertation titled "On the Life and Work of Patriarch Dositheus of Jerusalem." He was ordained a priest in 1932. The Theological Academy in Sibiu did not have a professor of dogmatics at one point, so he was asked to help the Department of Dogmatics as its rector. It was then that he began to translate from Androutsos' *Dogmatics*, and later he undertook the translation of St Gregory Palamas' work, surpassing Androutsos, for at that moment he began to write a neo-patristic dogmatic theology.

My first conclusion is that Fr Stăniloae's calling to become a priest was deeply connected with his mother's prayer. We do not always realize the importance of prayer because very often we are tempted to engage in a more didactic, more scholastic theology. However, each of us represents a spiritual array of gifts received from others. We acquire them from parents, teachers, colleagues more pious than us, believers meeker than us; and this energetic, spiritual presence of others in our own spiritual formation is immense. Yet, how we receive, restructure, or build inside our soul that which we have gathered from others makes us who we are as a person, as a distinct way of being and of processing the influences we have garnered. Personally, I believe that Father's propensity for prayer came from his mother's prayer. So, faith is transmitted energetically and spiritually to an extent as well, and not only didactically. The person who prays in the family influences the others, even if there is no theologizing. The one who prays exerts an influence on others by his or her own presence as a prayerful being.

There is a well-known story about St Seraphim of Sarov and a young student who went to see the saint because he had a very serious problem. The student found St Seraphim sleeping in a clearing, near the skete. He did not wake the saint up, but he watched him, prayed, waited, and suddenly arrived at the solution of his problem. He made his way back without arousing the saint from his sleep, for he had found the resolution to his matter. What was it that inspired him? The presence of the prayerful person! That was Fr Stăniloae's case with the advice from his mother's dream of gifting the Church with priestly vestments!

The second testimony comes from what Fr Dumitru Stăniloae said about his years in prison. A delegation of the World Council of Churches, on behalf of the Faith and Order Commission headed by Lukas Fischer—who was the committee's coordinator for twenty years—came here to Romania in 1963. Lukas Fischer asked, "Where is Fr Stăniloae?" Father had just been released, and he went to meet the Western theologians. It was, according to Fischer, a very emotional atmosphere, but there could not be too much talking or too many questions put because there were all kinds of observers around. The Westerners asked him, "So, how was it in there?" Father replied, "As it is in there."

Father worked for a while as a proofreader of theological journals until someone in the Department of Religious Affairs read his article "Thou Shalt Not Kill" and asked, "Who wrote this article? Have him come here. How is the man just a proofreader when he is so talented? We ought to give him a different job; look how well he writes."

After he was released from prison, Father was "rehabilitated" after a while. Once, when he was allowed by the communist establishment to represent Romanian theology at international gatherings, he was asked, "What marked you the most during your years of detention?" Fr Stăniloae replied, "In prison I learned to pray," which shocked the audience. So prison became for him a school of prayer. The dialogue continued: "How so—you didn't pray before?" "I did," Father said, "but I prayed out of custom, out of habit. In jail, when you do not know whether you will get out alive or not, connection with God is your only chance not to lose your identity and hope, so then true prayer really becomes the vital breath of the soul, not in a metaphorical sense but in an existential one." So, it is a type of existential prayer, made from one's inmost being; it is not superficial, mechanical prayer.

The third confession I wish to make about Father as a man of prayer was inspired by an Orthodox meeting in France, which took place in Amiens near Paris in the autumn of 1977. It was a congress of Orthodox Christians in Western Europe that was organized—if I am not mistaken—every year or once every two years. Fr Stăniloae was invited as the keynote speaker at Amiens. After the congress, we went together to the St Sergius Theological Institute in Paris, where many young Romanians later studied, some of whom are hierarchs today.

This institute had two or three modest buildings, with dormitory rooms for about twenty students. That weekend, some of the students of the St Sergius Institute were on campus, while others had gone home. Father and I, citizens of socialist Romania, had no money to pay for a hotel. As such, we asked for accommodation there in the two-bed dormitory room of a couple of students who had gone home for a few days. So we shared the room, and right before bedtime Fr Stăniloae said, "Let's pray." And we prayed. In the prayer position, Father said the Trisagion prayers, but because we did not have a Horologion with us, he began to pray freely. A simple, profound, delicate prayer without any elaborate theological ideas. He said only, "Lord, help us! Lord, be with us! Lord, forgive us!" just as a child talks to his father—a simplicity that can be seen only in country people who have never gone through a theological school but who pray with much conviction and faith in stunning intimacy and familiarity with God.

The next day, I dared ask him, "Father, forgive me, but you really surprised me when you prayed so simply last night." He replied, "The greatest temptation is to theologize during prayer, because then you are not talking to the Lord; you are talking with yourself about him." Later, over the years, I asked Fr Cleopas of Sihăstria Monastery about the temptation of theologizing (theological discourse) during prayer. And he clarified it for me based on quotes from the holy fathers of the Church. So I would say that Fr Stăniloae prayed like a student who is not a theologian. But it is precisely this form of prayer that shows us that, no matter how much theological learning we possess, if the prayer learned at home in our childhood endures in our soul, that is a sign that our prayer is authentic, and that our stance before God the Father is akin to that of a child before the parent.

I had the opportunity of seeing Fr Dumitru Stăniloae celebrate church services several times as a priest. There was such a stunning contrast between his lofty theology and his humble way of serving! At first glance there was nothing impressive, but upon contemplating his way of serving, one could see just how remarkable his authenticity was. He served as if he were a simple village priest with very modest theological training. Fr Stăniloae was not at all concerned with his appearance, his gestures, or how his voice sounded—he had a very faint chanting voice. He was very natural, lowly, humble, and when he preached, he would deliver a substantial but simple catechesis, so that anyone could understand the essence of faith as life in God. He greatly emphasized God's love for us. This truth resurfaced again and again in his sermons. He would then point out just how helpful prayer is. His homily would be a meditation with practical, easy tips from which anyone could gather that attending the prayers of the Church is a great gain for the spiritual life.

Reflecting on the way Father served, I realize that the most salient characteristics of his manner of serving as a priest were humility and simplicity. But his humility arose from his being overwhelmed by the presence of God. It is a great gift to feel the presence of God's holiness when one serves in the holy altar! In addition, when celebrating services, Fr Stăniloae conveyed a strong conviction which revealed him to be the bearer of a grace palpably present—yet it was not a spectacular presence, forcibly imposed on others, but a spiritual one perceived as pacification of the soul.

Sometimes I compared Fr Stăniloae to two other fathers of Romania, whom he resembled astoundingly when he served as a priest. He was much like Fr Sophian [Boghiu], who was not a great speaker either, but whose spiritual advice was mighty because of Christ's Spirit indwelling him. Fr Stăniloae had something in common with Fr Paisius [Olaru] of Sihăstria as well. So what Fr Stăniloae shared with Fr Sophian and Fr Paisius was the pacifying and hallowing word, the bearer of the Holy Spirit. I realize that in his liturgical ministry Fr Stăniloae lived very intensely in the presence of Christ, in his mystical love of the Church during the Divine Liturgy. Every so often he expressed his regret for not having been a parish priest for a while longer, saying, "If I had been a parish priest for a long time, that would have influenced my theology even more."

In his testament to the youth from the end of his life, sometime in 1992–1993, Fr Stăniloae revealed that he realized in his old age that he should have linked his theology more to the importance of philanthropic work, to the service of his neighbor. Continuously dissatisfied with his accomplishments, with great humility he regretted that he had not sufficiently merged his spiritual theology with missionary theology. However, we now know the great contribution his profound theology brought to the formation of our parish, monastery, and university priests.

In a way, the theology of Fr Stăniloae can be called a theology of prayer in its entirety, as we find in his works numerous references to its importance, its benefits, and its necessity. For example, in his book *Spirituality and Communion in the Orthodox Liturgy*, he affirms:

> Prayer is the mystery of people's union with God. It is a mystery that comes about every time a person prays attentively. The one who arrives at unceasing prayer lives this mystery continually. Through prayer, the individual dives into the endless depths of God, who, as a loving Person, remains distinct from the one who prays, and keeps him distinct as well. That is why prayer endows people with immeasurable and endless strength, even strength for more prayer, just as people receive strength—to an infinitely smaller degree— even from the fellows with whom they partake of communion. It is akin to our own being supported by the presence of another person

communicating his or her own spirituality. How much more does the presence of God strengthen us in prayer! When people make the effort to pray, God welcomes them, increasing their effort and drawing them into the depths of his divine life and power, from which they gain new strength.

We must remember then that prayer is the work of God in those who seek him. Prayer is not only our activity, because when we are in communion with God, *prayer becomes his working presence in us.* This truth is expressed in the Orthodox Liturgy, first performed by Christ, who also co-opts us into holy service. "For you are the *One who both offers* and is *offered,* the *One who is received* and is distributed," prays the celebrant priest during the chanting of the Cherubic Hymn. The moment we place ourselves in communion with God, he works in us and through us, for us and for others.

In this regard, in his *Brief Spoken Dogmatics: Dialogues at Cernica* (2nd rev. ed., Sibiu, 2000), Father speaks about his personal experience with prayer:

> I have sought God in the people of my village, then in books, ideas, and symbols. But that gave me neither peace nor love. One day, I discovered in the holy fathers of the Church that it is truly possible to meet God in prayer. And I heard him say to me, "Dare to understand that I love you." Then, patiently, I set out to work. Thus, I gradually understood that the Lord is near, that he loves me, and that by brimming with his love, my heart opens to others. I understood that love is communion with God and my neighbor. And without this communion, the world is nothing but sadness, ruin, destruction, massacre. If the world only knew to dwell in this love, then it would truly know life eternal.

In closing, it can be surmised that the work of Fr Dumitru Stăniloae is a liturgy of the mind and heart in many respects, a theology of prayer and communion with God, and he remains for us all *a teacher of prayer.*

PART II

The Communion of Saints is a Fount of Romanian Unity in Thought and Feeling[1]

B eloved pilgrims,
    We live today moments of special blessing and spiritual joy granted to us by the Holy Spirit by the prayers of Saint Demetrius the New, the protector of Bucharest, and of St Callinicus of Cernica (1787–1868), who reposed 150 years ago.

The holy hierarch Callinicus of Cernica was born on October 7, 1787, in the city of Bucharest, in the parish of St Bessarion's Church. The mother of the saint, the very pious Flora, instilled in her children love of God and zeal for the spiritual, her two sons choosing to don the angelic habit of the monastic life. Toward the end of her life, she became a nun and was given the name Philothea at Pasărea Monastery, where she reposed in the Lord on November 8, 1833.

In March 1807, at the age of twenty, the young Constantine followed his inner calling and joined the community of Cernica Monastery, receiving the name Callinicus at his tonsure. Cernica's spiritual atmosphere was animated by the hesychast movement of St Paisius

---

[1]Patriarch Daniel, "Comuniunea sfinților este izvor de unitate românească în cuget și simțiri" [The communion of saints is a fount of Romanian unity in thought and feeling], October 25, 2018, Basilica News Agency, accessed November 26, 2019, https://basilica.ro/patriarhul-daniel-catre-pelerini-comuniunea-sfintilor-este-izvor-de-unitate-romaneasca-in-cuget-si-simtiri/. In his October 25 address to the pilgrims, His Beatitude Patriarch Daniel emphasized that present at the patronal feast of the patriarchal cathedral were the relics of "two guardians of our capital," the communion of saints being "a fount of Romanian unity in thought and feeling."

(Velichkosvky, d. 1794) of Neamţ, which was subsequently maintained by the disciples of Abbot George of Cernica (d. 1806).

On October 14, 1818, the brethren of Cernica elected the venerable Callinicus as their abbot, especially appreciating his qualities as a true shepherd of souls. During the thirty-two years (1818–1850) of his abbacy, he founded the new church of the monastery, dedicated to St George, and the whole assembly of cells; he restored and painted the church of St Nicholas from the monastery's great islet; and he built new monastic cells, a new church, and a library, so that during his tenure Cernica became an important center of Orthodox culture and spirituality.

His virtues and accomplishments paved his way to becoming a hierarch, but St Callinicus repeatedly refused the metropolitan dignity. However, at the insistence of the ruler Barbu Dimitrie Ştirbei (1849–1856), he was enthroned bishop of Râmnicu Vâlcea, his ordination as hierarch being celebrated in Bucharest's metropolitan cathedral on October 26, 1850—168 years ago.

The luminous image of the holy hierarch Callinicus of Cernica remained enshrined in the people's reverence as one of the wisest Romanian shepherds of the nineteenth century for the way in which he blended the tradition of the holy hesychasts' uninterrupted prayer with the missionary fervor of holy founders and builders of holy places, of Christian culture and philanthropy.

A shepherd and an ardent man of prayer, a miracle worker and a healer, a wise spiritual guide and a compassionate priest, St Callinicus was also a learned man, a good organizer, a talented builder of churches for monasteries and parishes, a founder of Râmnicu Vâlcea's diocesan cathedral, a devout Romanian patriot, and an eager activist for the union of the Romanian Principalities in 1859.

Beloved pilgrims,

The shrine holding the holy relics of St Callinicus of Cernica was deposited next to the shrine with the relics of St Demetrius the New, the protector of Bucharest. Therefore, we have two protectors of our capital, who, despite not knowing each other during their lives, share the same spiritual work of healing and guidance through unceasing prayer before the throne of the Holy Trinity for all who venerate their relics in faith and reverence.

In this year, 2018, in which we honor the unity of faith and nation and commemorate the founders of the Great Union of 1918,[2] we can enjoy this moment of unity in prayer and the intercession of the two great saints for the salvation of our souls.

A profound and complete celebratory centennial of the Great Union can only be achieved through joint prayer, joy, and spiritual peace, all of which are gifts that God bestows upon us not only through the mediation and care of the Church's saints but also through our fruitful co-practicing of Christian virtues for the good of the Romanian people.

We ask the holy hierarch Callinicus of Cernica and St Demetrius the New to give help and health, peace, and joy to all the pilgrims for their living faith, confession, profound devoutness, and love of the Church. At the same time, we pray that God will bequeath his rich mercy to our brothers in suffering and need and give us all much courage to confess our faith and to confront the trials of life.

Through the prayers of our saints Callinicus of Cernica and Demetrius the New, the guardians of Bucharest, Lord Jesus Christ, our God, have mercy on us and save us. Amen!

---

[2] The Great Union of 1918 refers to the unification of Transylvania, Bessarabia, and Bukovina with the Kingdom of Romania.

Savant and Saint:
The Venerable Dionysius Exiguus, Father of the Christian Era[1]

Your eminences and graces, reverend and venerable fathers, distinguished guests, beloved brothers and sisters in the Lord,

With the choicest of joy, we are pleased to announce that the Holy Synod of the Romanian Orthodox Church, in its working session of July 9, 2008, has approved the canonization as a saint of the holy Dionysius Exiguus, "the Humble," or "the Little," after examining the report drawn up by the Synodal Commission for the Canonization of Romanian Saints, in connection with referral no. 5113/2008 of the Metropolitanate of Muntenia and Dobruja.

The glorification of St Dionysius Exiguus, bearing our signature, is based on supporting arguments of a canonical, historical, pastoral, and missionary nature that highlight the Orthodoxy of his faith; his pure and holy life; the sustenance he gave to the monasticism of Dobruja; and his erudition and contribution to the knowledge and exchange of values between Eastern and Western Christianity through the translation of the holy fathers and of the holy canons, and even to chronology, being acknowledged as the father of the Christian era.

[1]Patriarch Daniel, "Savant și Sfânt – Cuviosul Dionisie Exiguul, Părintele Erei Creștine" [Savant and saint: The venerable Dionysius Exiguus, father of the Christian era], November 2, 2009, Basilica News Agency, accessed November 27, 2019, https://basilica.ro/cuvantul-preafericitului-parinte-patriarh-daniel-adresat-participantilor-prezenti-la-proclamarea-locala-a-canonizarii-sfantului-cuvios-dionisie-exiguul-constanta-2-noiembrie-2008/.

Sermon addressed to the participants at the local proclamation of the glorification of Fr Dionysius Exiguus, Constanța, November 2, 2008.

St Dionysius Exiguus lived between AD 465 and AD 545 and was a great personality of Romanian Christianity. He marked universal culture by proposing the reckoning of years beginning with the birth of Christ, the Redeemer of the world. Researchers who have studied the theological contributions of this monk from Dobruja have characterized him as a "Dacian-Roman scholar" or an "adornment of our ancestral Church." The canonization of this erudite Dobruja monk represents both the confirmation of his Orthodox faith and holy life as well as the acknowledgment of his contribution to the history of Christianity.

The fact that St Dionysius Exiguus was a native of Dobruja is beyond any doubt. In addition to the unambiguous testimony of the historian Cassiodorus, we have evidence from his monastic brethren, the community of Scythian monks, with whom Dionysius Exiguus kept a close connection throughout his life. In this respect, we also have his own testimony in the preface to the translation of the *Synodal Epistle of St Cyril of Alexandria* addressed to his spiritual father along with whom and as a result of whose "holy striving" he secured the path to the divine truths.

His exceptional theological preparation "recommended" that he be summoned to Rome by Pope Gelasius (r. 492–496), who needed someone who had a great command of the Latin and Greek languages, something which is of great relevance, considering that his erudition had become known as far away as Rome.

In the winter of 496 and 497 and shortly after Pope Gelasius' death, Dionysius arrived in Rome, where he was received at St Anastasia's Monastery. The abbot of the monastery, who was in charge of the pontifical chancellery and archive maintenance, entrusted him with the responsibility of the chancellery archives, which St Dionysius Exiguus reorganized, becoming the "new founder of the pontifical archives." His activity as an archivist was the foundation of his later work as a translator, canonist, and archive organizer.

Ever since the beginning of his scholarly activity, the venerable Dionysius Exiguus testified faithfully to the Orthodox faith by translating from Greek the holy fathers and the holy canons of the first four ecumenical councils.

Three great virtues embellished the life of St Dionysus Exiguus: the Orthodox faith, preserved with piety throughout his life; the humility of his heart; and his love of God and men.

Cassiodorus, a former prime minister of King Theodoric, wrote about the humble Romanian forefather with the precision of a chancellor, offering a characterization of unparalleled beauty, marked primarily by respect, appreciation, and admiration, and also as a message for future generations:

> Even today the universal Church gives birth to illustrious men who shine with the adornment of true dogmas. For there lived in our day Monk Dionysius, by birth a Scythian, but a Roman in character, most learned in both languages, proving through his deeds the spiritual steadiness he had gathered from the Lord's books. He researched the Scriptures with such great zeal and understood them so, that whenever he was asked, he had the answer ever ready, giving it without any hesitation. . . . In him there was much simplicity together with wisdom, humility together with admonition, temperance together with eloquence; yet he considered himself the lowliest of servants, although he was undoubtedly worthy of royal companionship. May he, who used to pray with us, now intercede for us that we may be helped by his merits, with the prayer which strengthened us here on earth.

Even during his lifetime, Dionysius Exiguus had become a recognized authority, always assuming the same stance: the consolidation of the links between Christian and Roman values, the clear and orderly translations of the most important documents of the time, the paschal calculation, and especially the proposal that time be measured from the birth of our Lord Jesus Christ. Thus, as the initiator of Christian chronology, St Dionysius Exiguus is considered the father of the Christian age; and as a Latin translator and presenter of the holy canons, he is also considered the "Father of Church Law." He departed to the Lord, probably at the Vivarium in Calabria, Italy, in the year 545.

The Chronological System of St Dionysius Exiguus: The Chronology of the Civilized World

St Dionysius Exiguus proposed a new chronology of the history of the world, beginning with Christ and not with Diocletian. The reason was, he said, that while Diocletian persecuted Christians, Christ is "the beginning of our hope" and "the cause of our redemption" through his salvific suffering. In this respect, in 526 he answered the official call of the papal court, reaffirming the authority of the Council of Nicaea and the dates set by it, and established the beginning of calculating the years from the birth of the Savior. The chronological system of St Dionysius Exiguus, calculated and proposed during his lifetime, thus became the chronology of the civilized world.

From among the multitude of hierarchs, monks, and lay Christians native to the blessed land of Dobruja and known for the strength of their faith, who followed in the footsteps of the Apostle Andrew, St Dionysius Exiguus ("the Humble") is, along with St John Cassian, a personality of the universal Christian Church. If we only considered the reformation of chronology through the introduction of a new reference point in the counting of years from the birth of our Lord Jesus Christ, the Redeemer of mankind, the universality of this contribution would suffice in making the name of St Dionysius Exiguus known to all Romanian believers. But besides this contribution springing from his erudition, there was his unchanging humility that illuminated his holy life, a quality that was recognized and greatly cherished by his contemporaries.

Because St Dionysius called himself *Exiguus*, meaning "the insignificant" or "humble," thus shrouding his virtues with humility, our Church has added to her calendar him who considered himself "insignificant," hence signifying his holiness and wisdom for having greatly appreciated time united with Eternity and people united with Christ, the divine Wisdom.

The local proclamation in Constanța on November 2, 2008, of the canonization of St Dionysius Exiguus after the solemn proclamation in Bucharest on October 26, 2008, is a special blessing for Dobruja 130 years after its return to the Motherland, Romania (1878–2008). We pray that the Lord, who "is the same yesterday, today, and forever" (Heb 13.8), will bless Dobruja and the entire Romanian nation, the bearer and cultivator of the apostolic faith received from St Andrew the Apostle, to the glory of God and the salvation of mankind. Amen!

† DANIEL, Patriarch of the Romanian Orthodox Church

Politics Enlightened by Faith: Neagoe Basarab, a Christian Pedagogue Prince[1]

N eagoe Basarab (1512–1521) ascended to the throne of Wallachia during a very turbulent period when all Christendom feared the Ottoman Empire, which threatened the freedom of so many peoples.

The turmoil and confusion in the Ottoman Empire created by the battles between Bayezid II and Selim for the title of sultan somehow made it easier for Neagoe Basarab to be enthroned.

The new prince of Wallachia had much to do in the country; but first, he had to silence the murmuring voices alleging that he was not "of royal blood" and that the princely throne was not rightfully his.

Yet, the thorniest issue in his diplomatic work was external in nature. Given the muddy circumstances of that time, the voivode sought, on the one hand, to maintain peace with the Turks by paying a tribute, which impeded their interference in the domestic affairs of the country; on the other hand, he maintained intense diplomatic relations with all the political forces hostile to the Ottoman Empire, such that Wallachia would not have been isolated if they were to face the Turks and could have received, should it have been necessary, help from those Christian powers that were traditionally allies of the Romanian principalities in the fight against the Ottoman Empire. Such a situation was obviously quite difficult, but perhaps the most promising in the complex circumstances of that era. In this respect,

---

[1]Daniel, Mitropolitul Munteniei si Dobrogei, *Dăruire și Dăinuire: Raze și chipuri de lumina din istoria și spiritualitatea românilor* (Iași: Trinitas, 2005).

the relations with the Kingdom of Hungary and with Transylvania—which held a special, almost autonomous position within the Kingdom of Hungary—constituted the outstanding concern of Neagoe Basarab's foreign policy in the Christian world. The Wallachian lord forged a relationship of friendship and good neighborliness with Louis II Jagiellon, King of Hungary, who bequeathed him the domain of Geoagiu de Jos along with about twenty villages on June 9, 1517. The cities of Sibiu and Brașov had economic and commercial ties with Wallachia during the reign of Neagoe Basarab as well. From his correspondence with the Saxons of Sibiu, it appears that he also provided them with some political information. Most of the letters, however, address issues of commercial interest, as the Saxons were sophisticated silversmiths at that time. Thus, the master craftsmen John and Celestin were commissioned to create seventeen silver-gilt chalices in Wallachia. The prince had similar relations with the people of Brașov, whom he invited, in a letter dated April 24, 1520, to the second opening of Argeș Monastery, as during its first opening the exterior had not yet been completed.

Neagoe Basarab sought to establish diplomatic ties with other states interested in the anti-Ottoman fight, and two of them were the Venetian Republic and the Papal States. Thus, in 1518, Hieronymus Matievici was sent with a message to Venice, where he was welcomed with great warmth. That was the first time a messenger from the land of Wallachia journeyed to the Republic of St Mark. The West recognized in Neagoe Basarab a force that could enter its political combinations and interests, and not a docile subject to the Turks.

From what has been said so far, it can be surmised that the voivode's main interest lay in the country to whose throne he had acceded, and that he could not be indifferent to the unrest in and expansionist plans of the Crescent.

Still, Neagoe Basarab remains in the history of the Romanian people as an important figure, especially through his cultural and religious activity, a realm in which he excelled. The Wallachian prince's resoluteness on this front had a political substratum as well, and that was to strengthen the unity of the Orthodox Christians in their struggle against the Turks.

There is no exaggeration in affirming that Neagoe was the supporter of all the Orthodox, from the Carpathian Mountains to Syria and from the Ionian Sea to Egypt. The name of the Romanian voivode was commemorated at the time in countless monasteries in the Balkans, in Greece, and in Asia Minor.

In the *Life of St Niphon, Patriarch of Constantinople,* the chronicler Gabriel, *protos* (first/premier monk) of Mount Athos, referred to the donations given by Neagoe Basarab to numerous Eastern monasteries by writing:

> What might we add more especially, apart from the things and the monasteries that he has sponsored? Let us say that all of them, in Europe, Thrace, Ellada, Achaia, Illyria, Campania, Ilisos, Mysia, Macedonia, Tetulia, Sirmium, Lugdunum, Paphalgonia, Dalmatia, and far and wide from the east to the west, and from the south to the north—all the holy churches were nourished by him and were bestowed a great deal of mercy all around. And he was kind not only to Christians but also to the heathen, proving to be a merciful father to all, akin to the heavenly Lord, who makes his sun rise and sends his rain upon the good and the evil alike, as the holy Scriptures show.

What is particularly impressive is the support given by the prince to the monasteries of Holy Mount Athos. He renovated and granted gifts, items of worship, and annual donations to monasteries such as Koutloumousiou, the Great Lavra of St Athanasius, Iviron, Pantokrator, Vatopedi, Xeropotamou, Chilandar, Rossikon, Xenophontos, and Zografou. The annual sums of money were very generous—for example, Vatopedi and Iviron received a yearly donation of 200 thalers; Chilandar, 7000 asprons every year at Epiphany; Koutloumousiou,

10,000 asprons; Zographou, 3,000 asprons annually; Xenophontos, 2,000 asprons; Rossikon, 4,000 asprons annually.[2]

Moreover, in Constantinople he covered the church of the patriarchate and renovated the monks' cells; he also provided Jerusalem, Mount Sinai, Meteora on the rocks of Thessaly, Treskavec, Kosinitza, and Cathesca-Cuceina Monasteries with many and various benefits. In Ascalon, in Syria, he reinforced the fortress with an armed observation tower.

In his homeland, Neagoe Basarab gave donations to some monasteries and renovated others. He covered the roof of Tismana Monastery in lead; finished the construction of Dealu Monastery; helped the monasteries of Cotmeana, Vişina, Dobruşa, and Cozia; and brought the icon of St George from Constantinople to Nucet Monastery.

He also brought to Wallachia the relics of St Niphon, patriarch of Constantinople and former metropolitan of Hungaro-Wallachia, who, because of a conflict with Prince Radu the Great, had had to leave the country and had gone to Mount Athos, where he fell asleep in the Lord at Dionysiou Monastery. The translation of the relics of St Niphon, the former teacher of Neagoe Basarab, is described in detail by the same Gabriel, protos of Mount Athos, in the *Life of St Niphon, Patriarch of Constantinople*. The holy remains were brought from the Holy Mountain in a solemn procession and placed above the grave of Radu the Great at Dealu Monastery, after which intercessory prayers for forgiveness were offered in an all-night vigil. They were then sent back to Dionysius Monastery enshrined in a silver-gilt reliquary bejeweled with precious gems and enamel—a most resplendent gift from Neagoe.

In gratitude to their benefactor, the monks of Dionysiou presented the prince with the head and hand of St Niphon as holy relics, "and he [Neagoe]," Protos Gabriel wrote, "received them with great joy as Moses had received the tables of the law and took them wherever he

---

[2]The size and value of these monetary units varied over several centuries, but the thaler was the more valuable of the two, and at one point it was worth 40 asprons; purchasing power also varied, but one example is the sale of an orchard for one thaler in 1594, and another is the sale of a house for 2,110 asprons in 1485.

went, in the courtyard and in the church; and on the road he carried them as Israel carried the ark of the covenant."

The culmination of Neagoe Basarab's reign, something which resounds through the ages, is, of course, the construction of Argeș Monastery, which was consecrated with great festivities on August 15, 1517. Its consecration was an occasion for the meeting of many hierarchs—shepherds of subjugated nations—and effectively contributed to the strengthening of Christian solidarity.

The festivity of the consecration was beyond description. Along with Prince Neagoe, Lady Despina, their royal children, and all the boyars, an impressive synaxis participated as well: Theoleptus, patriarch of Constantinople; four metropolitans of the East; Metropolitan Macarius of Hungaro-Wallachia; many abbots from Mount Athos, led by their protos, Gabriel; and numerous clergy members of the nation.

Gabriel the protos wrote, "And when the Divine Liturgy ended, he gave a great feast in which all rejoiced, and he bestowed gifts upon them all, the great and the small, the poor and the widows . . . and to all he fitly gave alms."

Indeed, Curtea de Argeș Monastery is not a mere foundation of a ruler; it is a masterpiece of the Romanian people's artistic spirit, which represents the endless resources of our nation, its elegance and harmony, its mastery and skill.

As a witness to the consecration of this monastery, Gabriel the *protos* states about it, "And so we can truly say that it is not as big and sobornical as either Solomon's Zion or St Sophia erected by Emperor Justinian, but that it surpasses them both in beauty."

When he visited the church in the middle of the seventeenth century, the Syrian Paul of Aleppo, deeply enchanted by its beauty, characterized it as "a marvelous object for the mind and unlike any other monastery of this principality."

Therefore, the church of Argeș Monastery is and will be a testimony of the creative genius of a nation that loves beauty. The special concern of the voivode for this precious artifact of Romanian culture can be seen in the inscription on the stone slab laid on his tomb, where, among other things, is written, "I entreat those whom God shall wish to come after us, to safekeep this place of rest for my bones, that it may be undefiled."

Curtea de Argeş Monastery is the true crown of Neagoe Basarab, the halo that time cannot blot out, the most important testimony of his cultural and religious preoccupations. He recorded his military, political, and cultural vision in his most important work, the only work of its kind in the Romanian culture, *Învăţăturile lui Neagoe Basarab către fiul său, Teodosie* [The admonitions of Neagoe Basarab to his son, Theodosius], which further contribute to the shaping of this ruler's personality and to the better knowledge of his reign.

A leading contemporary researcher, Dan Zamfirescu, states:

> These *Admonitions* are at once a work of instruction and of religious and moral education, a breviary of Eastern ascetics and mysticism, an anthology of pedagogical texts selected and organized according to the general purpose of the work, a treatise of the political theory of Byzantine monarchy by divine right, an original manual of the theory and technique of modern authoritative governance, a synthesis of Romanian diplomatic experience and thought, a book on military tactics and strategy, and one of the most authentic and valuable literary creations in Romanian culture.

Neagoe Basarab's choice ecclesial instruction allowed him to quote from St John Chrysostom and other church fathers and to use information from the holy Scriptures with amazing ease. "He," Nicholas Iorga affirmed, "is the first Romanian prince deeply imbued with Byzantine culture."

Indeed, Neagoe Basarab had a broad vision and he honored the Byzantine heritage, which represented the past, but he was also a prince of his time, an innovator with ties to the new culture of the Renaissance. Although he never had to defend his nation with the sword as St Stephen the Great had, Neagoe Basarab—through his rich and continuous activity and concern for Christianity in the Orient and the Balkans—emerges as a fighter of the spirit who supported European culture and the legacy of brilliant Byzantium.

In 1521, after a nine-year reign, the voivode took up his habitation in the kingdom of God, leaving behind abundant light, whose rays reach us today. His body was laid to rest in the burial chamber of his magnificent Curtea de Argeș edifice.

Regarded in the context of its epoch, the reign of Neagoe Basarab can be considered a Romanian spiritual rebirth. The prince was a worthy son of the country to which he belonged and for whose cultural advancement he labored greatly. He will forever live on through the heritage he bequeathed to posterity and as an exhortation for the generations of today and tomorrow to serve the Romanian nation.

Curtea de Argeș Cathedral: A Paschal Torch through the Ages[1]

The 500th anniversary of the Cathedral of Curtea de Argeș Monastery (1517–2017) is a great occasion to offer pious thanks to God for the gifts abundantly poured over this holy place and to commemorate with gratitude and reverence the founder of this edifice, the holy voivode Neagoe Basarab.

The reign of the right-believing Wallachian voivode Neagoe Basarab (1512–1521) was marked by his wise, diligent, and generous spirit for preserving the Christian faith in times of burdensome Ottoman domination. He was the founder and benefactor of many places of worship in Wallachia, such as the Cathedral of the Dormition of the Mother of God in Curtea de Argeș, the Metropolitan Cathedral of the Ascension in Târgoviște, Snagov Monastery's Church, Ostrov-Călimănești Hermitage, Dealu Monastery, Tismana Monastery, Cozia Monastery, Glavacioc Monastery, and others.

A magnanimous supporter of Christians in the Orient and the Balkans, of the monasteries of Mount Athos, of Mount Sinai, and of Meteora perched on the precipices of Thessaly in Greece, of the Patriarchate of Jerusalem, and of the Patriarchate of Constantinople, St Neagoe Basarab remains in the consciousness of our nation's history and that of the Orthodox Church in general as a great Orthodox Christian

---

[1] Patriarch Daniel, "O făclie de Înviere peste veacuri – Catedrala de la Curtea de Argeș" [Curtea de Argeș Cathedral: A paschal torch through the ages], September 26, 2017, Basilica News Agency, accessed November 26, 2019, https://basilica.ro/o-faclie-de-inviere-peste-veacuri-catedrala-de-la-curtea-de-arges/. Homily on the 500th anniversary (1517–2017) of the Cathedral of Curtea de Argeș, founded by St Neagoe Basarab.

prince with a broad vision, a defender of the Byzantine heritage, and a great connoisseur of the Western European culture of his time.

Still, the culmination of his reign, which echoes over the centuries, is the building of the church of Curtea de Argeş Monastery, located in the heart of the old capital of Wallachia's first rulers. Built in the first half of the sixteenth century, between 1512 and 1517, on the site of the metropolitan church's old chapel founded by Voivode Vlad the Dragon, the church of Neagoe Basarab was consecrated with great festivity on August 15, 1517, on the feast of the Dormition of the Mother of God, the patronal feast of the metropolitanate's old church, which was preserved and then passed on to the new foundation.

A reflection of Neagoe Basarab's fascination with the beauty of Byzantine art, the church of Curtea de Argeş Monastery is a valuable architectural masterpiece owing to the skill of the master craftsmen who knew how to combine and harmonize different structures and designs with precious materials and splendid decorations in a distinctive style that ensured the church's uniqueness.

The interior painting, of rare artistic beauty, was completed by the Romanian painter Dobromir of Târgovişte in 1526. Fragments of this masterpiece are kept at the National Museum of Art in Bucharest. Repaired several times throughout its history, the church today represents the image of the restoration completed in 1885 by the French architect André Lecompte du Noüy, who later settled permanently in our country and was buried in the cemetery of the Holy Voivodes of Flămânzeşti Church, Argeş.

An ancient monastic hearth, a brilliant princely edifice, a royal necropolis and episcopal seat, the Cathedral of Curtea de Argeş has proven through the ages that it has the vocation of interweaving time with eternity, art with spirituality, and national ethos with openness to the universal.

Starting in 1914, the kings and queens of Romania were laid to rest in the cathedral of Curtea de Argeş: Carol I and Elisabeth, Ferdinand and Mary, and, not far from the church, King Carol II.

The communist regime did away with Curtea de Argeş Cathedral's status as a cathedral in 1948, so the old princely edifice was relegated to being a simple monastery. However, in 1990, after the Church was given the freedom to express and organize herself according to her calling, the Holy Synod of the Romanian Orthodox Church decided to re-establish the Episcopate of Argeş, and His Eminence Callinicus Argatu, who today bears the title "Argeşeanul" [of Argeş], was elected and enthroned bishop of this diocese (November 18, 1990), with the patriarchal mandate of reorganizing the newly re-established diocese with its headquarters at Curtea de Argeş Monastery.

With great striving and missionary zeal, the new bishop of Argeş carried out in this diocese rich pastoral, liturgical, cultural, educational, social, and missionary activity, serving "in season and out of season" (Tim 4.2) the Church of Christ of the house of Basarab.

In 2009, as a result of our proposal and with the Holy Synod's approval, the Diocese of Argeş and Muscel was raised to the rank of archdiocese, and His Eminence Callinicus became the archbishop of Argeş and Muscel on September 26, 2009, a date which coincided with the local proclamation of the canonization of the holy voivode Neagoe Basarab, of St John of Vicina, and of St John the New of Muscel. The three glorified saints were a ruler, a hierarch, and a hesychast monk, for whose canonization His Eminence Archbishop Callinicus keenly tended to the composition of the services, the painting of the icons, and the printing of the documentary material.

Today's feast, replete with ecclesial and Romanian significance, urges us to preserve the Orthodox faith of our saints and forefathers and to pass it on to future generations with piety and love of Church and nation by prayer and good works; by raising children and the youth in the Orthodox Christian faith; by building holy places of worship; and by helping our fellow humans in poverty, sorrow, and loneliness.

On the occasion of the celebration of St Neagoe Basarab's feast and the 500th anniversary of the Cathedral of Curtea de Argeş, we congratulate Archbishop Callinicus, all his collaborators from the eparchial center, all the priests and deacons, monks and nuns, and all the faithful of the diocese, wishing them much health, peace, joy, and help from God in all good deeds.

May our merciful Lord, by the prayers of the holy voivode Neagoe Basarab and all the saints, bless all of you present at this great feast: hierarchs, clergy, officials, and pilgrims; and may he reward your striving and generosity, your reverence and desire for renewal and sanctification of life with many and happy years!

† Daniel,
Patriarch of the Romanian Orthodox Church

Holy Martyr Constantine Brâncoveanu: A Model of Sacrificial and Steadfast Love for Christ and the Romanian People[1]

A mong the events occasioned by the commemoration of the right-believing martyr Constantine Brâncoveanu on the 300th anniversary of his tragic martyrdom, shared with his sons and the counselor Ianache, one significant event is the national symposium titled "Constantine Brâncoveanu and His Contribution to the Enhancement of the Cultural, Educational, Spiritual, and Social-Philanthropic Heritage of Wallachia in the European Context of the Eighteenth Century," organized by the Romanian Patriarchate in cooperation with the Patriarch Justinian Faculty of Theology at the University of Bucharest and with the generous support of the State Secretariat for Religious Affairs.

This event embodies the close connection between religion and culture, between academic research and spiritual life, as it reflects both liturgical-missionary and scholarly dimensions. Its liturgical-missionary character was manifested in the solemn procession with the relics of the holy voivode Constantine Brâncoveanu, undertaken in Bucharest on May 21 of this year, and in the all-night vigil service for the martyrs Brâncoveni at the Church of St George. Its academic aspect is reflected in the presentations and debates at this national symposium.

[1] Patriarch Daniel, "Sfântul Domnitor Martir Constantin Brâncoveanu – model al iubirii jertfelnice și statornice față de Hristos și de neamul românesc" [The holy martyr Constantine Brâncoveanu: A model of sacrificial and steadfast love of Christ and the Romanian people], May 22, 2014, Basilica News Agency, accessed November 27, 2019, https://basilica.ro/sfantul-domnitor-martir-constantin-brancoveanu-model-al-iubirii-jertfelnice-si-statornice-fata-de-hristos-si-de-neamul-romanesc/. Address given at the opening of the national symposium titled "Constantine Brâncoveanu and His Contribution to the Enhancement of the Cultural, Educational, Spiritual, and Social-Philanthropic Heritage of Wallachia in the European Context of the Eighteenth Century," Bucharest, Patriarchal Palace.

In the Christian and national consciousness of the Romanian people, Prince Constantine Brâncoveanu (1688–1714) remains a symbol of complete sacrifice and dedication to God and the Romanian nation, a living epitome of the courage to confess faith in Christ and of national dignity. He was a true statesman, a wise and visionary diplomat in the politics he conducted in an extremely difficult international context that was marked by multiple pressures and the antagonistic interests of the great powers. Under the difficult conditions of that historical period, the Romanian ruler consistently pursued Wallachia's interests, proving his wisdom, temperance, and ability to assess with great sophistication the ties with the different powers of the time.

St Constantine Brâncoveanu, a founder of holy places in the country and abroad, a lover of the Romanian cultural heritage and of art specific to the Romanian tradition, a defender of Orthodox ecclesial life in Transylvania and the Eastern patriarchates, and, above all, a martyr for the Christian faith, endures in the memory of the Romanian soul as a luminous confessor of the faith lived in Christ and as a promoter of the values specific to the Romanian Christian patrimony and culture.

Having been formed in a scholarly environment and ever conscious of the need for national unity—reflected especially in his overseeing the translation and printing of the Bucharest Bible of 1688—St Constantine Brâncoveanu also supported the development of the Princely Academy, which was housed in the precincts of St Sava's Monastery in Bucharest. In addition to the intensification of the cultural and educational activities of the academy, he organized schools within monasteries, in which the classes were conducted in Romanian and Slavonic. That is how the schools of St George's Old Monastery and Colțea Monastery in Bucharest functioned. Several Romanian schools were also instituted in Wallachian towns and villages. In some monasteries renowned libraries were established containing works from the great Western cultural centers.

As soon as he became a ruler, St Constantine Brâncoveanu encouraged the printing of works of theological and lay culture. He entrusted the princely printing house in Bucharest to a Georgian monk and future metropolitan, St Anthimus of Georgia. Through its intense cultural development, Bucharest became a significant spiritual and cultural center in southeastern Europe because of this Wallachian ruler, who was a truly keen guide of culture and education.

St Constantine Brâncoveanu remains in the consciousness of the Church and nation as a founder of monasteries and churches, building new edifices and restoring or endowing older ones. Hurezi Monastery (the largest ensemble of medieval architecture in Wallachia) and Sâmbăta de Sus Monastery of Făgăraş are emblematic. Among the churches, we mention the Church of St George of Bucharest (consecrated on June 29, 1707, by Patriarch Chrysanthos Notaras of Jerusalem), where later, in 1720, the founder's bones were finally laid to rest through the efforts and care of his wife, Princess Consort Mary.

Beyond all his outstanding political, cultural, educational, and social achievements, St Constantine Brâncoveanu illustrates the condition of the martyr who accepts his vocation to confess Christ at the cost of his life and that of his own beloved sons. On August 15, 1714, when Christians were celebrating the feast of the Dormition of the Mother of God, the ruler—who was turning sixty years old on that very day—his sons Constantine, Stephen, Radu, and Matthew, and the counselor Ianache Văcărescu were beheaded in Constantinople before Sultan Ahmed III and a great audience of dignitaries and Ottoman and European officials.

An eyewitness to the execution, Anton Maria Del Chiaro, wrote the following in his work *A History of the Modern Revolutions of Wallachia* (Venice, 1718): "When Brâncoveanu saw the executioner wielding the sword, he prayed briefly and addressed his sons with the following words: 'My sons, be brave! We have lost everything we had in this world. Let us save our souls and wash away our sins by our blood!'"[2]

[2] Anton Maria Del Chiaro, *Revoluţiile Valahiei* [A history of the modern revolutions of Wallachia] (Bucharest: Basilica Press, 2012), 139.

For his martyr's death and his steadfastness in the Orthodox faith, this founder of culture and generous supporter of the entire Eastern Orthodox Church was glorified by the Romanian Orthodox Church on June 20, 1992, with the feast day of August 16.

Trusting that the papers and debates of this national symposium will contribute to raising the awareness of St Constantine Brâncoveanu's model of sacrificial and unfaltering love for the Church and nation in our contemporary environment, which is marked by secularization and the relativization of national values, we eagerly beseech the Lord to bless the organizers and participants in this symposium.

† DANIEL, Patriarch of the Romanian Orthodox Church

The Saints of Putna: Humble Men of Prayer and Brave Fighters for Their Faith and Nation[1]

During the working session of June 6–7, 2016, the Synod of the Romanian Orthodox Church approved the glorification of Metropolitan Jacob of Putna, a godly and wise hierarch with a pure and holy life, a defender of the true faith, a worthy teacher and spiritual father, a great founder and tireless shepherd of his Christian flock, who was very much attuned to the social and economic problems of his time. During the same session, the canonization of the venerable fathers of Putna Hermitage, Silas, Paisius, and Nathan, three of the disciples of Metropolitan Jacob of Putna, was also approved. They were monks steadfast in the Orthodox faith and ascetic life, true models of fervent prayer, humility, self-restraint, mercy, and wise spiritual guidance.

Metropolitan Jacob of Putna was born on January 20, 1719, into a pious family from Bukovina. He was raised in the spirit of true godliness, and at the mere age of twelve he entered the monastic life. He was spiritually formed in the community of Putna Monastery and Putna Hermitage, being a disciple of Metropolitan Anthony of Moldavia (1730–1740). Owing to his "elder's wisdom" and choice life, he was ordained a priest at the age of seventeen, then elected abbot of Putna

[1]Patriarch Daniel, "Sfinții Putneni – rugători smeriți și luptători curajoși pentru credință și neam" [The saints of Putna: Humble men of prayer and brave fighters for their faith and nation], May 22, 2014, Basilica News Agency, accessed November 27, 2019, https://basilica.ro/sfintii-putneni-rugatori-smeriti-si-luptatori-curajosi-pentru-credinta-si-neam/. Homily given at the proclamation of the canonization of the holy hierarch Jacob of Putna, Metropolitan of Moldavia, and of Sts Silas, Paisius, and Nathan of Putna Hermitage.

Monastery at the age of twenty-five. In 1745 he was elevated bishop of Rădăuți, and during his episcopacy he printed a Slavonic-Romanian Liturgy book and set up a school for the Slavonic, Greek, and Romanian languages. After only five years, in 1750, he was enthroned metropolitan of Moldavia in Jassy. As metropolitan, he engaged in intense pastoral and social activity between 1750 and 1760, promoting Romanian culture and overseeing the translation of soul-profiting books. He set up a printing house, and over a period of ten years he published more than fifteen ecclesial and schoolbooks in Romanian, which were of great use to the churches and monasteries in all the lands inhabited by Romanians.

For the Romanians in Transylvania, who threatened to renounce their forefathers' faith, the metropolitan of Moldavia printed books defending the Orthodox faith, ordained priests, and sent antimensions to parishes in the regions of Maramureș and Cluj, where there was no bishop.

St Jacob was grieved by the benighted state of his flock, for he believed that "from the education of children—as from good or bad roots—grows the rest of their life." For this reason, in 1755 he printed *Bucvarul* (The Primer)—the first alphabet book published in Moldavia—and founded the first rural school in Moldavia for the children of Putna. He began the translation of the lives of the saints, succeeding in translating the first six of twelve volumes.

Besides his stewardship of Putna Monastery and its settlements, Metropolitan Jacob also helped other monasteries and churches: Doljești Monastery, St Demetrius' Church in Suceava, the diocesan cathedral in Suceava, the metropolitan cathedral in Jassy, St Spyridon's Monastery and Hospital in Jassy, and other holy places.

During Phanariot rule, he intervened with the country's other hierarchs to abolish serfdom in 1749 and some burdensome taxes (such as the wine tax in 1756 and especially the cattle tax in 1757), placing a curse on any ruler who would try to reinstate them.

A peacemaker and protector of the nation, Metropolitan Jacob of Putna asked the Tatar khan in 1758 to cease the plunder of Moldavia, and in the following year he was able to quell a popular uprising, requesting that the ruler meet some of the demands to restore peace in the land. He often rebuked several unjust rulers of his time, because of whom he eventually decided to step down from the metropolitan see in 1760, refusing to accept the reimposition of burdensome taxes on the populace.

Living the last part of his life at Putna Monastery, St Jacob continued the restoration work he had begun during his time as metropolitan, thus becoming Putna's second great founder, strengthening it both spiritually and materially. Consequently, the monastery became one of the pillars of Romanian Orthodoxy in the difficult times that would befall the country with Bukovina's occupation by the armies of the Habsburg Empire in 1774 and the recognition of this situation by the Ottoman Empire and the Russian Empire in 1775.

The withdrawal to Putna Monastery was an occasion for Metropolitan Jacob to grow deeper in purifying and soul-illumining prayer. In this sense, he said that "divine prayer, bringing the light of Christ into our soul and casting out the darkness that harms it, makes man much more luminous than the sun, for it is known that he who converses with God is already above death and corruption."

Feeling the end of his earthly life drawing near, after the holy Pascha of 1778, he went to Putna Hermitage and was tonsured into the Great Schema by his confessor, Fr Nathan, receiving the name Euthymius. Four days later, on May 15, 1778, he reposed peacefully in the Lord. He was laid to rest in the porch of Putna Monastery's church, as he was its new founder.

Having borne with diligence and worthiness his hierarchical cross and with meekness and humility the cross of those persecuted for righteousness' sake, having sacrificed himself for his flock, the holy Metropolitan Jacob put all his life in the service of the Church for the enlightenment of his people through schooling and print, through defending those who had been wronged, and through spiritual counseling on the path of salvation, thus enduring in the memory of the faithful as "the shepherd of the poor and humble, who led the life of a saint."

In the eighteenth century, Frs Silas, Paisius, and Nathan strove spiritually at Putna Hermitage, a skete of strict asceticism and tranquility to which monks who loved prayer and spiritual toil often retreated.

Fr Silas was born in 1697, in the Botoşani region, to Orthodox parents, John and Joanne. He entered Orăşeni Hermitage (in Cristeşti, Botoşani County) as a novice at a very tender age and from there, in 1714, at the age of seventeen, he went to Putna Hermitage, where he was tonsured a monk by Abbot Theodosius. Upon the repose of Abbot Theodosius, the new spiritual father of the hermitage, Abbot Dosoftei, ordained him to the holy diaconate and the priesthood, and shortly thereafter he was invested with the Great Schema. As a disciple and assistant to Abbot Dosoftei, Hieroschemamonk Silas cared for more than thirty years for all the needs of the monastic community, while celebrating church services and fulfilling his cell prayer rule. In the fall of 1753, after Abbot Dosoftei fell asleep in the Lord, Fr Silas was named abbot by Metropolitan Jacob of Putna.

As the spiritual father of the community, he renewed the spiritual life of Putna Hermitage. Endowed with great husbandry skills, with the blessing of Metropolitan Jacob of Putna, he built a new stone church dedicated to the feast of the Annunciation, adorned with all that was required, as well as a new refectory and monks' cells. Having become a well-known spiritual guide and confessor, the venerable Silas was honored by both simple believers and the rulers of Moldavia—such as Constantine Cehan Racoviță and Gregory Calimachi—as well as high officials, hierarchs, and abbots, whom he guided with wisdom on their path to salvation. Under the sage leadership of the holy abbot Silas, the monks of Putna Hermitage undertook the calligraphy of manuscripts that included holy services and important writings of the holy fathers. The venerable father Silas spent his last years in hardship and scarcity, owing to the occupation of Bukovina by the armies of the Habsburg Empire in 1774 and the restrictions imposed by the new regime. Putna Hermitage did not have the necessary supplies for the monks and was forced to borrow money and food. Knowing his earthly end was upon him, Fr Silas invested Fr Nathan (in 1781) as abbot of Putna Hermitage, then asked for forgiveness from all. On April 23, 1783, after nearly seventy years of spiritual struggle at Putna Hermitage, the holy hiero-schemamonk Silas reposed peacefully in the Lord, whom he had loved and served his whole life.

St Paisius was born in 1701 and entered the monastic life at a very young age. On account of his worthiness, he was ordained a deacon, then a priest, and became the abbot of St Elijah's Monastery near Suceava, and from there he later went to Râşca Monastery. After a while, he went to Putna Hermitage, where he lived a life of deep humility. He was never abbot of Putna Hermitage, but he was a monk of ardent prayer, strengthening many in the Orthodox faith, especially in the time of foreign domination. God also granted him the gift of clairvoyance and foreknowledge, which, together with his other virtues, gained him the esteem of all, who considered him a great spiritual father. Together with Abbots Silas and Nathan, Fr Paisius witnessed firsthand the difficulties of the years of foreign domination, but he proved to be a fervent spiritual struggler. He passed away in peace on December 16, 1784.

The venerable Fr Nathan was born in 1717, in the Paşcani region. He lived and became ecclesiarch at Putna Monastery, where he was ordained a deacon, then a priest. Longing for greater solitude and peace for the sake of prayer, he retired to Putna Hermitage, where he received the Great Schema and the name Nathan. Fr Nathan was a very wise confessor, being the spiritual father of the great Metropolitan Jacob of Putna. At the same time, the monks of the monastery, his spiritual co-strugglers, together with the pious laypeople, honored him as a true shepherd and guardian of good Orthodox order. He also worked extensively on manuscript calligraphy and on the compilation of the diptychs of the monastery's founders. In 1781 he was appointed abbot of Putna Hermitage by the venerable father Silas, almost two years before the latter's repose. Despite his old age, Hieroschemamonk Nathan continued, with great zeal and sacrifice, the spiritual work of his forerunner, Fr Silas, shepherding the community entrusted to him for three and a half years, despite the scarcities and struggles that were increasing as a result of the foreign occupation. Having led a life dedicated to God, fraught with material poverty but rich in spiritual purity, after bearing the heavy burden of illness with patience and unceasing prayer, the holy hieroschemamonk Nathan gave up his soul to the Lord the day after the Nativity of Christ, on December 26, 1784.

Shortly after the three holy hieroschemamonks Silas, Paisius, and Nathan departed to eternal life, Putna Hermitage was left desolate because of the adversity of the times. More than two hundred years later, at the beginning of Great Lent in 1990, a monk of Putna who had retreated to the site of Putna Hermitage's former foundation saw a heavenly light above the narthex of the old church's ruins, a light that encircled the church, then disappeared. Shortly thereafter, on April 24, 1990, when the rebuilding of Putna Hermitage began, the tombs containing the fragrant, honey-colored relics of Sts Silas, Paisius, and Nathan were discovered. In the following years, the hallowed remains of the venerable fathers worked many wondrous healings.

So, today we solemnly honor St Jacob of Putna, metropolitan of Moldavia, together with his disciples, Silas, Paisius, and Nathan. St Jacob's feast day will be celebrated every year on May 15, the day of his repose, and the commemoration of his disciples Silas, Paisius, and Nathan will be on the following day, May 16, so that they may be celebrated immediately after their spiritual father.

The four saints of Putna, whose canonization was officially proclaimed on this day blessed by God, are added to the other—more than a hundred—Romanian and proto-Romanian saints in the calendar of the Romanian Orthodox Church, wherein there is no month without at least one Romanian saint. Through the numerous Romanian saints, glorified throughout the years (1950–1955, 1992, 2005, 2007, 2008, 2009, 2010, 2011, and 2016), our nation understands and rejoices in having so many intercessors before the Holy Trinity, intercessors who help with the preservation of the Orthodox Christian faith as the foundation of salvation, so that it may be handed down to younger generations, to foster holiness of life and deeds of merciful love. That is why, as Romanians, it behooves us always to thank God for the gifts the Holy Spirit has bestowed upon the saints of our country, gifts that they have cultivated by faith, forgiveness, and suffering through prayer and works of humble and merciful love.

The holy intercessors in heaven from all times and places, especially the saints of our nation, helped us through the great and painful trial of faithfulness, or fidelity, to Christ—namely, the persecution by the communist regime. But after sufferings and humiliations innumerable, with the help of the Holy Trinity, of the Mother of God, and of all the saints, most of the Romanian people remained faithful to Christ. When in the year 1950 the Holy Synod of the Romanian Orthodox Church, owing to the initiative, perseverance, and wisdom of Patriarch Justinian Marina, canonized many saints (proclaimed solemnly in 1955), then, in fact, the Romanian people were mystically preparing for a painful spiritual struggle that would soon begin, the struggle of the difficult years of communist persecution against belief in God. In those days of hostility to the Church and religion in general, many Romanian Orthodox professed their faith in the crucified and risen Christ at the cost of losing their freedom or even their lives. For this reason, the Holy Synod of the Romanian Orthodox Church proclaimed 2017 as the "Commemorative Year of Patriarch Justinian and of the Defenders of Orthodoxy during Communism" in the Romanian Patriarchate. Among these confessors and defenders of the faith during communism, alongside Patriarch Justinian, there were many hierarchs, theology professors, students, monks, and Christian intellectuals, but above all over 1,800 Romanian Orthodox priests who were arrested and investigated, judged in mock trials and thrown in jail, and sent to work on the Danube-Black Sea Canal, where many suffered and died in terrible conditions.

The many witnesses and martyrs of the faith during communism urge us not to forget how great their long-suffering was, so that the Orthodox faith and the dignity of the Romanian Christian people may be kept alive in times of terror and persecution.

After 1990 the late Patriarch Theoctistus of blessed memory, apprentice of Patriarch Justinian, believed that those to whom God has granted the gift of saving and illuminating holiness must be continuously commemorated. Thus in 1992 numerous saints were glorified from all over the country, but especially from here, from Moldavia, such as St Paisius of Neamț; St John Jacob of Neamț and Chozeba; St Theodora of Sihla; St Stephen the Great; St Leontius of Rădăuți; and St Daniel the Hermit, the spiritual father of the great voivode Stephen the Great. More consecrations of Romanian saints followed, so that in the Metropolitanate of Moldavia and Bukovina alone we have as many as twenty-two new saints added to the calendar from 1992 until now, eighteen of whom were canonized before 2016. To them we add the four saints of Putna proclaimed on June 6–7, 2016, and consecrated today, May 16, 2017, at Holy Putna Monastery.

The canonization of new saints in these times is not accidental, as today there are renewed endeavors to preserve the Orthodox faith and the unity of the Church. More specifically, today we especially need the prayers of the saints because we are engaged in an unseen spiritual war called secularization, which is the organizing of the life of man and society as if God did not exist. These times of secularization as spiritual impoverishment and aridity, or the lack of humble and merciful love, lead us to ask for the saints' aid. Why? Because the warfare waged by the evil spirits that seek to tear people away from Christ cannot be fought against solely by individual will or by the exclusive trust of people in their own power; rather, spiritual victory is always acquired primarily with the help of the Holy Spirit and of God's saints, our teachers and intercessors.

So that our love may rekindle and grow, we also need the prayer of others for us and especially the prayers of the saints. Sometimes we pray more, sometimes less; sometimes we pray more carefully, sometimes more superficially. That is why St Mark the Ascetic teaches us, "At the times when you remember God, increase your prayers, so that when you forget him, the Lord may remind you" (*On the Spiritual Law* 25). Behold why we need prayer, especially in times of waning faith!

Let us entreat the saints of Putna, all the saints of the Romanian nation, and all the saints of the universal Orthodox Church, to enlighten, warm, and strengthen our souls more abundantly with their prayers, that we may step onto the path of salvation, which is the union of the individual with God, the Source of life and eternal happiness!

We thank the distinguished hierarchs who answered the invitation of His Eminence Archbishop Pimen of Suceava and Rădăuți to be present today at Putna Monastery for the proclamation as saints of the great hierarch Metropolitan Jacob of Putna and his three disciples, Silas, Paisius, and Nathan.

We thank the venerable monks and nuns who came to share their joy in the canonization and proclamation of the four Putna saints.

We thank the parish priests present here and those who, out of their love for Christ and in obedience to the Church, keep the faithful on the path of salvation.

We thank Abbot Melchizedek of Putna Monastery, Abbot Nectarius of Putna Hermitage, and all the fathers from these two holy monasteries, as well as all the sponsors and donors who contributed to the organization of this great event of proclaiming the canonization of the four saints. We thank all the officials and all of you, our beloved brothers and sisters in Christ, who have prayed with us today.

With holy gratitude, let us always rejoice in the blessing of God and the prayers of the saints, to the glory of the Most Holy Trinity and the good of Christ's Church. Amen!

The Unity of Faith and Nation Is Strengthened by the Saints' Light and Prayers[1]

The Holy Synod of the Romanian Orthodox Church, in the working session of October 5–6, 2017, approved the glorification of Metropolitan Joseph Naniescu of Moldavia and Suceava (1875–1902), who was a compassionate hierarch of holy life and theological culture, a wise teacher and spiritual father, a founder of holy edifices, and a tireless pastor of the faithful.

In the same working session the Holy Synod approved the canonization of the pious layman George the Pilgrim (1864–1916), who venerated the holy places and was an example of sacrificial love, restraint, humility, and spiritual guidance.

Today, by the will of God, the blessing and joy begotten of the glad tidings of the feast of the Annunciation are enhanced by the blessing and joy of proclaiming the canonization of the holy hierarch Joseph the Merciful, metropolitan of Moldavia, and that of St George the Pilgrim as intercessors and saints of the Romanian people before the throne of the Most Holy Trinity.

---

[1]Patriarch Daniel, "Unitatea de credință și de neam se întărește prin lumina și rugăciunile sfinților" [The unity of faith and nation is strengthened by the saints' light and prayers], March 25, 2018, Basilica News Agency, accessed November 26, 2019, https://basilica.ro/unitatea-de-credinta-si-de-neam-se-intareste-prin-lumina-si-rugaciunile-sfintilor/. Homily on the proclamation of the canonization of the holy hierarch Joseph the Merciful, metropolitan of Moldavia, and of St George the Pilgrim at the Metropolitan Cathedral of Jassy.

It is significant to note that St Joseph the Merciful was born in Bessarabia (the village of Răzălăi) two hundred years ago (1818) and lived in Jassy, Buzău, Bucharest, Argeș, and then again in Jassy; St George the Pilgrim was born in Transylvania (the village of Șugag) in 1864 and lived in Moldavia at Piatra Neamț until his departure to the Lord in 1916. These two saints symbolically show the spiritual communion of Romanians living in different provinces but united by the same faith and the same love of nation.

Taken together, the two faithful sons of the Romanian land and saints of our Church show us the light of Christ's gospel that bore the fruit of these rays and countenances of light in the midst of the Romanian people just as our Savior Jesus Christ said: "The righteous will shine forth as the sun in the kingdom of their Father" (Mt 13.43, cf. Dan 12.3). They sanctify the time and communion across generations, because in them "Jesus Christ is the same yesterday, today, and forever" (Heb 13.8).

These two saints now join more than one hundred proto-Romanian and Romanian saints registered in the calendar of the Romanian Orthodox Church, so that there is no month without the commemoration of at least one Romanian saint.

Our nation recognizes and rejoices in the Romanian saints glorified at different times (1950–1955, 1992, 2005, 2007, 2008, 2009, 2010, 2011, 2016, and 2017). These intercessors before the Holy Trinity help the Romanian people to safekeep the Orthodox faith needed for gaining salvation and to transmit it to younger generations, to nurture holiness of life and works of mercy and love.

The noun *holiness* and the adjective *holy*, together with the verb *sanctify*, represent the most specific and most prevalent language of the Orthodox Church. In a general sense, the Church is holy and sanctifying, for she is the mysterious Body of Christ, the Holy One of God, who summons to holiness soul and body, people and works, household and nature, time and eternity.

Yet when we ask what holiness is in and of itself, the answer is not easy to find. Holiness is praised, hymned, desired, and sometimes perceived existentially, but its conceptual definition remains a difficulty: it cannot be defined in its essence but can only be described in its manifestations, in its fruit.

Holiness manifests itself in this world in God's creation, but it does not rise from this world, for holiness is the Holy God himself, present and working in the world but at the same time being above the world. Therefore, all that appears to be holiness or holy in the created world has its unique source in God the Creator, the only one holy in himself and through himself.

The holy Scriptures tell us that "God is wondrous in his saints" (Ps 67.36). This primarily means that God—the one source of holiness—shares his holiness with people as they seek him and fulfill his will in their lives.

For this reason, the holy Apostle Paul exhorts us, "Pursue peace with all people, and holiness, without which no one will see the Lord" (Heb 12.14). The Church of Christ the crucified and risen one, founded by him through his salvific work and established as a divine-human institution or community through the descent of the Holy Spirit at Pentecost, is at the same time the experience of seeking holiness and receiving holiness by people.

Therefore, the primary purpose of the Church is to realize the communion of saints of all ages and all places in the kingdom of heaven, which is "righteousness and peace and joy in the Holy Spirit" (Rom 14.17).

The saints are the closest friends of God and the most prayerful among people. A saint is the bearer of Christ's humble love for the world and the dwelling place of the Holy Spirit, who, with unutterable groanings, desires that every believing individual grow spiritually toward the likeness of God (cf. Rom 8.26–30).

The Orthodox Church honors the saints, recognizing in them "the grace of the Lord Jesus Christ, and the love of God, and the communion of the Holy Spirit" (2 Cor 13.14). The veneration of the saints is therefore not a lessening or diminution of God's righteousness but, on the contrary, is an exaltation of his merciful love for people and his work of raising the human person toward the Most Holy Trinity's eternal beauty and glory.

In relation to the world, God is not wondrous in living in loneliness or eternal isolation but is wondrous in his saints, that is, in the communion of those who partake and rejoice in his love and glory. It is for this reason that the righteous Church cultivates the veneration of the saints, as a work of God's sanctifying grace in people.

Since people were created in the image of God, the Eternal and Holy One, and called to his likeness (cf. Gen 1.27), holiness is the true life, or fulfillment, of a person. In this sense, we are all called to holy living, according to the word of the Lord Jesus Christ, who urges us to "be perfect, just as your Father in heaven is perfect" (Mt 5.48).

All people are called to become holy, but only those who respond to the call of God and cultivate their communion with him, the Holy One, become saints.

The Orthodox Church honors the saints as icons of the Holy Spirit's work in people and as the most dependable teachers and closest friends of people, for they are the closest friends of God.

As we face today's phenomenon of secularization, the saints teach us that if we forget God, we will quickly forget the eternal and unique value of every human being, for the holy purpose of the human person's life on earth is to seek first eternal life in the kingdom of heaven (cf. Mt 6.33).

In the face of the temptation of amassing material wealth, the saints teach us to practice almsgiving—that is, to discover the spiritual force of being generous and merciful as our merciful Father (cf. Lk 6.36).

In the face of the temptation of affirming ourselves through the selfish love of dominion over others, the saints teach us to learn the humble love of Christ for all people.

The saints constantly and persistently teach us to discover through prayer the joy of communion in the Church of Christ as a foretaste of the joy in the kingdom of God (cf. Rom 14.17).

The life and holiness of God the living and holy present in the world can be seen in the saints whose life therefore is an icon of Christian life. For this reason, it was affirmed in the early Church that "The saints are (truly) alive. And living are the saints."[2]

Since without holiness no one will see the Lord (cf. Heb 12.14), neither will anyone fully understand without the saints the meaning or the purpose of the Church in the world as the antechamber, or foretaste, of the kingdom of heaven, a truth lived deeply especially through partaking in her holy mysteries.

We beseech the recently canonized saints of Moldavia, Metropolitan Joseph the Merciful and George the Pilgrim, and all the saints of the Romanian people and of the universal Orthodox Church to enlighten our minds, to warm our hearts, and to strengthen our will to love Christ and his Church in the light, peace, and joy of the Most Holy Trinity.

We thank the distinguished hierarchs present here today to honor the newly canonized saints and to cultivate the eucharistic communion in Jesus Christ.

We thank the monastics who came to Jassy, the capital of Moldavia, to rejoice in the consecration of the holy hierarch Joseph the Merciful, the metropolitan of Moldavia, and of St George the Pilgrim.

We thank the parish priests who are here as a sign of love for Christ and his saints and in obedience to the Church whose flock they guide on the salvific path of God.

We thank His Eminence Theophan, metropolitan of Moldavia and Bukovina; the collaborators from the Diocesan Center of the Jassy Archdiocese; all the fathers from the Metropolitan Cathedral of Jassy; the professors from the Dumitru Stăniloae Faculty of Theology in Jassy;

---

[2]Olivier Clément, *Sources: Les mystiques chrétiens des origines; textes et commentaires* [Sources: Origins of Christian mysticism; Texts and commentaries] (Paris: Stock, 1982), 238.

and all those who contributed to the organization of the great event of the canonization of Sts Joseph the Merciful and George the Pilgrim.

We thank the officials present, and we thank you, beloved faithful, in prayer with us today.

May we always rejoice in the blessing of God, in the help and communion of the saints, to the glory of the Most Holy Trinity and for the salvation of humankind. Amen!

PART III

The Mission of the Church in the Religious-Moral Education of Children and Young People[1]

The Romanian Orthodox Church is constantly concerned with the moral and spiritual education of children and young people, contributing fully to their formation and training through responsible involvement in the life of society. Orthodox Christian education must be tailored to and realized in accordance with the spiritual needs specific to each age, having, as such, an informative function that presents to children and young people a body of Christian moral knowledge reinforced by a pronounced formative character of internalization and transposition into life of religious precepts, for "now we have received, not the spirit of the world, but the Spirit who is from God, that we might know the things that have been freely given to us by God. These things we also speak, not in words which man's wisdom teaches but which the Holy Spirit teaches, comparing spiritual things with spiritual" (1 Cor 2.12–13). Therefore, Orthodox Christian education will not be limited to transmitting information, but it will particularly emphasize the moral and spiritual formation of children and young people and the alignment of their lives with the ideal of Christ's gospel of love

---

[1]Patriarch Daniel, "Misiunea Bisericii în educaţia religios-morală a copiilor şi a tinerilor" [The mission of the Church in the religious-moral education of children and young people], *Credinţa şi educaţia: Principalele lumini ale vieţii* [Faith and education: Life's leading lights] (Bucharest: Basilica, 2019), 91–92. Message addressed to the participants in the sixth iteration of the national congress "Christ Shared with the Children," organized by the Romanian Patriarchate in collaboration with the World Vision Romania Foundation (Caraiman Monastery, September 16–18, 2013).

and service to the neighbor, of respect for parents and teachers, of fidelity to the values and traditions of the Romanian nation: "For no other foundation can anyone lay than that which is laid, which is Jesus Christ" (1 Cor 3.11). In this sense, in complementarity with the religious education system in schools and in collaboration with the Ministry of National Education and the World Vision Romania Foundation, the Romanian Patriarchate has implemented in recent years a series of educational projects and programs such as "Christ Shared with the Children," "Children Learn Christ's Merciful Love," "Choose School!," and more recently, "The Way of Salvation" (The Way).

The projects and programs of the Romanian Patriarchate are addressed to all children and young people, with the hope of opening the path for Christian faith and moral values. The national congress "Christ Shared with the Children," organized by the Romanian Patriarchate and the World Vision Romania Foundation, has reached today its sixth iteration. Through the results obtained over time, this project has shown that well devised and structured catechetical programs can offer educational alternatives, increasing knowledge and wisdom in the hearts and souls of children and young people from families, parishes, and communities in Romania and the diaspora.

We congratulate and bless all those who, with great responsibility and self-dedication, have been involved in these projects for the success of a fruitful moral-spiritual education.

With love and fatherly blessings,
† DANIEL
Patriarch of the Romanian Orthodox Church

The Orthodox Youth: Confessors of Christ and Missionaries of the Church[1]

It is such a great spiritual joy to greet all the young Orthodox Christians who have arrived in these days in Cluj-Napoca—the 2015 European Youth Capital—for the Meeting of the Orthodox Youth of Europe, which also includes young Orthodox from Palestine, Jordan, Syria, and Africa.

Learning the real situation of our Christian youth today and gaining a deeper understanding of their spiritual vocation are necessary priorities of the Church's missionary work in the world.

In this fleeting world, youth is a symbol of the beauty of life eternal, so God has planted in people, from their early years, a longing for an ideal, for a holy love and eternal life, as we see in the life of the rich young man from the Gospel, who found that full happiness is not given by ephemeral material goods, but by the eternal love of God (cf. Mk 10.17–21; Lk 18.18).

The holy Gospel shows us that our Lord Jesus Christ greatly cherished the young. The three resurrections from the dead that he performed during his life on earth were resurrections of several young people—namely, the son of the widow of Nain; the daughter of Jairus; and Lazarus of Bethany, Jesus' friend. He resurrected these young

[1]Patriarch Daniel, "Tinerii ortodocşi – mărturisitori ai iubirii lui Hristos şi misionari ai Bisericii" [The Orthodox youth: Confessors of Christ and missionaries of the Church], in *Credinţa şi educaţia: Principalele lumini ale vieţii* [Faith and education: Life's leading lights] (Bucharest: Basilica, 2019), 161–166. Homily given at the Meeting of the Orthodox Youth of Europe (Cluj-Napoca, September 4, 2015).

people because he also wanted to show that youth is a symbol of eternal life's beauty in the kingdom of heaven (cf. Mt 22.30).

It is also significant that many of the disciples who followed Christ were young. Some of St Paul's disciples were young as well. They were named Tychicus, Trophimus, Tertius, Timothy, and Titus. The last two became bishops in Ephesus and Crete, respectively. To his disciple Timothy, the Apostle Paul said, "Let no one despise your youth, but be an example to the believers in word, in conduct, in love, in spirit, in faith, in purity" (1 Tim 4.12).

The holy Apostle and Evangelist John, Jesus' youngest disciple, addresses the youth with this advice, or exhortation: "I have written to you, young men, because you are strong, and the word of God abides in you, and you have overcome the wicked one. . . . And the world is passing away, and the lust of it; but he who does the will of God abides forever" (1 Jn 2.14; 17).

Truly, when this limited and transient material world is used selfishly and idolatrously as if it were the only reality and the only source of human happiness, then a profound spiritual crisis befalls society, and young people are, many times, those most affected by it.

Aspects of this crisis are manifest today in the tensions between secularized and spiritual people, between the rich and the poor, between the violent and the peaceful, between the avaricious and the generous, between the honest and the corrupt.

In the current secularized and individualistic European society, more and more young men are not getting married, and more and more young women do not want to birth children! That is why presently Europe is the only aging continent.

In a secularized society in which faith and spiritual values are marginalized and freedom is no longer associated with responsibility, many young people are confused and find themselves without ideals, without a desire to study or work, preferring to be indefinitely supported financially by their parents. In many of them there is a spiritual ignorance, or a superficial approach, to information regarding the activity of the

Church and the spiritual life of people. Also, there are more and more young people whose main intellectual or cultural concern is reduced to surfing the internet. For this reason, many of them become victims of all kinds of manipulation, induced by certain media that promote sensationalism and non-values.

At the same time, however, there are many faithful and hardworking young people today, who participate intensely in the Church's life and missionary activities on a spiritual, educational, cultural, and social-philanthropic level, either individually or through youth organizations. All of them are a great joy and a great support for the Church!

1. The crisis of ideal and spiritual orientation of human life, which dramatically cuts through secularized European society, represents for the Church a challenge and a call to action to deal more carefully with the problems and aspirations of today's youth.

The harried youngsters of today face difficulties that are economic (material poverty, unemployment, professional discomfiture, uncertainty about the future, depression), moral (liberty, violence, drugs, alcoholism, human trafficking), and spiritual-religious (sectarianism, fanaticism, and religious proselytism). The Church is called to pay special attention to young people, defending their innocence, sincerity, courage, desire for renewal, and all the values of this age blessed by God, and to help them to develop human dignity and a healthy life while seeking salvation and eternal life.

Consequently, more intense and broader pastoral and missionary work by the Church is needed in practice, to guide and support young pupils, students, married couples, those who work hard for little money, and those who are unemployed; to offer spiritual, pastoral, and social and charitable assistance both to those in Romania and to those outside its borders.

2. We are called today to help poverty-stricken young people who are in danger of dropping out of school; to help young people who are forced to migrate to other countries to support themselves; and to learn how to offer more brotherly and parental love to orphaned

children and young people, especially those abandoned by their family and by secularized and individualistic society. Let us work together to intensify the love of parents for children and of children for parents and to strengthen the friendship, pure love, and respect among young people while preserving the Orthodox faith and life we have inherited, as Christians, from our parents and ancestors over the centuries.

3. Today, the Church, the school, and the family must work together to achieve a comprehensive education—scientific and spiritual, professional and moral—especially for rearing our children and our youth in the Orthodox faith, in the love of their neighbor, and in holiness. Let us teach the young generations to find in prayer the fount of pure love and to live their lives on earth in the light of the blessing of our Heavenly Father and of the Church of his Son, our Lord Jesus Christ, so that they may feel the light, peace, and intense joy of the Holy Spirit.

4. With much joy and motherly love, the Church of Christ calls on her youth to be witnesses of Christ's love for humanity and her missionaries in the world, as in times past the Lord Jesus Christ called his disciples to the apostolate.

The true meaning of young people's mission in the Church today is the same as it was during the time of the holy apostles: "to pursue peace with all the people, and holiness, without which no one will see the Lord" (Heb 12.14). And the pursuit of holiness, which is the human person's strongest connection with the Holy One, ought to begin in childhood, at the early, tender age of youth, which is a time of searching and exploration. In a secularized and individualistic society, a young person in search of holy love and life in communion with God can become an example for his or her peers, a young confessor and missionary of great use for the life of the Church and for the good of society!

5. Let us defend and cultivate in Europe and in the world the eternal values of the gospel of Christ's love and of the dignity of the human person created in God's image. Let us sanctify creation (the surrounding natural world) through prayer and resourceful activity and not

destroy it by selfish and irrational pollution and exploitation. Let us promote peace and cooperation among nations, not violence and deadly conflicts.

Let us pray that our Savior Jesus Christ may help us all, so that together with the young believers who love Christ and the Church, we may preach the gospel of love and his resurrection in today's world, to the glory of the Holy Trinity, to the joy of the Church, and to the good of the contemporary society.

† Daniel
Patriarch of Romania

Children's and Young People's Education: The Most Valuable Investment[1]

The Holy Synod of the Romanian Orthodox Church declared 2016 "The Year of the Orthodox Christian Youth and the Commemorative Year of the Holy Hierarch Martyr Anthimus of Georgia and of the Church Typographers."

Taking into account the crisis of ideal and spiritual orientation of young people in today's secularized and consumerist society, the Church, together with the family and the school, has a duty to intensify her work in their spiritual formation and Christian education, so that they may acquire the "perennial moral and spiritual values of cultivating love, friendship, self-respect, and neighborliness."[2]

Reduced only to the immediate and the necessary, the contemporary person is alone and defenseless, both in the face of technical and economic manipulations and in the face of the blind forces of instinct, aggression, and violence. The consumerist mindset and the media "completely seize the work and the time of the people, who, for the

---

[1] Patriarch Daniel, "Educația copiilor și tinerilor—cea mai valoroasă investiție" [Children's and young people's education: The most valuable investment], May 30, 2016, Basilica News Agency, accessed November 27, 2019, https://basilica.ro/educatia-copiilor-si-tinerilor-cea-mai-valoroasa-investitie/. Address delivered at the opening of the spring session of the pastoral and missionary conference of the clergy of the Archdiocese of Bucharest, Patriarchal Palace, May 30, 2016.

[2] The Holy Synod of the Romanian Orthodox Church, "Chancery Report," (Bucharest, October 28–29, 2014).

sake of verbs such as *consume, see, have fun,* forget to conjugate the essential verbs *be, live, think, care for, pray.*"[3]

School abandonment, family breakdown, poverty, unemployment, parents leaving for work abroad, youth delinquency and violence, insecurity for today, and uncertainty about the future are major causes of the education crisis in the school and family.

The Church cannot remain indifferent to the current challenges of the world because her mission is precisely to proclaim the gospel of Christ's merciful love in the world and the way of life that is in accord with it. The educational-formative activity of the Church was ordained by the Savior Jesus Christ himself when he said, "Let the little children come to me" (Mk 10.14), and by the words of his holy apostles, as constant spiritual growth: "Grow in the grace and knowledge of our Lord and Savior Jesus Christ" (2 Pet 3.18).

The religious education of the Orthodox Christian youth is one of the missionary and pastoral priorities being carried out in the parishes of the Romanian Patriarchate. The parish, as a church family of conjugal families, must take care of people of all ages, but it must take a special interest in children and young people because they are the hope of our nation and because, owing to social challenges, this age presents the most acute problems and determines the continuity or discontinuity of the Church's traditions in the life of our society.

As spiritual parents, priests need to pay greater attention to the spiritual growth of children and young people. During one's youth, one experiences a strong desire to give and receive the love of others and also to ascribe meaning to one's life. The Church ought to be careful and sensitive to the lives of young people. Some of them often experience fear, disappointments, illnesses, emotional breakdown and pain, crises of trust in their peers, and difficult communication with parents and teachers. They are thirsty for the authentic and the essential. They are in search of spiritual guidance that has the potential to teach them

---

[3]"Globalizarea: Mutații și Provocări" [Globalization: Mutations and challenges], *Gândirea Socială a Bisericii: fundamente, documente analize, perspective* [*Social thought of the Church*], ed. Ioan Ică, Jr. and Germano Marani (Sibiu: Editura Deisis, 2002), 487.

to live in a communion of love and give meaning to their present and future lives.

The educational and religious activities carried out in the parish and youth organizations must be a chance for young people to rediscover the Church today as a place where they are welcome, respected, and loved; a place of communion and selfless friendship, of reconciliation and rediscovery of the profoundly Christian meaning of life; of the beauty of prayer; of mutual sharing of the joys of faith; of experiencing inner peace and meeting with God; a place of life and creative spirituality.

The Department of Culture and Media Communications and the Department of Education and Youth Activities of the Bucharest Archdiocese have paid special attention to this topic this year by publishing a volume containing pastoral dialogues about the Church's mission among young people, meant to also be a guide of good practices for all priests engaged in educational activities with the youth within the parishes they serve or within the Orthodox Christian youth organizations they coordinate.

The abovementioned volume, published by Cuvântul Vieţii (The Word of Life Publishing House) of the Metropolitan Church of Muntenia and Dobruja, highlights a multitude of activities through which religious education can be transmitted to young people within parishes.

Instilling the love of participating in the holy and divine Liturgy and in other weekly services and prayers in the parish church; confessing and communing as frequently as possible; regularly conducting weekly catechesis and organizing spiritual conferences; collaborating with schools from various parishes; setting up "forums for young people," after-school programs in churches or parish houses, and educational-recreational workshops near the church; and generally stimulating creativity through literary-artistic activities (setting up plays, poetry contests, choral activities, painting workshops, etc.), and organizing pilgrimages or summer camps at Orthodox monasteries and thematic trips to cultural objectives, are some of the educational activities in which young people engage within and outside the Church.

Fostering solidarity or philanthropy in the face of suffering by visiting young or old people in orphanages, hospitals, or penitentiaries; offering food to the elderly at their homes; donating blood; strengthening communion through gatherings after the Divine Liturgy, during agape meals, and sports events; participating in the "March for Life"; and creating websites and media portals and encouraging communication through them are also some other possibilities to ensure the presence of young volunteers in the Church and to integrate them into the parish family.

In meeting the enthusiasm of young people in all these actions, the priest must behave in an open and warm manner; he ought to be sensitive and receptive to the needs and turmoil specific to their age; and above all, he ought to demonstrate a spirit of sacrifice, self-giving, patience, and generosity.

The family, the place wherein parents, children, and young people cultivate their Christian faith, has the vocation to be truly the "little church" in which the love of the Most Holy Trinity, acquired through prayer, becomes a source of love, peace, and joy for all the members.

Christian families should be encouraged to rear their children in faith and love for God and others. We remember St John Chrysostom's lasting words addressed to parents on the education of their children: "I shall not cease exhorting and begging and supplicating you before all else to discipline your sons from the first. If you do care for your son, show it thus, and in other ways too you will have your reward. . . . Raise up an athlete for Christ and teach him though he is living in the world to be reverent from his earliest youth."[4]

Together with the Church and the family, the school has the vocation of being active and creative in the education of children and young people.

[4]St John Chrysostom, "The Right Way for Parents to Bring up Their Children," quoted in Sister Magdalen, *Sfaturi pentru o educație ortodoxă a copiilor de azi* [Reflections on children in the Orthodox Church today] (Sibiu: Editura Deisis, 2006), 136.

Life's fundamental truths are learned and consolidated from an early age. So, it is imperative that kindergartens form in the pre-school-age child, in addition to specific competencies, a series of attitudes regarding the religious dimension of the child's personality. Time spent with preschool children for religious education can become a long-term investment for the betterment of the world.

Religious education is fundamental to the formation of a child's personality and involves a great responsibility on the part of religion teachers to instill in the children faith in God, which must be planted in their souls as a light for life. Through the educational-formative approach employed in religion classes in elementary, middle, and high school, the religion teacher comes to the aid of the students, giving them the chance to gain a gradual and dynamic knowledge of God's love, manifest in Jesus Christ. Religious education promotes values of Christian faith and morality such as friendship, love, peace, justice, reconciliation, responsibility, solidarity, and cooperation among people, as basic principles of Christian life.

The university education system has not only the mission of the young generations' training and intellectual development but also the vocation of their moral formation and growth. Scientific values must be inextricably correlated with spiritual and moral values. The students' activity within Christian organizations such as the Orthodox Christian Student Association of Romania and the League of the Romanian Orthodox Christian Youth and their participation in the liturgical life in the chapels of universities help them to discover the beauty of spiritual life lived in a communion of love with God and people.

In complementarity with the religious education offered at different school and university levels, this year, the theological-educational department of the Romanian Patriarchate organized a national creative contest named "The Church and School of My Soul," carried out within the national program "Christ Shared with the Children," addressed primarily to children in catechetical groups; coordinated the project "Choose School!" meant to prevent school dropout; and executed the national catechesis project for young people and adults entitled "The Way of Salvation." Also, between September 4 and 7, 2016, the theological-educational sector of the Romanian Patriarchate will organize an international congress of theology titled "The Religious Education of Young People in the Context of Today's Secularization."

The Bucharest Archdiocese also conducts specific programs, contests, and youth camps for youth activities, such as the following: "Youth in the Areopagus: Religious-Cultural Dialogues," "Young People: Solidarity in the Face of Suffering," "The Pilgrimage: A Path to Knowledge and Strengthening in the Faith," "Let's Adopt a Grandparent!," "The Joy of Multiplying the Talents!," "Joy in Communion," "Nature: God's Gift to People," and "Life in Christ: The Path to True Happiness!," which are all positive examples of the Church's missionary work with young people. The Archdiocese of Bucharest, in collaboration with the theological-educational department of the Romanian Patriarchate, will organize the International Meeting of Orthodox Youth between September 1 and 4, 2016, an event which expects 2,500 young people from Romania and abroad.

We bless and urge all priests and deacons in the Archdiocese of Bucharest to pay special attention to the activities of children and young people through the pastoral and missionary programs they organize and to promote intense cooperation with the families and schools within the parishes for the joy and benefit of all.

† Daniel
Patriarch of the Romanian Orthodox Church

Religious and Theological Education: Training for Life[1]

In the year 2016, declared by the Romanian Patriarchate as the "Solemn Year of the Religious Education of Orthodox Christian Youth" and the "Commemorative Year of the Holy Hierarch Martyr Anthimus of Georgia and of the Church Typographers," the theological-educational department of the Patriarchal Administration, in cooperation with the Patriarch Justinian Orthodox Faculty at the University of Bucharest, organized the international congress of theology entitled "The Religious Education of Young People in the Context of Today's Secularization." This academic event brought together representatives of state institutions, hierarchs, priests, education sciences specialists from Romania who are responsible for the religious education of the youth, and delegates from sister Orthodox Churches.

The international congress of theology unfolds as a continuation of the International Meeting of Orthodox Youth, which took place in Bucharest between September 1 and 4, 2016, and is meant to give the guests the opportunity to learn about the conclusions reached by the young people gathered in Bucharest and and analyze them.

This congress is an opportunity to share the experience of the participants regarding our youth's religious education in an international

---

[1]Patriarch Daniel, "Educația religioasă și teologică – formare pentru viață" [Religious and theological education: Training for life], in *Credința și educația: Principalele lumini ale vieții* [Faith and education: Life's leading lights] (Bucharest: Basilica, 2019), 399–The address was given at the international congress of theology "The Religious Education of Young People in the Context of Today's Secularization" (Bucharest, Patriarchal Palace, September 3–7, 2016).

context; to increase the knowledge of educational projects carried out within sister Orthodox Churches; to identify current challenges and educational perspectives in order to find solutions and to improve the information and training of young people for an integrative education; to become aware of the importance and necessity of the Orthodox Church's specific mission of the spiritual formation of young generations; to develop joint educational projects at national and international levels; and to capitalize on the cooperation between the family, Church, and school for the religious education of young people.

In the context of the current secularization, when traditional values are belittled and education is subject to paradigm shifts, young people need the support of the family, the Church, and the school, as only through proper guidance and the promotion of authentic models will they be able to discern their current challenges and future prospects.

In the field of education, the Romanian Orthodox Church has played a significant role throughout the history of our people, contributing to the organization and enrichment of national education and culture. The Romanian school began in the Church's porch and continued to exist and develop in close connection with the Church.

In what follows, we will present aspects of Romania's religious education as it relates to religion classes [in the K–12 school system], pre-university theological education, university and post-university theological education, educational-catechetical programs and projects, and youth activities.

1. Religion classes

Religious education in public schools offers an integrative spiritual horizon, a binder that links and incorporates knowledge from other school disciplines, to form together a luminous and uplifting spiritual guide for a life lived in a communion of love and responsibility for the common good.

In most European countries, the subject of religion is taught within the public education system and holds a recognized and appreciated role in society. In our country, until the adoption of the law on public instruction (November 25/December 7, 1864), Romanian education was conducted almost exclusively within the Church, and through this law, the school subject of religion was given an important place in elementary, middle, and high school instruction.

The education reform decree of 1948 removed religion from schools. The hard years of the communist dictatorship—whose humiliating atheism was imposed on public schools, contrary to the will of a spiritual nation—taught us that we no longer want a culture without faith, science without spirituality, matter without spirit, knowledge without communion, philosophy without hope, and, in particular, a school without a soul, meaning an education without religion, especially during the age of existential questions and the spiritual formation of young generations.

After the fall of communism in 1989, "moral-religious education" classes were reintroduced in elementary and middle schools, starting with the academic year of 1990–1991 (as per a protocol concluded in 1990 between the Ministry of Education and Science and the State Secretariat for Religious Affairs).

Regarding this school subject, the Constitution of Romania, approved by the national referendum of December 8, 1991, provides that the state ensures the freedom of religious education, according to the specific requirements of each denomination. In public schools, religious education is organized and guaranteed by law (article 32, paragraph 7).

Religion classes have maintained their compulsory character to this very day in the curricular offering of schools. Since 2014, following the publication of decision no. 669 of Romania's Constitutional Court, registration for attending this class is done freely by the written request of students aged eighteen or above, or of the parent or legal guardian of minor students. At the beginning of 2015, from a reporting base of 2,371,697 students, 2,167,485 applications were registered in the Integrated Information System of Education in Romania—that is, an application rate of 91.39 percent.

In support of the discipline of religion, the Parents for Religion Classes Association and the Association of Religion Teachers were established in 2015, and the Romanian Patriarchate issued a document named the "Strategic Plan for Increasing the Quality of Religious Education." To develop the cooperation that would support and improve religion classes, 5,642 partnerships between parishes and schools were established, during which various school and extracurricular activities took place.

One of the biggest challenges for religious education has to do with the need to develop a unitary educational and religious path appropriate to the set of spiritual values, and a suitable way of conveying them. In this respect, the religion curricula and textbooks are reviewed periodically. The new Orthodox curriculum for the elementary school years was put together by the Ministry of National Education and Scientific Research in collaboration with the Romanian Patriarchate between 2012 and 2014. Currently, new school curricula for the middle school years are being prepared. At the same time, during the selection process for school textbooks organized by the Ministry of National Education and Scientific Research in 2015 and 2016, the Romanian Patriarchate endorsed and approved new textbooks for elementary school education. These textbooks are available in print and digital versions.

In support of students and religion teachers, ensuing the entry into application of new religion school curricula, auxiliary teaching materials for elementary education were published by Basilica Press of the Romanian Patriarchate.

The discipline of religion has always played an important role in the process of forming competencies and moral and social attitudes within the public education system. Therefore, religious education cannot be absent from the Romanian school curriculum, precisely because the study of religion corresponds to the need of local and national Romanian communities to preserve their spiritual wealth and identity and to transmit permanent values to young generations.

2. Pre-university theological education

Positioned as the continuation of religious education in public schools and the Church, theological seminaries[2] anticipate the advanced and specialized training to be received in faculties of theology. The general education acquired in theological seminaries, through its common body (set) of disciplines, offers students the opportunity to attend the courses of any faculty in Romania.

In 1803, Metropolitan Benjamin Costachi established the first Orthodox theological seminary in Moldavia, at Socola Monastery near Jassy. Subsequently, Orthodox seminaries were set up in Bucharest, Buzău, and Argeş (1836); Râmnicu Vâlcea (1837); Huşi (1852); and Roman (1858).

In the communist period that lasted from 1948 to 1989, theological education was marginalized; thus, until 1989 only the following six theological seminaries were operating: Bucharest, Buzău, Neamţ Monastery, Cluj, Craiova, and Caransebeş.

The fall of the communist regime in December 1989 brought the reintegration of pre-university theological education into public education. The enthusiasm of the 1990s together with the freedom that the Church began to enjoy meant that in addition to the existing seminaries, those that had been abolished were reopened and new ones were established.

Currently, twenty-eight theological seminaries and seven Orthodox theological high schools operate within the Romanian Orthodox Church, with the following specializations (for vocational paths): Orthodox theology, cultural heritage, and religious tourism.

Theological seminaries aim to develop competencies and skills that facilitate young people's access to culture, civilization, and information, in accordance with the values of authentic Christian morality. In the general context of a lay education that often emphasizes intellectual

[2]In Romania, theological seminaries are secondary schools, for grades 9 through 12. In addition to all disciplines of lay education, the students take intensive courses in theology. Higher theological education takes place in theological faculties or departments of theology in universities.—Ed.

formation to the detriment of spiritual and moral formation, theological education correlates intellectual and spiritual formation with the liturgical and practical experience of faith. Remaining faithful to its own religious traditions and taking into consideration the concrete problems of the contemporary world, theological education proposes solutions oriented toward consecrated values, as lights of life in the eternal love of the Holy Trinity.

3. Undergraduate and post-graduate theological education

Theological institutions of higher education have the role of cultivating the personal vocation of the young person who aspires to spiritual and academic training. The graduates of Romania's theological faculties are called to become servants of the holy altars, teachers of religion, social workers, church painters, curators, and restorers of sacred art.

Currently, eleven faculties of Orthodox theology operate within the Romanian Patriarchate in the cities of Bucharest, Constanța, Târgoviște, Pitești, Jassy, Sibiu, Alba Iulia, Cluj-Napoca, Oradea, Craiova, and Arad. There are also four theology departments within some faculties in Galați, Baia Mare, Timișoara, and Caransebeș. These faculties and departments of theology offer the following specializations: pastoral theology, didactic theology, social theology, sacred art, religious music, and educational sciences. At the same time, theological education at the university level organizes masters and doctoral courses.

Through the partnerships between the Romanian Patriarchate and different educational institutions from abroad, Romanian students of theology also benefit from opportunities to study overseas. Correspondingly, young people from abroad have the opportunity to study at the faculties of Orthodox theology in Romania.

The Romanian Patriarchate seeks to highlight the importance and necessity of religious and theological education, so it periodically organizes national and international congresses and symposia.

A genuine theological education involves the careful cultivation of spiritual and edifying reference points and living models of holiness, especially through participation in the liturgical life and social mission of the Church. Faculties of theology also have the role of analyzing and promoting possible solutions to the challenges and existential problems of today, such as the phenomena of secularization; globalization; migration; the ecological crisis; economic, social, and moral problems in society, etc.

4. Catechetical educational projects and programs

Since 2005 the Romanian Orthodox Church has intensified the educational-catechetical activities for children and young people, by initiating local, regional, or national programs, projects, and competitions. As of 2008, one of these programs, "Christ Shared with the Children," has become the national program for catechizing children and young people, by the decision of the Holy Synod of the Romanian Orthodox Church.

For the development of this national program, biblical catechesis guides (for children between six and seventeen years old) and guides for catechumens have been published. These catechetical tools were distributed to parishes in all dioceses, and priests and teachers/catechists were trained in their use and for organizing catechetical activities at the parish level.

In order to energize these activities and to identify the best solutions for the implementation of the national program "Christ Shared with the Children," a countrywide congress has been organized yearly since 2008 and is attended by eparchial inspectors who are responsible for catechetical activities at regional levels and who are specialists in education sciences.

As some of the children participating in the aforementioned program face the danger of school dropout, a project that aims to prevent and correct the phenomenon of ill-timed school abandonment was needed as well. Thus, starting in 2009, the Romanian Patriarchate, in partnership with the World Vision Romania Foundation and the

Metropolitanate of Moldavia and Bukovina, has carried out in four stages the educational project named "Choose School!"

The "Choose School!" project, funded by the European Union through the Sectoral Operational Program for Human Resources Development, was meant to provide equal opportunities for education to 30,929 students and to develop remedial and corrective actions for 418 people who dropped out of school. The project was implemented in 3,309 parishes.

Within the project, 103 "Choose School!" educational centers were established and were well supplied with the office equipment and materials needed to carry out educational activities with children and young people from disadvantaged areas of the country. An educational curriculum was developed, consisting of seven modules adapted to the academic needs of the educational system and to the needs of the labor market. Based on it, "school-after-school" activities and lessons were developed, during which groups for reading and mathematical computation were formed. A number of 247 training sessions were organized for priests and teachers, and counseling and information services were provided for parents or guardians of pupils at risk of school abandonment, to inform them of the importance of educa-tion. Several competitions with prizes for all the children enrolled in the project and free camps for 11,793 children were organized as well. The awards amounted to more than four million lei (approximately one million euros) for the 33,488 prizes conferred in the competitions organized in all four stages of the project. The following awards were given as well: 11,793 prizes for the creativity camps; monthly financial aid for 2,075 families with difficulties in caring for their children; and grants for 418 children and young people participating in the "Second Chance" program.

At the same time, two virtual educational platforms, www.alegescoala.ro and www.alegscoala.ro, have been created, containing information on the activities performed in the project in general and in each center in particular, an interactive map, and an online discussion forum. As a result of the research undertaken within the project by professors from the Faculty of Psychology and Educational Sciences at the Babes-Bolyai University in Cluj-Napoca, a complex and integrated psychological study on the risk factors of school dropout was published, which presents the impact of the activities on the children who benefited from the project.

Studies and specialized reports confirm that the flexibility of "second chance"–type programs that involve the school, the family, and the Church simultaneously, greatly reduces risk factors and increases the reintegration likelihood of children who abandon school.

The world of childhood, along with its values, offers students the opportunity to be creative in various fields and to develop their imagination, skills, and talent. Through the "Choose School!" project, we set out to understand this world of children and to know better the current generations of children and young people's concerns, interests, and aspirations, while giving them the opportunity to highlight and develop them.

5. Youth activities

The Romanian Orthodox Church, through its available infrastructure, offers young people the necessary space and opportunity to develop their capacity for active and assumed participation in a creative process, with a purpose well determined by the formation of their personality. Within the Church's youth programs, they have the chance to get to know one another and to become aware of the cultural heritage and richness of the traditions specific to Romanian and universal Orthodoxy. Owing to the fact that this process of intra- and interpersonal knowledge and development unfolds with the support and guidance of the Church, young people come to understand her importance and role in daily life.

The dynamizing of youth activities is a priority for the Romanian Patriarchate, and it has the following objectives: to provide a framework conducive to the personal development of young people as members of the Church, in which they learn to communicate, interact, and develop harmoniously; to offer an alternative to the ways of spending leisure time furthered by contemporary society; to promote social responsibility among the youth; to involve young people in coordinating volunteer activities in their dioceses; to organize teams for developing youth programs under the guidance of eparchial centers; and to familiarize young people with the specifics of each area of Romania.

In our country, there are two organizations—the Orthodox Christian Student Association of Romania and the League of the Romanian Orthodox Christian Youth—that operate with the blessing of the Holy Synod of the Romanian Orthodox Church. Also, in some dioceses there are well-structured youth organizations, such as the Association of Orthodox Young People, especially present in Transylvania and Moldavia. Within dioceses, numerous youth activities are implemented and carried out, with specific partnerships developed in this respect. The youth camps organized in some monasteries in Romania (Caraiman, Tismana, Buciumeni, Durău, Neamț, Putna, Sâmbăta de Sus, Oașa, Nicula, Rohia, etc.) play a special role.

To sum up, the aspects presented above highlight different ways of organizing religious education in the Church and in the Romanian school system, as well as the importance of achieving integrative education of children and young people, with the prospect of their spiritual and practical formation as young members participating in the life of the Church and society. Certainly, all the activities presented so far require continuity and unceasing improvement.

We thank the participants in this international congress of theology, which we believe will contribute to a better understanding of the importance and role of the religious education of young people in today's context of secularization, as a light for life in the family, in the Church, and in society.

† DANIEL
Patriarch of the Romanian Orthodox Church

The Meeting of Orthodox Youth from All over the World: The Joy of Communion and the Dynamics of Christian Mission[1]

D uring these days we have the joy of being together with 2,500 young people from different countries of the world, who, between September 1 and 4, 2016, are our guests at the Meeting of Orthodox Youth, an event organized by the Bucharest Archdiocese and the Romanian Patriarchate, in the context of the "Solemn Year of the Religious Education of Orthodox Christian Youth."

Our meeting endeavors to train young people through participation in educational, spiritual, cultural, and artistic programs in Bucharest. The event's program is a rich one and includes the first Divine Liturgy at the site of the Cathedral of the Romanian People's Salvation; a spiritual conference; two workshops, whose theme is the importance and activity of young people in the Church; artistic events; and sightseeing in Bucharest. The workshops are meant to create an appropriate framework in which you, our guests, identify the specific problems of your generation and propose possible solutions.

---

[1]Patriarch Daniel, "Întâlnirea Tinerilor Ortodocși din Toată Lumea, București 2016 – bucuria comuniunii și dinamica misiunii creștine" [The Meeting of Orthodox Youth from All over the World, Bucharest 2016: The joy of communion and the dynamics of Christian mission], in *Credința și educația: Principalele lumini ale vieții* [Faith and education: Life's leading lights] (Bucharest: Basilica, 2019), 183–186. Address given at the opening ceremony of the International Meeting, Bucharest, September 1–4, 2016.

Young people face many challenges in a secularized and globalized society that is impoverished of spiritual values and is subject to permanent changes and economic and moral crises such as emigration, alcohol consumption, drugs, libertinism, violence, etc. As a result, they represent an additional reason to raise awareness of the role and importance of the family, the Church, and the school in the formation of young Christians. The young generation's aspirations for the good and the beautiful must be supported by the whole of society, which holds the responsibility of guiding young people and cultivating their confidence to love perennial spiritual, moral, and cultural values. The family, the Church, and the school have a duty to provide a Christian education to the young, so that they may promote faith as a light of daily life and love for God and for people.

The Romanian Orthodox Church tries to respond to the formative needs of youth through programs and projects such as the national catechetical program "Christ Shared with the Children," the educational project "Choose School!," pilgrimages, scholarships, and many social parish activities that take place both at home and abroad and are adapted to each community. Through all these, we cultivate self-confidence and self-respect, deference and love for people and nature—God's creation—and we strengthen the young people's life of communion, Christian solidarity, friendship, affiliation with and respect for the Church, and national identity and dignity in international dialogue.

Yet what is and remains essential in all these activities ought to be the happiness given by uniting young people with the love of Christ both in prayer and in action, in working together to bring joy to people. Because the risen Christ is "eternal joy," "the light of the world," and "the Good Shepherd," the Apostle to the Gentiles urges us, "Rejoice in the Lord always. Again I will say, rejoice" (Phil 4.4).

At the same time, we encourage you to gladly cultivate love for the Christian family, which can only be discovered in the Church—as the place wherein the family gains the value of an icon of Christ's love for humanity and where the saints, who represent models of a life lived in Christ, raise prayers for the world's youth.

With these thoughts, we welcome you to the International Meeting of Orthodox Youth, and we pray that the Most Holy Trinity grant you holy joy in brotherly communion and friendship.

† DANIEL,
Patriarch of the Romanian Orthodox Church

Only Jesus Christ Gives People Complete Liberty[1]

"Stand fast therefore in the liberty by which Christ has made us free, and do not be entangled again with a yoke of bondage."
(Gal 5.1)

1. Liberty: a constant concern of humanity

Liberty has preoccupied not only philosophers of ancient times such as Plato or Socrates but also those of modern times such Immanuel Kant, Nicholas Berdyaev, Jean-Paul Sartre, and many others. Liberty was also the concern of those intellectuals who reflected on the relationship between individual freedom and social order, based on laws, rights, and obligations.

Today, in the capitalist context of new secularist ideologies, priority is given to individual rights or liberties, without any reference to the values of faith in God and to the vocation of the human person to live an eternal life.

Although the theme of liberty, as a permanent aspiration of people and peoples, has preoccupied humankind throughout time, there is no common definition of liberty, the essence of which is difficult to define. However, a distinction is often made between the *natural liberty* of the

---

[1]Patriarch Daniel, "Numai Iisus Hristos oferă omului libertate deplină" [Only Jesus Christ gives people complete liberty], in *Credința și educația: Principalele lumini ale vieții* [Faith and Education: Life's Leading Lights] (Bucharest: Basilica, 2019), 189–194. Address delivered at the International Meeting of Orthodox Youth (Jassy, September 1–4, 2017), whose theme was "The Young Person in Search of Freedom."

human person, as the free will to choose between good and evil, and *social liberty*, as the freedom granted to individuals by the society in which they live.

Indeed, *natural liberty* and *social liberty* have a certain value for all people, but for Christians they do not represent the *full spiritual liberty* that was revealed to the world by Jesus Christ and bestowed upon those who believe in him.

2. The liberty of the human person was damaged (perverted) by the fall from the communion of life with God, the Creator of the universe and humankind

The liberty of people, created in the image of God (cf. Acts 1.26–27), has been severely impaired, corrupted by the disobedience to God of our foreparents Adam and Eve, when man wanted to be like God, but in forgetfulness of and separation from him (cf. Gen 2). Since all human beings inherited the fallen nature of the old Adam (cf. Rom 5.12), their liberty on earth is perverted by sin—understood as a selfish and possessive mode of existence—which prevents them from fully and permanently loving God and all people: "For the good that I will to do, I do not do; but the evil I will not to do, that I practice," notes St Paul in Romans 7.19.

Human liberty is also perverted by the spirits of evil (demonic powers), which often urge a person to unbelief and disobedience to God, as well as to hatred of other people. Therefore, the Christian fights "against . . . the spiritual hosts of wickedness in the heavenly places" (Eph 6.12).

Finally, the greatest obstacle to human liberty is death, for it is opposed to the human person's desire to live life permanently in relation to the seen world (fellow humans and nature). For this reason, the holy Scripture tells us that "the last enemy that will be destroyed is death" (1 Cor 15.26).

3. Jesus Christ—the new Adam—overcame sin, hell, and death, thus giving people complete liberty to love God and their neighbor

Jesus Christ, the eternal Son of God, became man precisely to liberate people from sin, from the spirits of wickedness and death, which are major obstacles to the individual's spiritual freedom. In this regard, the holy Apostle Paul says that the Son of God became man, "that through death he might destroy him who had the power of death, that is, the devil, and release those who through fear of death were all their life-time subject to bondage" (Heb 2.14–15). More precisely, the Lord Jesus Christ, the new Adam, by humble obedience to God even to death on the cross and by his resurrection from the dead, delivers people from the bondage of sin, evil spirits, and death, "into the glorious liberty of the children of God" (Rom 8.21). As a result of the salvific and redemptive work of Christ, through holy baptism, the new Christian is granted forgiveness of sins, the grace of adoption, and resurrection from death, meaning a new spiritual life, as Jesus Christ vouchsafed: "I am the resurrection and the life. He who believes in me, though he may die, he shall live" (Jn 11.25). And the new life of those who believe in Christ is cultivated in the Church of Christ by the grace of the Holy Spirit for the acquisition of eternal life in the kingdom of God.

Therefore, the complete spiritual liberty in Christ of the human person is the complete freedom to love God and people in time and in eternity.

Referring to this freedom, the Lord Jesus Christ teaches us thus: "You shall know the truth, and the truth shall make you free" (Jn 8.32). Here, the truth is the divine-human Person himself, who fulfills within his very Person the communion of the eternal love of God with humanity. That is why, later, Jesus Christ states, "I am the way, the truth, and the life. No one comes to the Father except through me" (Jn 14.6), meaning Christ is the way to Truth, and the ultimate truth is life eternal in the kingdom of the Holy Trinity. Since the spirit of truth is the Holy Spirit (cf. Jn 14.26; 15.26; 16.13–14), the Apostle Paul testifies that "where the Spirit of the Lord is, there is liberty" (2 Cor 3.17). But the holy Apostle Peter warns that the liberty of those who believe in Christ, given to them by the Holy Spirit, is not liberty to do evil, but liberty to do good "as free, yet not using liberty as a cloak for vice, but as bondservants of God" (1 Pet 2.16).

This spiritual liberty of the individual to do good as a manifestation of a humble love of the Lord and compassionate (godly) love for people is in fact the full freedom acquired by saints through prayer, repentance, and fasting after struggling for a long time with selfish passions, evil spirits, and the fear of death. And these saints are not only monks but also a lot of faithful martyrs who founded families, gave birth to children, and raised them in faith and in love for God and for people. Therefore, this full liberty is God's gift received through baptism in water and the Spirit, but it is also the constant spiritual struggle of the believers with their own selfishness, to abide permanently in the state of humble love of God and of generous love toward people.

4. The liberty to be permanently in a communion of love with God and with people is cultivated in the Church

The concrete environment for cultivating this spiritual liberty offered by Christ is his Church, the spiritual house of the Holy Trinity. For this reason, the Church gladly welcomes all young people who seek true liberty and imparts to them the following, through the holy mysteries and holy feasts: the paternal love of the heavenly Father, who rejoices not only in his obedient (devout) spiritual children but also in the "prodigal sons" who repent; the healing and redemptive love of the Savior Jesus Christ, the physician of souls and bodies; and the *hallowing love* of the Holy Spirit, the comforter, treasury of goodness and giver of life.

Spiritual liberty received through faith in Christ and cultivated in the communion of prayer and fraternal love becomes a fount of peace, joy, and happiness. In this sense, Fr Stăniloae notes that "[t]he liberty given us by the Holy Spirit goes hand in hand and grows with our spiritual life. He is the Spirit of liberty because he is the Spirit of life; by calling us to liberty and helping us to grow in it, he becomes our cause (source) of life."

We find today that in the family, in religion classes at school, in the parish, in pilgrimages to monasteries, in theology schools, in Orthodox educational and cultural centers, young people greatly enjoy feeling God's love and that of other people; and when they are encouraged, in return, they also love God in prayer and their neighbors through works of generous love.

And when young Orthodox Christians carry in their souls the love, peace, and joy bestowed upon them by Christ, they can become confessors and missionaries of his love in the world, sharing it with other young people seeking to ascribe a deep spiritual meaning to their lives and with those in difficulty (abandoned by family and friends, faced with poverty, unemployment, loneliness, confusion, and other problems). In this regard, the Church greatly appreciates the spiritual, humanitarian, and missionary activities of the youth.

Upon pursuing liberty in their many stages of life, all people on earth, young or less young, ask themselves the essential question of existence: What have I done with the liberty I have found? If this liberty has helped me to love God and people more, then I have found true liberty. If the liberty I have found has removed me even farther from God, people, and myself, then I am not truly free.

Here is an example: during the atheist communist regime, although they were tormented and tortured in prison, many young people, and especially the clergy and lay intellectuals, acquired, through suffering and prayer, a great freedom of the soul to confess their faith and to forgive those who persecuted them, akin to the martyrs of the early Christian centuries. That was the liberty and peace given to them by the crucified and risen Jesus Christ himself. That is the liberty to love God and people not only in a favorable context but also in a hostile or oppressive environment. This is the liberty of the soul which, by

God's grace, transforms the suffering of the cross into the joy of the resurrection.

In closing, we congratulate His Eminence Theophan, metropolitan of Moldavia and Bukovina, and all those who have endeavored to organize this international meeting of Orthodox youth in Jassy.

And as for you, dear young people, we hope that you may spend these days in fraternal communion and friendship. May the Most Holy Trinity, the source of life and joy eternal, bless you with peace, light, and love!

† DANIEL
Patriarch of the Romanian Orthodox Church

Children: God's Gift to the Family, Church, and Society[1]

K nowing the real situation of the Christian family today and understanding its spiritual vocation more deeply are priorities of the Church's missionary work in society. To this end, the Holy Synod of the Romanian Orthodox Church established in 2009 that the first Sunday in June would be dedicated to parents and children.

The family is the crown of creation and the place, or environment, in which the human child begins to understand the mystery of God's parental love for all people.

Today, given the weakened bond of love between people and God because of secularization, the family is in a deep spiritual crisis. In this context, a Christian education is ever more needed, so that generous love and responsibility in the family can be enhanced.

The family can never be reduced to its earthly biological, legal, psychological, sociological, or cultural aspects, because it encompasses and transcends them through the communion of holy faith and love and through its vocation to represent the world in the cooperation between people and God for the acquisition of eternal life.

Children born into a family and baptized into the Church in the name of the Most Holy Trinity can become citizens of the eternal heavenly kingdom if during their earthly life they cultivate the spiritual gifts

---

[1]Patriarch Daniel, "Copiii – daruri ale lui Dumnezeu pentru familie, Biserică și societate" [Children: God's gift to the family, Church, and society], in *Credința și educația: Principalele lumini ale vieții* [Faith and education: Life's leading lights] (Bucharest: Basilica, 2019), 133–138. Homily given on International Children's Day (June 1, 2018) and the Sunday for Parents and Children (June 3, 2018).

received at baptism, as shown by the families who have given many saints to the Church and are now recorded in her synaxarion.

In order to contribute more to the spiritual growth of the Christian family, the Romanian Patriarchate pays special attention to the religious education of children and young people, offering them the opportunity to develop their capacity for vigorous participation in the life and activity of their parish communities.

Through educational, cultural, and artistic programs, children and young people have the chance to become better acquainted with one another and to learn the permanent values of the Christian faith and Romanian spirituality.

We find that in the family, in religious classes at schools, in the parish, in pilgrimages to monasteries, in theology schools, in the Church's educational and cultural centers, all children and young people rejoice in God's love and in the love of other people, and so they become encouraged to love God in prayer and their neighbor through works of compassionate love. And when young Orthodox Christians carry in their souls the love, peace, and joy bestowed upon them by Christ, they become confessors of his love and missionaries to their peers, especially helping those in distress.

The year 2018, which the Holy Synod of the Romanian Orthodox Church declared the "Solemn Year of the Unity of Faith and Nation" and the "Commemorative Year of the Founders of the Great Union of 1918" is a good opportunity to increase the cooperation of the Church, family, and school in the formation and education of children, offering them the prospect to develop permanent spiritual values inspired by the faith and the living tradition of the Romanian people.

On the International Children's Day and the Sunday for Parents and Children, we urge all parents to give more time to their children, to help them not to lose their health and innate gifts, and to cultivate the freedom to do good and to bring joy to those around them.

We urge children to love their parents more and to pray for them, for it is through parents that God gives children their lives and helps them grow and be formed as wise, compassionate, and loving people, created in the image of God, the good and holy (cf. Acts 1.26–27).

On this day we particularly pray to God, the Father of light, from whom we receive "every good gift and every perfect gift" (Jas 1.17) to give the Romanian parents and children here and abroad peace, health, and much help in life, to the joy of the family, the Church, and the Romanian people.

† Daniel

Words of Blessing to the Young Participants at the International Meeting of Orthodox Youth, Sibiu, 2018[1]

D ear young people,
    With great spiritual joy I send a benediction to you, young participants in Sibiu—in the heart of Romania—at the International Meeting of Orthodox Youth.

This event is organized between September 6 and 9, 2018, by the Archdiocese of Sibiu, with the theme of "unity, faith, and nation," in the context of the "Solemn Year of the Unity of Faith and Nation" and of the "Commemorative Year of the Founders of the Great Union of 1918."

The Mother of God is the icon of the Church and the Protectress of the family

It is particularly significant that, in the Romanian Orthodox Church, these international gatherings of young Orthodox Christians are held in communion of faith, prayer and song, dialogue and friendship, at the beginning of the new Church year, which calls us to the sanctification of our life on earth as a time of salvation.

---

[1]Patriarch Daniel, "Cuvânt de binecuvântare pentru tinerii participanți la ITO 2018 – Sibiu" [Words of blessing to the young participants at the International Meeting of Orthodox Youth, Sibiu, 2018], in *Credința și educația: Principalele lumini ale vieții* [Faith and education: Life's leading lights] (Bucharest: Basilica, 2019), 197–200. Address delivered at the opening ceremony, Thursday, September 6, 2018, Great Square, Sibiu.

In this sense, the first great feast of September is the Nativity of the Theotokos (September 8), the Mother of the Lord being the icon of the Church, for she is the human being through whom the eternal Son of God, Jesus Christ, becomes man in human history to give eternal life to mortal people (cf. Jn 11.25). The number eight symbolizes the eternal life and infinite light of the kingdom of heaven.

Children and young people are a holy gift and a great blessing for the family and the Church, for the country and the people.

Young people are eager to live in a communion of love—to love and to be loved in the family and in society—but also to cultivate an ideal and to give meaning to their present and future lives through the accumulation of new knowledge and creativity.

In this respect, they represent not only the future of the Church and society but also their dynamic and innovative present at a national and international level.

By participating in the youth programs supported by the Church, young people have the chance to get to know one another better, to forge new friendships, to cherish more the cultural heritage and the richness of the traditions specific to Romanian Orthodoxy from different cities of Romania, and to learn new information about the spiritual richness of universal Orthodoxy.

If the meeting last year in Jassy had "liberty" as its main theme, this year, the 2018 meeting in Sibiu calls us to think about and live more intensely the connection between "liberty and unity"—in the family, in the Church, and in society, following the luminous example of the founders of the Great Union of 1918.

Liberty and unity are two essential and permanent components of human life, because the human person was created to live in a communion of love, in the image of God—or of the Trinity of distinct Persons, free and undivided, living in perfect unity—who is love (cf. 1 Jn 4.16).

In this sense, the healthy state of human life, in which the liberty of the distinct persons is harmonized with the unity among them, is expressed in a communion of love.

This communion of love bears the fruit of peace and joy; mutual respect; dialogue and cooperation; and solidarity and co-responsibility in the family, the Church, and society. This is the human life blessed by God and beneficial to the individual and the community.

But when because of sin—which is a person's selfish, possessive, and aggressive attitude and action in relation to the neighbor—liberty is asserted against the unity or communion of love, it then becomes destructive liberty.

This is how disputes in the family and society arise and how conflicts and violent wars of conquest begin, followed by revolts and wars of liberation of occupied and oppressed peoples.

The Most Holy Trinity is the fount of unity and liberty in a communion of love

We understand, then, that although the sin of selfishness divides people and nations, the merciful love of God, or the grace of the Most Holy Trinity, still brings together different people and nations, or different ethnic groups (cf. Acts 2).

Therefore, in the Church of Christ, Christian life begins with baptism in water and the Holy Spirit, performed by the Church *in* the name of the Father and of the Son and of the Holy Spirit—that is, in a spiritual relationship with the Holy Trinity's eternal love.

Afterward, the Christian life develops through the participation of Christians in the liturgical and social and philanthropic life of the Church, so that through prayer they may receive and subsequently transmit through good deeds the Holy Trinity's humble and generous love in family, community, and social life.

In every holy Orthodox eucharistic Liturgy, we confess our common faith in God the Father, the Son, and the Holy Spirit (the Orthodox

Creed), and we thank the Holy Trinity for the gift of life and "for every good and perfect gift."

Then, by partaking of the Body and Blood of Christ, the one who was crucified and resurrected, we receive in our soul "the grace of the Lord Jesus Christ, and the love of God, and the communion of the Holy Spirit" (2 Cor 13.14). And toward the end of the Divine Liturgy we sing, "We have seen the true light; we have received the heavenly Spirit; we have found the true faith, worshiping the undivided Trinity, for the Trinity has saved us."

In fact, the whole of Orthodox liturgical life is rhythmed by the sign of the holy cross and the doxology: "Glory to the Father and to the Son and to the Holy Spirit, now and ever and unto the ages of ages. Amen!"

The belief in the love of the crucified and risen Christ has strengthened the love of the nation and the solidarity between Romanians

For the Orthodox Christian people, faith in the Most Holy Trinity has been a source of holy love in the Church, family, and society throughout the centuries. And the sign of the holy cross, as a sign of suffering but also of victory through the resurrection, has been a call to sacrificial love for the Church and the nation in the struggle for liberation from unjust and oppressive rule, and in the fight for the defense of ethnic identity and achievement of national unity.

In this sense, it is significant that in Transylvania the patronal feast of several eparchial cathedrals is the feast of the Most Holy Trinity (Sibiu, Arad, Baia Mare, Blaj [Greek Catholic] and in particular the Cathedral of the Nation's Reunification of Alba Iulia), thus emphasizing the desire of Romanians for liberty and national unity.

Through the books of worship printed in the Romanian language and through the love of nation of her servants, the Church contributed greatly to the fostering of the national consciousness of Romanians when they lived in three Romanian principalities under foreign domination: Moldavia and Wallachia, under Ottoman rule, and Transylvania, under the Habsburgs.

In this sense, a humanist chronicler, a member of the Hungarian elite, noted at the end of the sixteenth century that Michael the Brave's victory in Transylvania was also prepared "by the surreptitious work of priests and monks."[2]

Also, the Orthodox chaplains present in the front line alongside the Romanian soldiers in the First World War (1916–1918) instilled in them great courage and faith in achieving the ideal of the Great Union of Romanians from all provinces.

National identity is cultivated even in international cooperation

Today, however, because of secularization, or the weakening of faith in God—the source of undying love—the communion of love between people, family, and society has declined.

Thus, it is often found that without a mutual relationship of humble and sincere love in the family, its members' liberty and unity quickly turn into conflict and separation between husband and wife or between parents and children.

Also, without the love of country and nation, freedom and national unity gradually turn into self-alienation, and natural patriotism is often replaced by the desire for immediate material profit: *patria ubi bene* (my homeland is where it is well with me).

Yet beyond this wilting cultivation of national values, we are convinced that these values—namely, national identity, freedom, and unity—will not disappear but will be fostered by nations even in the course of their international cooperation.

Why? Because these national values are identity-affirming values that express the special character (or uniqueness), wealth, and dignity of each nation in relation to other nations.

---

[2]Cf. *Istoria Transilvaniei* [History of Transylvania], vol. 2 (Cluj-Napoca: Editura Academiei Române, 2007), 100.

The young Orthodox are missionaries of Orthodox unity and communion between nations

Dear Orthodox Christian youth from Romania and abroad, you are apostles and your nations' missionaries of freedom and unity, of communion between ethnic groups, and of cooperation between countries, especially when you promote generous love in the family, in your friendships, in the parish, in the diocese, in society, and in all national and international Orthodox meetings, for the joy of Orthodoxy as a whole and communion between the peoples of the world.

We entreat God to bless you, so that you may use your stay in Sibiu as a time of cultivation of the Orthodox Christian faith, of dialogue, of friendship and unity, to the glory of the Most Holy Trinity, the good of the Church, and the joy of all!

We invite you all to Bucharest, on November 25 of this year, to be present at the consecration of the National Cathedral!

† Daniel
Patriarch of the Romanian Orthodox Church

Young People: Seekers of Enduring Values and Promoters of Communion among Generations[1]

The national council of the Orthodox Christian Student Association of Romania (ASCOR), organized in 2019—the year designated by the Holy Synod of the Romanian Orthodox Church as the "Solemn Year of the Romanian Village (embodied by priests, teachers, and diligent mayors)"—represents a good opportunity for a meeting of its members from all over the country, who generously dedicate themselves to youth activities.

As the Savior Jesus Christ once called his disciples to the apostolate, so does his Church today call young people to mission, or holy work, for salvation.

The true meaning of the young people's mission today in the Church is, just as it was for the holy apostles of old, "to pursue peace with all people and holiness, without which no one will see the Lord" (Heb 12.14). And the pursuit of holiness—the human person's strongest connection with the Holy One—ought to begin in childhood, the age of searches.

Only a young person seeking eternal life in God's love can truly become a young missionary of great service to the life and mission of

---

[1]Patriarch Daniel, "Tinerii – căutători ai valorilor netrecătoare și promotori ai comuniunii între generații" [Young People: Seekers of enduring values and promoters of communion among generations], July 12, 2019, Basilica News Agency, accessed November 26, 2019, https://basilica.ro/tinerii-cautatori-ai-valorilor-netrecatoare-si-promotori-ai-comuniunii-intre-generatii/. Address at the National Council of the Romanian Orthodox Christian Students' Association, Bucharest, July 12–14, 2019.

the Church of Christ. The young person who strives for everlasting invaluable spiritual values shows that youth can be, in this transient world, a symbol of eternal life's beauty.

Steadiness and fidelity in friendship; individual freedom united with responsibility for community life, as maturity of the spirit; and brotherly help given to other young people, are major benchmarks for maintaining, promoting, and transmitting the permanent values of the Christian faith from one generation to another.

We are glad that young people pay special attention to their continuous formation by participating in events wherein they have the opportunity to develop their capacity for active involvement both locally, in the life of the parish communities to which they belong, and nationally, in the Romanian Patriarchate's projects. Through educational and cultural programs, young people have the chance to get to know one another better and to become aware of the immortal values of the Orthodox faith and of Romanian spirituality.

The year 2020 will mark thirty years of the association's existence and activity. Its members will have the opportunity to relive the emotions of an anniversary moment and to evaluate, with joy and responsibility, the activities carried out so far and their impact.

We entreat God to protect all the young believers of our ancestral Church by giving them health and help in their missionary work of Christ's love, to cultivate communion, joy, and holy peace in the family, in the Church, and in society!

With fatherly blessings,
† Daniel
Patriarch of the Romanian Orthodox Church

Young People Are a Blessing and a Joy for the Nation[1]

With great spiritual joy we address a word of blessing to you, young participants in the International Meeting of Orthodox Youth, organized this year by the Archdiocese of Craiova.

Youth is a symbol of eternal life's beauty in this fleeting world, so God has seeded in young people a yearning for the ideal, for holy love, and for everlasting life, just as we can see in the example of the rich young man of the Gospel. He learned that complete happiness comes not from transient material goods, but from the eternal love of God (cf. Mk 10.17–21; Lk 18.18).

Jesus Christ loves children and young people

In the Scriptures we find that our Lord Jesus Christ paid special attention to and had appreciation for children and young people. He said, "Let the little children come to me, and do not forbid them; for of such is the kingdom of God" (Mk 10.14), thus emphasizing the value of their innocence and purity. While on earth, Christ raised three young people from the dead: the son of the widow of Nain (cf. Lk 7.11–16), the daughter of Jairus (cf. Mt 9.18–25; Mk 5.22–42; Lk 8.4–56), and his friend Lazarus of Bethany (cf. Jn 11.1–46). The Lord resurrected them

---

[1]Patriarch Daniel, "Tinerii sunt binecuvântare și bucurie pentru popor" [Young people are a blessing and a joy for the nation], in *Credința și educația: Principalele lumini ale vieții* [Faith and education: Life's leading lights] (Bucharest: Basilica, 2019), 205–214. Address delivered at the opening of the International Meeting of Orthodox Youth, September 5–8, 2019, in Craiova.

to show that youth is a symbol of the beauty of unending life in the kingdom of heaven (cf. Mt 22.30).

In a secularized and ever-changing world, young people need to feel the bountiful love that God and the Church have for them.

The Church is continuously called to rejuvenate herself through the new generations of young people as well, because Jesus Christ, the One who "is the same yesterday, today, and forever" (Heb 13.8), desires that she testify about him at all times.

And the renewal of the Church's spiritual life is also achieved through young people who always cultivate the three great Christian virtues: faith, hope, and love.

Faith in God, hope, and love are the fundamental qualities of the Christian's life

Faith cannot manifest itself without hope and without love. The Christian believes, hopes, and loves all at once. But that which makes the human person resemble God most closely is the virtue of humble and generous love.

In his Epistle to the Hebrews, the Apostle Paul defines faith as follows: "Faith is the substance of things hoped for, the evidence of things not seen" (Heb 11.1). In other words, faith is the foretaste of hoped-for realities and the confirmation of realities unseen. The same apostle teaches us that "the things which are seen are temporary, but the things which are not seen are eternal" (2 Cor 4.18). In this sense, faith is spiritual knowledge that transcends the senses.

Faith is the spiritual capacity of a person to see with the eyes of the soul and to feel with the heart the presence of God in creation and his work in people's lives.

Therefore, faith is not just an intellectual conviction that God exists somewhere in heaven, but it is the beginning of a new relationship, or rapport, of the faithful with God the Creator and Redeemer of the world. St Paul tells us that by faith we understand that God made heaven and earth (cf. Heb 11.3); by faith Abraham departed from his native country to an unknown land promised to him by the Lord (cf. Heb 11.8); by faith Moses was not afraid of Pharaoh's wrath but endured "as seeing him who is invisible" (Heb 11.27).

The Apostle Peter talks to the Christians about Christ, "whom having not seen you love. Though now you do not see him, yet believing, you rejoice with joy inexpressible and full of glory" (1 Pet 1.8). For this reason, we can say that the Christian's life is illuminated by "faith working through love" (Gal 5.6).

A young Romanian theologian, who also studied physics, philosophy, and medicine, contends in a recent book:

> By faith we see the cosmos and our world as a Church, by faith we feel our neighbors to be brothers in the Lord, and by faith we receive the world's gifts and riches as goods for sacrifice. In the light of faith, the powerless are healed; in the shadow of Christ's cross all hardship, suffering, and shortcomings are filled with light.
>
> Through the grace imparted by the mysteries of the Church, our faith in Christ, his life, and the saints' lives renew the intellective powers of the mind in each of us, giving us the power to free ourselves from the narrow habits of fallen nature and to see God's care everywhere in the setting of life and in past, present, and future experiences.[2]

Christian hope grows and bears fruit through the human person's co-working with God

Hope is a gift from God to people, a gift that ought to be nurtured. Therefore, Christians have a duty to fight, especially from a young age, against everything that can prevent them from loving God and their neighbor.

[2]Archdeacon Adrian-Sorin Mihalache, *Eşti Ceea Ce Trăieşti: Câteva date recente din neuroştiinţe şi experienţele duhovniceşti ale Filocaliei* [You are what you live: Some recent data from neuroscience and philokalic spiritual experiences], 2nd ed., rev. and exp. (Bucharest: Trinitas, 2019), 371.

The Church calls on young people to pay special attention to the renewal of spiritual life; to defend innocence; and to cultivate sincerity, courage, creativity, love, truth, and all the values of this age blessed by God, for the good of society.

The first step in the cultivation of spiritual life is young people's participation in the life and mission of parishes and other church institutions. Therefore, it is important that they belong to a community—it is not enough to pray at home alone, even if this prayer is necessary. In this sense, the Christian writer Tertullian wrote in the third century, "A single Christian is not a Christian"—that is, one is a Christian when in communion with other Christians in the Church.

The second step in cultivating spiritual life is family prayer. Even if our spiritual life is not intense, we can often be inspired by other members of our family or other practicing families who live their faith deeply. We can ask them to pray for us. St John Damascene said that a coal ignites when it touches another that is aflame. In other words, living faith communicates itself more quickly to others through prayer.

The third step in cultivating spiritual life is living the faith every day, not just on Sunday. We live in a civilization of technology and electronics, of excessive information, which often perturbs people so much that they become spiritually scattered and fragmented. For this reason, in the fight against stress, prayer as an expression of the living faith is a beneficial practice, especially the prayer of the mind and heart that invokes Jesus' name: "Lord Jesus Christ, Son of God, have mercy on me, a sinner."

Specific to monastics, this prayer has proved to be of great use to laypeople who wish to attain inner peace of soul. This prayer is simple and short but suited to today's hectic and disjointed life. It can restore the spirit to a state of watchfulness and love for God and others. In this regard, St Isaac the Syrian says that pure love is born of prayer.

The religious services in which young people participate also bring great inner peace and much joy. The countenance of those who partake intensively in the Church's services is no longer overwrought, and sadness and stress yield to light and gladness. It is Christ's peace that shines forth from the souls of those who pray deeply. Prayer is a gift we receive from God, but we must cultivate it especially as preparation for confession and communing in the Eucharist.

The Eucharist is not only the forgiveness of sins but also a source of spiritual power that inspires us, gives us courage, and plucks us from despondency. In this day and age, loneliness and life's difficulties induce, a feeling of meaninglessness, absurdity, and hopelessness that often causes depression. Yet prayer and especially the holy Eucharist give us the power to feel, through faith and hope, a foretaste of the resurrection—that is, the victory of love over solitude.

Young people love the beauty created by God and cultivated by humans

Nature trips develop the joy of seeing the beauty of natural creation and the joy of glorifying God, the Creator of the universe.

Pilgrimages to holy shrines and reading the lives of the saints sprout in the souls of the young the joy of seeing the beauty of ecclesial art and that of the saints' lives.

Youth camps have as their main purpose the cultivation of the beauty of communication and communion among young people at the parish, deanery, eparchial, or metropolitan levels—nationally and internationally—through common prayer and hymns, through common thought, through common action, through friendship and joy.

Cultural, social, and philanthropic—or charitable—activities are an opportunity to cultivate in the souls of children and young people the beauty of plentiful love, or the beauty of generosity, for the underprivileged, for orphans, for the sick, for the elderly, for the lonely and the sorrowful, for bereaved and helpless families.

All these activities, however, show us that the greatest beauty is the kindness of the soul who loves God and neighbor in the family, in the Church, in school, in society, and in the world at large.

In this regard, our Church encourages young people to become the hands of Christ's love for people—that is, to initiate spiritual and social projects and programs that meet the concrete needs of local communities.

It has been ascertained that many young volunteers beget joy from the joy they bring to those they help to feel loved and understand the dignity of being created in the image of God and called to fellowship with him and with their peers.

Our youngsters are eager to live in a communion of love—to love and to be loved—in the family and in society and also to cultivate an ideal, to give meaning to their present and future lives through the accumulation of new knowledge and creativity. Thus, they represent not only the future of the Church and society but also their very dynamic and renewing present.

The presence of youth in the liturgical, social, cultural, and missionary activities of the Church confirms the truth that young people are a blessing to the family, to the Church, and to society.

Dearest young people, by faith, hope, and love you become a cup of joy and apostles of the gospel of our Lord Jesus Christ, especially when you cultivate genuine love in the family, in friendships, in the parish, in the eparchy, in society, and in all the national and international Orthodox communities, to the joy of the whole of Orthodoxy and the communion between the nations of the world.

To conclude, we congratulate His Eminence Metropolitan Irenaeus of Oltenia and all those who have striven to organize this International Meeting of Orthodox Youth in Craiova.

We entreat God to bless you all, and may you use your stay in Craiova as a time to cultivate faith, hope, and love for promoting dialogue, friendship, and Orthodox Christian unity, to the glory of the Holy Trinity, the good of the Church, and the joy of all!

† Daniel
Patriarch of the Romanian Orthodox Church

PART IV

Brâncuşi:
Orthodox Christian Sculptor

In 2007 we commemorated fifty years since Constantin Brâncuşi reposed in the Lord (March 16, 1957) and one hundred years since the great Romanian sculptor created the first revolutionary works, or masterpieces, of his youth, *The Prayer* (1907) and *The Kiss* (1907), thus departing from classical and academic sculpture, which imitated nature, to inaugurate modern art through a "great plastic turning point" (C. Zărnescu). *The Prayer* was said to represent "the starting point of modern art" (V. G. Paleolog).

Paradoxically, Constantin Brâncuşi achieved this new orientation by valuing archaic folk art through the eternizing of profound meanings—"essences" or "key forms"—of the existence of the human person and the universe, as he himself said.

The year 2007 also marked the seventieth anniversary of the event during which the so-called "peasant demiurge," "peasant prince," or "prophet of modern art" personally supervised in 1937 the execution and placement of the forty-seven components of the monumental ensemble at Târgu-Jiu: *The Table of Silence*, *The Gate of the Kiss*, and *The Endless Column*, works that were completed, inaugurated, and later consecrated in his presence in 1938. The monumental ensemble at Târgu-Jiu remains Brâncuşi's most valuable achievement and his most profoundly artistic sculptural synthesis between spirit and matter, faith and art, the archaic and the modern, time and eternity.

It is fitting that this year, at the commemoration of more than fifty years since Constantin Brâncuşi's repose—a silent passing through the gate of eternal love into the endless light—we emphasize more intensely the presence of the Orthodox Christian faith and spirituality in his life and his work, especially since the pieces wrought and named by him *The Prayer* (1907) and *The Endless Column* (1937) were commissioned by Orthodox Christians to serve as funerary monuments, and were considered masterpieces of funerary sculpture of the twentieth century shortly after their public display.

In what follows, I will highlight the presence of Orthodox Christian spirituality in Constantin Brâncuşi's life and work, using, in a restructured and enriched form, the text of the lecture "Sculpted Matter: An Epiphany of the Creator's Light; Orthodox Spirituality in Brâncuşi's Work," which I gave on January 14, 2006, at the George Enescu University of Arts in Jassy, upon being awarded the title of *Doctor Honoris Causa*, for which I remain deeply grateful.

It is my desire that the publication of this text, now under a new title, *Brâncuşi – sculptor creştin ortodox* (Brâncuşi: Orthodox Christian Sculptor), be both a pious tribute to the memory of the famous Romanian sculptor,[1] long entered into the light of humankind's great artists, and a call to a more ample and profound knowledge of the spiritual meanings encompassed in the artistic work of this faithful and wise son of the Romanian Orthodox Church, who has made the unsurmised valences of the Romanian soul known worldwide.

We thank all those who gave us photographs of the life and work of Constantin Brâncuşi to illustrate the content of this volume, published now in a new edition by Trinitas Press of the Romanian Patriarchate, in the "Solemn Year of the Holy Emperor Constantine and Empress Helen," promoters of Christian faith and art.

---

[1]"The motivation of this tribute lies not only in my personal connection with Oltenia, as my father was born in this province of Romania, but also in the admiration I hold for the Romanian artist, who brilliantly linked tradition with novelty and influenced universal art like no other. And the fact that Joseph Brummer—an art lover who was born in Botoşani, Moldavia, and emigrated to the United States of America in 1912—made Brâncuşi known throughout the world through his art galleries urges me to contribute to a better understanding of Brâncuşi's work." Patriarch Daniel, *Brâncuşi – sculptor creştin ortodox* [Brâncuşi: Orthodox Christian Sculptor], 2nd rev. ed. (Bucharest: Trinitas, 2013), 7.

The father of modern art, Constantin Brâncuşi is a Romanian who entered the sphere of perennial universal values. The one to whom Henri Rousseau said, "You transformed the ancient into the modern," left Romania and settled in France, where he benefited from extensive information on art history and personal contacts with the world's greatest artists. His exhibitions in New York and other western cities brought him recognition and appreciation. Yet, although he left his homeland, he kept it permanently in his soul through the faith and tradition of his people, assumed in a creative form reflected artistically. Being at once a traditional Romanian and a universal modern artist, Constantin Brâncuşi did not alienate himself from his identity while among foreigners, because he always sought the "essence of things" beyond ephemeral appearances, and he discovered the spiritual space of creative freedom within any geographical space. He discovered the lights of eternal life beyond any sign of death in the passing material world. Brâncuşi united faith with art, the national with the universal, and the ephemeral with the eternal. Therefore, the *Endless Column* of his creation is also the column of his immortality!

He remains a guide for us all!

Orthodox Christian Spirituality in Brâncuși's Life and Thought

Many exegetes of Constantin Brâncuși's creations emphasized the truth that the old and rich tradition of Romanian folk art was a major source of his artistic and philosophical inspiration, but only a few discerned in his art the influence of the Orthodox Christian faith or that of the Byzantine liturgical tradition.

Among the latter are Dan Botta and Mircea Eliade. Dan Botta wrote about Brâncuși's art at the beginning of the 1930s:

> Brâncuși's Byzantine sculpture is the fruit of a dogma that forbids graven images, of a dogma that only prescribes the geometric sculpture, the flower, the symbol. The son of a peasant from Gorj County, Constantin Brâncuși expresses in this unparalleled plastic art this fact of our tradition. He is a sculptor of abstract forms. . . . A thousand years of an obscure . . . peasant art, a thousand years of carved geometry, are expressed in this great statuary's art. . . . But the line of force on which Brâncuși is situated is the royal way of the tradition he represents and furthers. Art is all the more valuable if it brings to the fore an older tradition and harmoniously integrates more varied cultural complexes. Brâncuși's sculpture participates in prehistoric art as well.[1]

And Mircea Eliade wrote in 1962, "Brâncuși had the wisdom of the Romanian peasant, which allowed him to find the source of Romanian folk art—that is, the worldview inherent to the Neolithic farmers. . . .

---

[1]Dan Botta, *Limite* [Limits] (Bucharest: Editura Cartea Românească, 1936), 56–63.

Rediscovering *matter* as the womb of religious epiphanies and meanings, Brâncuși found the emotions and inspirations of the archaic artist."[2]

However, the religious dimension of Brâncuși's work, sporadically noted by some exegetes or art critics, must be emphasized more thoroughly and more systematically based on the sculptor's own testimonies, expressed especially in his *Aphorisms*, and on the Orthodox liturgical universe in which he lived and worked. Without the perception of existence as a mystery or sacrament, and of art as a transfiguration of life into joy and eternal light, the key, the backbone of the exegesis of Brâncuși's work is lost.

Constantin Brâncuși was convinced of the deep connection, or the symbiosis, between religion and art in human history. In this sense, he confessed:

> For me—for Brâncuși—art in itself cannot exist. From its beginnings to its ultimate, contemporary acceptance, art has been a means of propagating religious ideas. The artist was that fanatic [enthusiast] who knew how to materialize the visions rendered by faith. The greatest masterpieces of the past emerged during periods of maximal religious fervor. Once they dwindled, times of decadence followed, and the most lackluster imitative realism arose invariably. . . . In other times . . . it was faith that ensouled art. . . . In the past, faith unconsciously [instinctively, unintentionally] gave birth to forms that matched the religious feeling.[3]

---

[2]Mircea Eliade, "A vedea lumea ca în clipa dintâi a Creației – Note pentru Pasărea Măiastră" " [To see the world as in the first moment of Creation: Notes on *The Măiastra Bird*], first published in *Cuvântul în exil* [The Word in exile] (1962) and reproduced in the collection *Împotriva deznădejdii: Publicistica exilului* [Against despair: The exile publications], ed. Mircea Handoca (Bucharest: Humanitas, 1992), 205–207, which also contains the pages dedicated to Dan Botta.

[3]Cf. Ion Pogorilovschi, coord., *Brâncuși, artist-filosof: Comunicări și antologie de texte* [Brâncuși, artist-philosopher: Communications and text anthology] (Târgu-Jiu: Editura Fundației "Constantin Brâncuși," 2001), 153–157.

Like all believers of old and of today, the sculptor Constantin Brâncuşi felt that he lived and created within the world created by God, the Maker of heaven and earth. For Brâncuşi, the work of the artist must be done in harmony and in cooperation with God the Creator:

> A block of marble or the trunk of an oak is a work of art in itself. Why carve perfect arms and legs into it and ruin the proportion to make parts of the human body that are themselves in proportions different from the divine ones? The swirls in the marble and the age line of a trunk should not be broken. The artist's carving and cutting ought to harmonize with the material's divine lines. . . .[4]

The abovementioned affirmation was expressed at another time by Brâncuşi in a single sentence: "The artist is but a humble tool in the hands of the Creator."[5]

And in one of his aphorisms he stated that closeness to God the Creator, or communion with him, is a condition of understanding his works, precisely because they offer pure joy. In the authentic religious experience, pure joy, very different from sensual pleasure, is the experience of the presence of divine grace in a person's life (cf. Phil 4.4 and Gal 5.22). Here are Brâncuşi's words on the relationship between faith in God the Creator and the perception of pure joy communicated by the art informed by this very belief: "Do not look for obscure formulas or mysteries. It is pure joy that I give you. Look at my works until you see them. Those closest to God have seen them."[6]

In another aphorism, Brâncuşi stated, "My statues are occasions of contemplation. Temples and churches have always been and remain places of contemplation."[7]

---

[4]Cf. Constantine Zărnescu, "Aphorism 121," *Aforismele şi textele lui Brâncuşi* [Brâncuşi's aphorisms and texts] (Cluj-Napoca: Editura Dacia, 2004), 112.

[5]Quoted in Barbu Brezianu, *Brâncuşi in România* [Brâncuşi in România] (Bucharest: Bic All, 1998), inside flap of dust jacket.

[6]Zărnescu, "Aphorism 5," *Aforismele*, 81.

[7]Zărnescu, "Aphorism 120," *Aforismele*, 112.

The Church, or her space and liturgical time, represented for Brâncuși a space of prayer and meditation, of communion with God and with people.

Since his childhood, he loved the peal of bells, especially those of Tismana Monastery—the old hearth of ascetic or hesychast monastics, lovers of prayer and unfading light. Later, while he was studying at the School of Arts and Crafts in Craiova, he was fond of the bells of the Obedeanu Church,[8] and he was an altar server and chorister at the Madonna Dudu Church in Craiova. Then, during his studies at the Faculty of Fine Arts in Bucharest, Brâncuși was a member of the choir of the Mavrogheni Church, where he masterfully chanted his " 'sustained and unique alleluias' in one breath and 'Lord, have mercy' modulated one hundred times, such that no one ever came close to that kind of vocal performance among those who joined him," according to V. G. Paleolog.[9]

Also, two years after he moved to Paris (1904) Constantin Brâncuși became a chanter and an altar server in 1906 at the Holy Archangels Michael and Gabriel Romanian Orthodox Church in Paris. As for his workshop, located near Paris (11 Impasse Ronsin), Brâncuși considered it a kind of metochion of Tismana Monastery: "I opened a lowly branch of Tismana [Monastery], here, at 11 Impasse Ronsin."[10]

Carola Giedion-Welcker, a distinguished Swiss intellectual and a good connoisseur of Constantin Brâncuși's life and work, noted a certain similarity between the spiritual elevation of the *Endless Column* and the Byzantine church music sung by Brâncuși in the Romanian Orthodox church in Paris:

In its monodic rise, in the rhythmic repetition of basic proportions, the *Column* is akin to the liturgical chanting of Gregorian [i.e., Byzantine] music, whose hymns were to accompany him all his life,

---

[8]Cf. V. G. Paleolog, *Tinerețea lui Brâncuși* [Brâncuși's youth] (Bucharest: Editura Tineretului, 1967), 98, with a preface by Petru Comarnescu, quoted in Calinic Argatu, *Frumusețea lumii văzute* [The beauty of the seen world] (Cluj-Napoca: Editura Dacia, 2002), 165.

[9]Paleolog, *Tinerețea*, 102.

[10]Cf. Petre Pandrea, *Brâncuși: Amintiri și exegeze* [Brâncuși: Reminiscences and exegeses] (Bucharest: Editura Meridiane, 1967), 65, 91; see also Zărnescu, *Aforismele*, 135.

from his early youth until the Parisian years; in the homeland and later in the Romanian Orthodox church in Paris, he intoned them during the Liturgy with his pure tenor voice. How deeply anchored in him this infinitely subtle monotony must have been, obtained only by elongation or accentuation of the syllables![11]

Brâncuşi's workshop near Paris was the space in which, for over forty years (1915–1957), he conversed and worked together in harmony with matter,[12] until matter displayed its "spiritual fluidity." It was also there that the wise artist met with people from all over the world, whom he impressed not only with his art but also with his spiritual presence and with the organization of his workshop as a creative space. And at the end of his life, Brâncuşi wanted his passing to eternal life to be a "meeting with the Good God" in the workshop he had once called a "branch of Tismana Monastery." In this regard, we recall here the most significant moments preceding his death. On January 6, 1957, on the feast of the Baptism of the Lord, Brâncuşi sprinkled his workshop with holy water. Later, when he was visited by Eugène Ionesco, together with his wife and daughter, Brâncuşi told them, "I am now very close to the Good God. I only need to extend my arm to touch him."

At the beginning of March 1957, Constantin Brâncuşi, aged and ill, called on Archbishop Theophilus from the Romanian Orthodox Church in Paris to confess him and to give him the holy Eucharist. The great Romanian artist intimated that he would die "spiritually dismayed"—"because I cannot breathe my last in my homeland." A few days before his death, Brâncuşi refused to go to the hospital, saying that he was awaiting God at home. He requested that his bed, above which an Orthodox icon was placed, be moved to his workshop, near the

---

[11]Cf. Carola Giedion-Welcker, *Constantin Brâncuşi* (Bucharest: Editura Meridiane, 1981), 72.

[12]"The intimate collaboration between the artist and the materials used, and the passion that unites the joy of the craftsman with the momentum of the visionary, bring him one at a time to 'essentialization,' to the form of the idea itself. . . . The sculptor must harmonize his spirit with the spirit of the material." Zărnescu, *Aforismele*, 85.

fireplace. From his workshop, Brâncuşi departed to the Lord on March 16, 1957, on a Saturday night, at two o'clock in the morning.[13]

Feeling his end upon him, he said, "I am now very close to the Good God; and I only need to reach out my hand to him, to touch him! . . . I will wait for the Good God in my workshop . . ."[14] It is worth noting that the expression "the Good God" used by Brâncuşi showed both his gratitude toward and his familiarity with God.

Three days after Brâncuşi's death, memorial services according to the Romanian Orthodox rites were celebrated for him, on March 19, 1957, in the same Romanian church in Paris where he had been a chanter and altar server in his youth. He was then buried in the Montparnasse Cemetery in Paris.[15] On that day the weather was splendid, full of sunlight, like his art. At the end of the funeral service, the great sculptor was eulogized in the church. One of the speakers (Salles) called Brâncuşi "the venerable Homeric shepherd amid his fabulous flock."[16] A French admirer of Brâncuşi, who had visited him shortly before his death, described him as follows:

> Brâncuşi, whom I saw yesterday lying on a small bed in a room that looked like a hunter's cabin in the far North; Brâncuşi, who would contemplate for hours on end the terrestrial glass globe suspended above him, murmuring, "I see other worlds beyond this world". . . . He said naught to convince you of anything—no matter what that might have been—and yet, separating yourself from him, you feel lighter, more serene, closer to the true and mysterious hierarchy of things. His presence acted upon us much like his works: through silence.[17]

---

[13]Cf. Alexandru Buican, *Brâncuşi: O biografie* [Brâncuşi. A Biography] (Bucharest: Editura Artemis, 2007), 546 and 548–550.

[14]Zărnescu, "Aphorism 252," *Aforismele*, 149.

[15]Giedion-Welcker, *Constantin Brâncuşi*, 114–117.

[16]Buican, *Brâncuşi*, 553.

[17]Alain Jouffroy, "A Visit to Brâncuşi Shortly before His Death" [in French], in *Une révolution du regard* [A revolution of the gaze] (Paris: Gallimard, 1964), quoted in *Memorialul Brâncuşi* [The Brâncuşi Memorial] (Craiova, 2001), 37 and 39.

Jean Cassou, a well-known French art critic, said of Brâncuși, "With his chisel he divided art history in two"—that is, in two stages: a classical one and a modern one. In fact, Constantin Brâncuși surprised and crystalized through his art the "essence" of creation, or its spirituality, confessing that the ultimate crux of existence is lasting, eternal life: "I am no longer of this world. I am far from myself, detached from my own person—I am within the essence of things."[18]

A staunch Christian, Brâncuși lived and confessed the biblical apostolic faith according to which "the things which are seen are temporary, but the things which are not seen are eternal" (2 Cor 4.18).

[18]Zărnescu, "Aphorism 254," *Aforismele*, 149.

Carved Matter:
An Epiphany of the Creator's Light

The "essence of things," which Brâncuși sought by his innate disposition, upon which he meditated with steadfast faith, and which he highlighted through artistic creation, became the essential truth of his life and oeuvre: "I have never set out to amaze the world—by whimsy! . . . I judged simply, as you can see, and I arrived at something equally simple, exceedingly simple: a synthesis that suggests what I wanted to represent. I extracted from bronze, wood, and marble that hidden gem—the essence."[1] "Reality lies in the essence of things. And if you get closer to the real essence of things, you reach simplicity."[2]

Brâncuși's entire repertoire is marked by these essential truths. More specifically, first of all the inner light of matter—which he grasped— is an epiphany or a garment created of the uncreated light, of grace, which brings together the beginning and the end of the universe. The chanter Constantin Brâncuși must have read Psalm 103 often during the vesperal service, in which the psalmist calls upon God, who "covers himself with light as with a garment" (Ps 103.2), and must have sung during the matins of Pascha that "all is filled with light: heaven and earth and the lower regions!"

A symbol of eternal light, created light appeared simultaneously with time at the beginning of the world and is the womb of matter and nourishment of life. It bears all that is created toward the uncreated light, toward the glory of God the Creator. In this perception of "essence," carved matter (wood, marble, stone, bronze, etc.) conveys

---

[1]Zărnescu, "Aphorism 79," *Aforismele*, 100.
[2]Zărnescu, "Aphorism 80," *Aforismele*, 100.

the relationship between light and meaning as a presence of the eternal Creator's grace in his temporal creation.

Secondly, Brâncuși presents the artist's (spiritual) inner exaltation in humility as joy and peace in communion with God the Creator of life. This is what Brâncuși says in this regard:

> Whoever does not detach himself from his ego never attains the Absolute and never deciphers life.[3]

> There is a purpose in all things. But to reach it, one must detach oneself from one's self.[4]

> The mission of art is to create joy, and one can create artistically only in balance and in spiritual peace.... And peace is attained through renunciation....[5]

> Our destiny is in the hands of the Good God. Our life remains important. Oh, our life endures as something truly so beautiful, so miraculous, and so divine that we could never replace it with absolutely anything, ever. Unite all forms into one and render it alive![6]

> Art is neither modern nor old—it is Art.... Art remains a mystery and a belief.... We must rid ourselves of ourselves and of all human impertinence—only thus can we rediscover the Beautiful.... I hear talk about all kinds of trends in art today. This is some sort of universal gibberish. Art developed only during the great religious epochs.... And everything that is created through philosophy [i.e., wisdom] becomes joy, peace, light, and freedom.[7]

Brâncuși strongly emphasized the necessary connection between humility and art, between reverence and spiritual beauty: "The human body is beautiful only insofar as it mirrors the soul."[8] In this sense, his

[3]Zărnescu, "Aphorism 35," *Aforismele*, 89.
[4]Zărnescu, "Aphorism 38," *Aforismele*, 90.
[5]Zărnescu, "Aphorism 55," *Aforismele*, 93.
[6]Zărnescu, "Aphorism 56," *Aforismele*, 94.
[7]Zărnescu, "Aphorism 67," *Aforismele*, 96.
[8]Zărnescu, "Aphorism 29," *Aforismele*, 88.

first sculpture that was spiritually laden was *The Prayer*, whose origin is explained by Brâncuşi himself: "*The Prayer*—an ordinary commission, much like any other. But it was my first clash with responsibility. The monument was supposed to represent a weeping woman. But how was I to carve a bare woman in a cemetery? So then, from the matter given me, I made a . . . prayer."[9]

The following was noted:

> To carve *The Prayer*, the funeral monument of Peter Stănescu in the cemetery of Buzău, Brâncuşi rented a more spacious workshop in Paris, at 54 Rue du Montparnasse. The piece indicated a decisive stage in his artistic evolution. On the one hand, it expressed the sculptor's desire for truth, his renunciation of the outer beauty of forms in favor of their inner dimension—and here Rodin's influence intervened—and on the other, it represented a tendency between stylization and generalization, which would greatly widen his artistic horizon.[10]

This is the novelty of Brâncuşi's sculpture:

> His work of art unveils the essence captured in the concrete forms of existence. It is, therefore, a synthesis of the universal force, which expresses what cannot be uttered and unites opposites in a harmonious whole. *The Prayer* opened this new way of looking at sculpted matter. Indeed, *The Prayer* takes on the form of an anonymous face that does not preserve the lineaments of a model. It is a concrete representation of a universal feeling: introspection in the face of death.[11]

Yet Brâncuşi's *Prayer* holds something more than "introspection in the face of death," because prayer is the state of a living spiritual communion of the human person with God, the Source of life, and also with those who, through death, "departed to the Lord" and "rest in the

[9]Zărnescu, "Aphorism 27," *Aforismele*, 87.
[10]Ionel Jianu, *Brâncuşi* (Cluj-Napoca: Editura Dacia, 2003), 38.
[11]Ionel Jianu, *Brâncuşi*, 38–39.

Lord," being united in their immortal souls with him by a faith stronger than death. The connection between Brâncuși's *Prayer* as a sculpture and the spiritual vision of Orthodox icons, which depict elongated and transfigured human forms as undertows of the human person's spiritual communion with God, was justly emphasized. Thus, it can be asserted that Brâncuși carved in fact "the woman-prayer, stylized for hundreds of years, first in paintings of Byzantine origin—on icons."[12] Today, a replica of Constantin Brâncuși's masterpiece is displayed at the Palace of the Council of Europe in Strasbourg, as a gift offered by the Romanian state to this European institution. Certainly, this creation is a well-chosen symbol representing the connection between living faith and creative art as a major feature of the Romanian people's identity and vocation. It must also be said that for Brâncuși the growth of trees, the flight of birds, the swimming of fish, the leap of a turtle,[13] the love in a person's kiss, and all the zest of life were contemplated and carved as an aspiration for relentless joy and a thrust toward heavenly light.

This truth can be perceived especially in Brâncuși's sculpted birds. They confirm that stylization in art strives for a spiritual message. For example, his *Măiastra Bird*,[14] akin to his *Birds in Flight* and *Golden Birds*, is a wingless bird that flies or rises vertically, about which Brâncuși himself said:

> This bird represents flight without pride, without defiance, without vainglory. I struggled for a long time to attain this form in which the elevation is done without pride, without egotism. I have toiled over the *Măiastra* since 1909 and it seems to me that, behold, I have yet to perfect it. I would like to represent the imponderable in a concrete form.[15]

[12]Zărnescu, *Aforismele*, 8.

[13]The author is alluding to Brâncuși's last sculpture, *Flying Turtle*.

[14]*Pasărea măiastră* is a mythical otherworldly bird—the queen of birds—of Romanian folklore, endowed with unique splendor, luminous plumage, enchanting song, and the miraculous powers of foretelling the future and reading people's hearts.—Trans.

[15]Zărnescu, "Aphorism 96," *Aforismele*, 105.

The *Măiastra*! . . . She struggles fiercely so that all I have accomplished to this day may ascend to heaven.[16]

I wanted my *Măiastra* to raise her head somehow without expressing through this movement pride, disdain, or hubris. It was one of the most difficult problems, and only after a long exertion did I manage to reproduce this motion—incorporated in the vim of flight.[17]

As a matter of fact we see that, in all of Constantin Brâncuşi's *Birds*, but especially in his *Măiastra* carved in marble (1911–1912), this flight is not primarily the effort of its wings, but the fruit of its inner spirit, of its impetus, as a response to a mysterious and fascinating heavenly call.

Brâncuşi thus surprised the mystery of the relationship between humility and exaltation. The *Măiastra Bird* shows that only in humility, in the receptiveness of searching and communion, lies true inner exaltation. This spiritual vision finds its profound origin in the words of the Savior Jesus Christ: "Everyone who exalts himself will be humbled, and he who humbles himself will be exalted" (Lk 18.14). The *Măiastra*, a symbol of the baptized human soul joined with the Holy Spirit—who descended as a dove at the baptism of the Lord in the river Jordan (cf. Mt 3.13–17, Mk 1.9–11, Lk 3.21–22, Jn 1.32–33)—unites in its wonderful form simultaneously the humility and dynamism of spiritual growth.

During matins services on Sundays, the chanter and sculptor Constantin Brâncuşi had the opportunity to reflect on the Orthodox liturgical chant: "Every soul is enlivened by the Holy Spirit and is exalted in purity," which contains a message similar to that of his art's humble flight.

In fact, all of Brâncuşi's *Birds*, especially those carved in bronze and then brought, through sanding and polishing, to the brightness of light, represent the soul united with the Holy Spirit[18] in its drive for

---

[16]Zărnescu, "Aphorism 99," *Aforismele*, 106.

[17]Zărnescu, "Aphorism 104," *Aforismele*, 104.

[18]Interpreting in verse the meaning of Brâncuşi's *Bird in Flight* (1926), the poet and philosopher Lucian Blaga wrote in his poem "The Holy Bird": "In the vaulted zenith of your late afternoons / Guess in its depths the complete mystery. / Ascend without end, / But never reveal to us what you see." Quoted in *Memorialul Brâncuşi* [The Brâncuşi Memorial], 19.

immortality, light, and love eternal. The wonderful birds' fascinating flight, signifying the elevation of the soul in undying light, was integrated in Brâncuși's *Endless Column*. They resemble a pack of golden cranes traveling to the heavenly homeland, thus symbolizing an eternal communion of the human souls united by the same longing for ascent in the joy and light of God's unceasing love.

From this perspective, the observation that "the *Endless Column* is a humanized bird"[19] is utterly befitting.

On the other hand, the *Kisses* carved by Brâncuși in 1907, 1910, 1919, and 1940 (1945?) as symbols of nuptial love yielding the fruit of human life, were integrated and transfigured in the pillars of *The Gate of the Kiss*—in those big and cordial eyes of an eternal love stronger than death—as love condensed in the immortal eye-soul, seer of the unceasing light of the heavenly Jerusalem, "prepared as a bride adorned for her husband" (Rev 21.2).

This spiritual perspective contained in the mystery of *The Kiss* also confirms the truth that Brâncuși's art is "a sculpture of light,"[20] in which "transparency becomes transcendence."[21]

Someone who tried to explain the peace and light that pervade Brâncuși's entire artistic creation came to the following conclusion: "Many will wonder where Brâncuși found the serenity and gentleness that abide in his work, when his very life was a constant struggle in times so difficult. That light came from within, from his genius that was not warped but ennobled by the suffering of life."[22] In other words, the light in the artist's soul is imparted to his art when he "pours his soul" into that which he creates, transfiguring loneliness in inner peace and suffering into the victory of joy.

---

[19]Mario de Micheli, quoted in Dan Grigorescu, *Brâncuși și secolul său* [Brâncuși and his century] (Bucharest: Editura Artemis, 1994), 45.

[20]V. G. Paleolog, quoted in Zărnescu, *Aforismele*, 54.

[21]Carola Giedion-Welcher, quoted in Zărnescu, *Aforismele*, 54.

[22]Dimitrie Pascotă, quoted in the collective work *Brâncuși inedit: Însemnări și corespondență românească* [Unpublished Brâncuși: Romanian notes and correspondence], ed. Doina Lemny and Cristian-Robert Velescu (Bucharest: Humanitas, 2004), 465.

PART V

The Believers Are the Wealth of Our Church[1]

TITI DINCĂ. The first and sixth patriarchs of Romania bear the same baptismal name: Elijah. Your Beatitude, we begin our discussion with a topic that has been intensely disseminated lately in the media—namely, the material state of the Romanian Orthodox Church two decades after the fall of communism. In fact, the wealth of the Church, whose ecclesiastical essence can only be spiritual in nature, is represented—in my opinion—by her believers. I invite you to start our discussion with this topic.

PATRIARCH DANIEL. First of all, yes, the faithful are the wealth of our Church. No matter how materially wealthy a church may be, if it is empty during services on Sundays or festal days, then it is spiritually poor. Material wealth can be a benefit or a temptation; it depends on how much we are bound to it. With just a piece of bread—if it is offered in brotherly love to a poor person—one can earn heaven. With many material riches—if they become the ultimate purpose in life—one can lose salvation.

That is why the Savior Jesus Christ teaches us to use the material goods of this world as an expression of our brotherly love. From this perspective, if matter is a symbol of communion, it becomes spiritual; it receives a spiritual meaning. If it blocks communion between us

[1]Patriarch Daniel, "Credincioșii sunt bogăția bisericii noastre" [The believers are the wealth of our Church], interview by Titi Dincă, Romanian Public Television, September 30, 2007, transcript published by the Basilica News Agency, accessed November 25, 2019, https://basilica.ro/credinciosii-sunt-bogatia-bisericii-noastre-interviu-acordat-de-patriarhul-daniel-jurnalistului-titi-dinca-in-anul-2007-integral/.

and God or among human beings as a dividing wall, matter becomes a danger.

Christ the Redeemer, observing a wealthy man who was too fond of his earthly riches and was in thrall to material goods as if they were the ultimate reality, said that his salvation would be difficult to attain. On the other hand, the holy Scriptures offer examples of rich people such as Abraham, Job in the Old Testament, or Barnabas in the New Testament, who funded many of St Paul's missionary journeys. The Church has a special prayer for the *hegumen*—the *hegumen stavrophore*, or crossbearer—which supplicates that he mete out, or gladly administer, the wealth of the Church, by invoking the holy disciple Barnabas's intercessions for his work.

TITI DINCĂ. With your permission, Your Beatitude, let us continue these ideas by discussing the social work of the Church, an institution that ranks at the top in credibility for Romanians.

PATRIARCH DANIEL. In terms of her wherewithal, the Romanian Orthodox Church is very poor. I know this from my own experience, from the many activities we started in Moldavia, in Jassy. We do not have the money we need to help the poor, effectively and efficiently. The Church is rich in the sense that she has many monasteries or works of art, but financially—in terms of a productivity that would immediately generate an income—she is very poor in relation to the needs for help.

For this we ask that people help the Church now, so that she can help the poorest, thus blending spirituality with the willingness to help the sick, the hungry, the underprivileged.

It has been said that the Church of Antioch fed three thousand people daily in the day of St John Chrysostom with the products or money given by a few families of wealthy people. If all the rich did this, said St John Chrysostom, then there would be no more poor people in the city. We do not always refer to the wealth that belongs directly to the Church, but to people of means, who, if they are reverent, can do a great deal of good, should the Church ask them to do so. We, as a Church, are very poor with respect to the current needs, but the generous wealthy people—sponsors or benefactors, as they were called in times of old—can complete what the Church lacks as an institution.

TITI DINCĂ. Appreciating your effort tonight, I invite you to move on to another registry of ideas. This recent period of time was marked by public debates in which the mentality of the future primate of the Romanian Orthodox Church was discussed: traditionalist or modernist. What is your opinion in this regard?

PATRIARCH DANIEL. I believe that the Orthodox Christian is by definition a traditionalist because he or she has the duty to transmit the received faith without diminishing its content. At the same time, however, we must bear in mind that a traditionalist can be static or dynamic. For example, the New Testament was written in Greek. If we read it only in Greek or celebrate the Divine Liturgy only in Greek or Slavonic, then we are static traditionalists.

If we translate the New Testament and the Divine Liturgy into Romanian—the content remaining the same—we adapt the understanding of this content for our contemporaries. This is what dynamic tradition means. The content remains the same, but the form of presentation, appropriate to our time, relies on the dynamics of tradition.

We cannot be against tradition, but we can represent it either statically, repetitively, or dynamically. For example, if he were contemporary with us, St Paul would use not only the ship but also the plane. But we cannot be modern in the sense of being secularized or radically breaking away from tradition.

TITI DINCĂ. The holy Scriptures and the holy Tradition have always represented the main treasure of the Romanian Orthodox Church. From 1925 to the present day, each primate of the Romanian Orthodox Church has especially tended to the printed publications. Your Beatitude, what do you think about the transmission of this treasure through modern means of communication (television, radio, daily newspapers)?

PATRIARCH DANIEL. We continue the tradition of printing because prayer or teaching books remain very necessary. But through modern means of communication, such as television or radio, the word extends and becomes more accessible to many people who have no money to buy books or cannot read extensively, but who want to participate in a more lively way in the life of the Church, to listen daily to the Divine Liturgy or various prayers, to hear the news from the lives of our dioceses.

From this perspective, television and radio are becoming modern means of complementing print, and not of contradicting it. Also, a daily newspaper is very necessary because people want to be informed without delay and every day about the Church's concrete life.

TITI DINCĂ. You talked about the challenge of secularization. What is the position of the Romanian Orthodox Church in relation to the phenomenon of the secularization of the individual and of modern society?

PATRIARCH DANIEL. Right at the outset, it is necessary that we define the term "secularization" from a theological standpoint. Secularization means building one's personal life and the life of the society without reference to God and religious values. Secularized people are not necessarily atheists, but they are rather more indifferent or nihilistic.

They forget about God but do not directly deny him as if to say that God does not exist. Instead, they do not understand the usefulness of prayer, church services, or participation in the life of the Church. From this point of view, secularization is an attitude of indifference to the presence of God and to the need of rhythming our lives and openness to eternity.

Remaining in the *saeculum* (in the world, in our time) as a closed reality without eternal purpose is a very great temptation. We attach ourselves to this world as if it were the final reality. There exists a phase of secularization in the form of alienation from traditional religion.

In France, since the 1960s, there has been a kind of denial of the traditional Roman Catholic or Protestant Churches. But this phase did not last long because university professors of chemistry and physics, of the sciences of the universe, began to search for a spiritual dimension in all sorts of syncretistic sciences and oriental religions, such as the occult African practices supposed to have the special charisma of foreseeing the future. *Le Monde* would post announcements about the possibility of reading the immediate future or predicting the chance of winning the lottery.

So secularization tends to turn into a search for a more diffused, chaotic spirituality than a systematically organized one. From this perspective, I believe that we, the Church, must delve deeper into our own tradition and not just stick to ritualism but explain the existential meaning of our services, of prayer, of worship, so that people can understand that, in fact, faith—assumed consciously and existentially—is a matter of life, not just a matter of repetitive tradition, of inherited tradition.

TITI DINCĂ. Because you mentioned the confrontation that exists in the West between syncretistic phenomena and authentic spirituality, I would like to open another line of discussion. With the passage of time, the millions of Romanians working in the West have been expressing an increasing need for autochthonous spirituality, tradition, and customs. Do you think this is part of the Romanian spirit?

PATRIARCH DANIEL. First of all, I think it is part of a life experience that risks losing its roots. These migrating people meet a different cultural environment, an environment of Christian spirituality different from the one at home, so they need guides. For those who migrate, the Church, the Romanian Orthodox community, is a guide. They want to maintain the connection with those at home, but at the same time they want to earn some money in the country to which the person or family has migrated. It is from this standpoint that we believe elderly people are in greater need of such guides.

But those born there adapt to the new context more easily than their parents, who came from another country. In terms of our conationals' specific nature, we believe that it is very difficult for a Romanian to be a convinced atheist. A Romanian believes that religion is part of his or her identity, even though not all Romanians are equally religious. This is probably because we were not Christianized by force or by an order, but the process of Christianization and the formation of the Romanian people occurred together.

Today, we can even say that the spiritual wealth of Orthodoxy determines us to compare our inheritance with what others have. People go to the West for material wellbeing, but whoever is accustomed to not giving up the spiritual side is not content with money alone. Money is necessary, but it cannot fill the soul of the individual, because we are made for a love of eternal communion with God. People cannot be filled with limited and transient things, even if these transient things mean a great deal of money.

TITI DINCĂ. In the last seventeen years, the Romanian Orthodox Church has entered the West with some difficulty. Over time, people gathered around the Church, and now, at the request of Romanians, there are numerous Romanian Orthodox parishes in the West. What, in fact, is the strategy of the Romanian Orthodox Church in terms of her care for these growing communities?

PATRIARCH DANIEL. We consider our strategy a positive one in view of the fact that we are setting up new parishes, and we already have several dioceses. But this strategy needs to be amplified. The number of Romanian Orthodox believers gone abroad is very high in relation to the existing parishes. Because in Western Europe, especially in Italy and Spain, there are two to three million Orthodox Romanians, more parishes should be founded. We also need new dioceses. Because of great distances, a bishop who is the metropolitan for half a continent cannot know these parishes or visit them often enough and take care of them.

Although legislation has common parts in the European Union, it respects the special character of each country, just as religiousness has its own special character. For example, the Nordic countries are mostly Protestant, while the southern countries around the Mediterranean Sea are predominantly Roman Catholic. We need to know the specifics and laws of each country so that we can assist these believers not only with Sunday services but also help them to be able to integrate, find a job, or, in the case of the very poor, have a canteen in the parish.

That is why we need more places of worship. For now, we celebrate the holy Orthodox Liturgy in liturgical spaces borrowed from different Roman Catholic, Anglican, and Protestant churches, with which we have good relations. But it is necessary that we build Romanian churches akin to the ones at home, with Orthodox iconography, with all the objects specific to Orthodox worship.

TITI DINCĂ. Your Beatitude, in the sermon delivered at the enthronement ceremony, you said that the first care is "preserving, cherishing, and cultivating the luminous spiritual inheritance left by His Beatitude Patriarch Theoctistus of blessed memory." Within this legacy is the Metropolitanate of Bessarabia. The emergence of this metropolitanate led to a formalism in the relations between the Romanian and Russian Orthodox Churches. What is the strategy for restarting the dialogue between these two sister Churches?

PATRIARCH DANIEL. We want to intensify this dialogue. Already, as a resumption of the dialogue, a meeting is planned for November in Moscow and, at the same time, from past experience, we believe that we have learned to think in a more nuanced manner. Certainly, Orthodox unity is territorial, but a territory's political affiliation is another matter. Now that the territory is declared independent, we have a new situation. The Republic of Moldova is part of neither the Russian Federation nor Romania. It is a new situation that needs to be understood, combined with the people's freedom to manifest their belonging to one patriarchate or the other.

We recognize that the Metropolitanate of Moscow has a structure there, but we mutually request the same for the metropolitanate that is connected to the Church of Bucharest. It is not easy to find solutions, especially when there is a fluctuation of priests moving from one metropolitanate to the other, but on both sides there is a intense desire to find a solution, to better understand the complex situation and, at the same time, to cooperate more on practical, pastoral, and missionary grounds.

As in other areas, there are many movements in the Republic of Moldova, even Protestant ones, which are much more active and efficient, while we often argue with each other. Therefore, we ought to move from dispute to dialogue, from confrontation to a more credible cooperation. We also have common problems in the diaspora. The Orthodox in the West need cooperation between sister Churches. From this point of view, we believe that a permanent dialogue with the Russian Orthodox Church, with the Greek Church, and, in particular, with the other Orthodox Churches that are part of the European Union, is necessary.

This is not just a matter of jurisdictions but of a common testimony that is to become more credible than when it is contradictory and isolated. After the conversations we have had with various hierarchs of the Russian Orthodox Church, we felt an openness, a desire to resume the dialogue and to solve the problems even if the solutions are not definitive but provisional.

TITI DINCĂ. Your Beatitude, we are entering a new stage of ecclesiastical life in Romania. Theological education, which has had a particular dynamic over the last seventeen years, has revealed its great capacity to generate educators meant to become the teachers of our future Church servants. Where are we at this moment? Are there enough priests? Are there enough people working in the social or philological field? What should the strategy of this theological education be?

PATRIARCH DANIEL. We first have to consider two aspects: theology is studied either with a concrete, practical purpose or because of its pleasantness, out of a desire to be informed. In France, I saw many pensioners enrolled in theology courses at Roman Catholic faculties, either part-time or by correspondence. They are aware that they will not be employed in the practical life of the Church, but from a beneficial desire to deepen their faith in a faculty of theology, they study theology for the sake of theology.

But as a Latin proverb goes: *Non scholae, sed vitae discimus* (we learn not for school but for life); we must ascertain the concrete needs of the Church and the life she leads in society. There was a great need for priests and teachers of religion because, following the interwar model, religion was reintroduced in schools. Now parishes have priests and the positions for teachers of religion have been filled, so there is no urgent need for such a large number of teachers.

From a social point of view, the new law for religious affairs also provides a solid basis, being an organic law. The cooperation of Church and State in the social field and the European funds coming in make it necessary to have many social workers. Regrettably, owing to a lack of employment, many of those who trained in the field of social work in faculties of theology went to Italy to care for the elders of families there for double the salary. So we do need more social workers to be integrated into these programs. In the formation of a social worker, science is not the only component—there is a spiritual dimension as well.

If we see a sick or aging person only as an individual or as a mere number, then social work no longer has the same depth as when we see in that person the face of Christ suffering or asking for our love and help in concrete circumstances. The spiritual dimension in social work is very important.

Going back to the current situation of theological education, it is necessary to speak not only in terms of numbers or quantity. We must improve the quality of studies at all levels and link scholarly, academic theological study with the Church's mindset of social and pastoral work. So we ought to have solid academic training but also mission-ary and pastoral purpose.

TITI DINCĂ. In the last seventeen years the number of monasteries in Moldavia has doubled. Monasticism brings to the fore a way of spiri-tual life that can be a model of moral life. What is the attention that the Romanian Orthodox Church must pay to a monasticism undergoing authentic growth?

PATRIARCH DANIEL. Having so many callings for monasticism was a vocation from God. The large number of monasteries and hermit-ages that were established after the Revolution of 1989 was beneficial, and they should be supported. Some of them face a very precarious economic situation. Some sketes are downright poor. Because scores of people left for the West, there aren't very many who continue to come to these hermitages and monasteries, and so they are no longer financially and morally supported. Hence, young monastics must be helped to deepen their spiritual life and learn theology.

I asked all the young monks from the Archdiocese of Jassy to attend either a seminary or a faculty of theology, and now we have several hundreds of them who have studied theology and enjoy it because they no longer have the complex of being mere monastery priests without a theological degree. Such a training is missionary in its nature as well.

Our monasteries do not allow time for study owing to the agricul-tural work needed for survival. Very often even the monastics' prayer is no longer profound because their time for study or prayer is filled with the immediate cares of survival, building cells, or completing the construction of a church.

At the same time, we ought to realize that the temptation of secu-larization, which touches all institutions, may sometimes affect some monasteries that are closer to the city, where it can be seen that a young monastic must struggle very hard in order to carry out the daily prayer rule. In this regard, I can tell you that many monks and nuns enjoy Trinitas Radio. Some have said that, in addition to their daily prayers, they also pray through the night along with the prayers broadcast on Trinitas Radio.

The monastery completes the liturgical life of the parish, so it is necessary to support monastic life. The most appropriate thing is cooperation, not competition, between the parish and the monastery. There are people in the city who are not content to participate only in the Divine Liturgy and wish to participate in vespers as well. Because not all parishes can celebrate vespers services on Sunday evenings, believers who are desirous of a deeper spiritual life can go to the monasteries in or near the city.

For this reason, we must think about our believers' spiritual needs. In fact, I have seen many priests who go together with their flock to the monastery to confess. This mutual aid between the parish and the monastery is very profitable.

TITI DINCĂ. Who is responsible for and what is the Church's strategy on generating thematic discussions on the need for a moral life in society and for honorable relationships, even in the field of business?

PATRIARCH DANIEL. I believe there is a need to develop a dialogue between clergy theologians and lay theologians on the one hand, but also between theologians and people of other professions on the other. For example, discussions between priests and doctors and between priests and educators are very necessary, especially because we have big problems with children who have remained in Romania while their parents went to earn money abroad to support them.

These children's behavior changes; it reduces their efficiency in assimilating educational information or even attending school. So it is necessary to think in terms of dialogue in a team of people with a common purpose but with different training. The fact that some theology students study other disciplines is particularly beneficial for a dialogue with the exact sciences, or the earth and natural sciences.

On the other hand, dialogue is not an end in itself, but the means by which we make tradition and faith relevant to everyday life, how we understand what the creed, icons, or prayer have to do with our daily lives. We need to know theology, but we also must heed the believers because, more often than not, a direct, correct, and academic discourse does not resonate with their immediate needs.

TITI DINCĂ. Large crowds of believers attend every major feast day. Feasts are landmarks that create a spirit of unity. But they also represent an occasion—in the good sense of the word—for hierarchs to actualize either the needs of the Church or Christians' relation to the Church. What is the role of the Christian feast day?

PATRIARCH DANIEL. First off, a feast day is an exercise in freedom. One who does not celebrate does not escape the trap of "growthism," measured in quantity or numbers. The gratuitousness and experience of God's grace are seen primarily in a feast, because in a celebration we do not produce something straightaway. This does not mean that it is not useful. During a feast we cultivate our relationship with God and with others. The cultivation of the soul is just as important as the cultivation of the land. When people come together, they talk to one another, they rejoice, they gather around the saints, and their communion is strengthened.

A life without feasts is a meaningless life. A celebration gives meaning to our existence because it is then that we show generosity, hospitality, and appreciation for the people we meet or for whom we pray, more so than the efficiency of toiling in a factory or plant production. I would say that the Church has turned feasts into moments of generosity and goodwill, not accumulation. In a celebration nothing material accumulates, but there occurs an inverse movement, one of generosity.

On great feasts we are urged to practice almsgiving. When we experience the feast as a time of sanctification of our lives, then we feel God's grace in the celebration. Feasts have been, both in the family and in the nation, the means of maintaining communion between people, between relatives from long distances. Many times, patronal feasts brought together Romanians from within or without the country's borders.

For this reason, we established the Sunday for Migrants, the first Sunday after the feast of the Dormition of the Theotokos. So the need for communion is as great as the need for physical nourishment and clothing, and from this point of view, the feast is time that is not wasted but sanctified.

TITI DINCĂ. Your Beatitude, we are in a world that, akin to a mosaic, displays the facets of diversity. What role does the Romanian Orthodox Church play in the dialogue with other denominations or minorities and in promoting the diversity of interhuman relations?

PATRIARCH DANIEL. Historically speaking, we have had many Orthodox Christians living in Africa or Asia. There are Orthodox Christians who have been coexisting for centuries with other denominations, and in our country, we have experienced centuries of peaceful cohabitation with those of other religions. A Romanian who is good at heart does not need to expend a great deal of diplomatic effort to be a tolerant person or to respect the identity of each individual.

In order to respect one's own religious identity it is necessary to respect the religious identity of others. We cannot engage in sincere dialogue if we do not respect and understand one another.

There are now many Romanian Orthodox believers who have entered Roman Catholic areas in which there had never been an Orthodox community. We spoke to a few Italians who confirmed that these Romanians pray three times more [than they do] and expressed their joy at having them in their midst. With a few small exceptions, most Romanians in the diaspora are good Christians; they are reverent and much admired by the locals. Likewise, we rejoice when we see the Coptic Orthodox believers in Egypt, who live in hostile conditions but are so steadfast in their faith without being fundamentalists. We cannot compare ourselves to them, because the practice of their faith is an existential one.

I can give you an example. When we received guests from abroad here at the patriarchate, His Beatitude Patriarch Theoctistus sometimes asked us to offer our cell for a few days. I happened to see that a delegation from the Church in Egypt did not use the bed at all; they slept on mats on the floor, and they prayed on those mats, by the beds, from 5:00 a.m. until 7:30 a.m.

This type of monastic life is part of the prayer rule of the first Orthodox monasteries in Egypt. So, if we cannot imitate them, the least we can do is appreciate and admire them. If we have a modicum of humility, then we can first grasp the light in others; this is how we can establish friendly relations with them even if they are from other confessions, provided that we retain our identity, of course.

TITI DINCĂ. I will go back now to your sermon at the enthronement ceremony, when you said that the first concern consists in "preserving, cherishing, and cultivating the luminous spiritual inheritance left by His Beatitude Patriarch Theoctistus of blessed memory." One of these legacies is the desideratum to erect a cathedral of our Romanian dignity. Is this still a desideratum of the Church?

PATRIARCH DANIEL. I think we have gone past the desideratum phase and into the phase of urgent need. We felt so ill at ease today that in the cathedral we could only fit our guests while the faithful had to stand outside. The patriarchal cathedral is very small and no longer meets believers' current needs. It was the church of a seventeenth-century monastery. So what we have at stake here is not an ambition or a pastoral necessity, but the very dignity of a European capital.

When the Romanian Athenaeum was built it was said, "Give a leu[2] for the athenaeum!" Now, we could say that we need a cathedral for the Romanian capital. It is unfortunate that this large, expanding city does not have a cathedral.

---

[2]Leu (lei, pl.): The basic monetary unit of Romania.—Trans.

TITI DINCĂ. I tried to define the agenda of the Church through the voice of the Romanian Orthodox Church's primate. What is the most urgent project you are considering?

PATRIARCH DANIEL. The continuation of everything that was begun. Together with the Holy Synod we will find new stages of missionary work, but we have commenced our pastoral work in so many directions that even its continuation requires an effort not only in terms of energy but also of material and financial support. The priorities are multiple, but first we must think about the spiritual life. If we develop social undertakings without spiritual support, we risk secularizing ourselves even if the intention of the social work is a positive one.

Therefore, we ought not to separate the liturgy from philanthropy and philanthropy from the liturgy, or social work from the spiritual life. Only in this way will we go on a safe path verified by the holy Tradition of our holy fathers who, to this day, have shown us that if we bring the spiritual and the material together, we bless God, both spiritually and materially.

TITI DINCĂ. We have reached the end of our show, and I must confess that I was especially honored by your presence. Thank you for giving this exclusive interview to the Romanian Public Television and Radio stations.

PATRIARCH DANIEL. I thank you and I am grateful that, as part of your shows, you have made known the legacy received from our late patriarchs of blessed memory: Myron, Nicodemus, Justinian, Justin, and Theoctistus, who enriched the treasury of the Romanian Church through their activity and work. I also thank the Romanian Television station for being a television station that does missionary work.

The National Cathedral: A Practical Liturgical Need and a Symbol in Honor of Our Romanian Heroes[1]

The old patriarchal cathedral on the Metropolitanate Hill in Bucharest was built as a monastery church by Prince Constantine Șerban Basarab, between 1656 and 1658.

The church was consecrated in 1658 and dedicated to the Holy Emperor Constantine and Empress Helen in a ceremony celebrated by the patriarch of Antioch, Macarius III Zaim.[2] At that time, Wallachia had only three hierarchs: Metropolitan Stephen I of Hungaro-Wallachia in Bucharest, Bishop Ignatius in Râmnic, and Bishop Seraphim in Buzău.[3]

Ten years later, in 1668, by a charter issued by Prince Radu Leon,[4]

[1] Patriarch Daniel, "Catedrala Națională – o necesitate liturgică practică și un simbol al cinstirii eroilor români" [The National Cathedral: A practical liturgical need and a symbol in honor of our Romanian heroes], November 26, 2018, Basilica News Agency, accessed on November 28, 2019, https://basilica.ro/catedrala-nationala-o-necesitate-liturgica-practica-si-un-simbol-al-cinstirii-eroilor-romani/.

[2] Paul of Aleppo, *Jurnal de călătorie în Moldova și Valahia* [A travel journal in Moldavia and Wallachia], ed. and trans. Ioana Feodorov (Bucharest: Editura Academiei Române, 2014), 416–417.

[3] Fr Mircea Păcurariu, "Listele cronologice ale ierarhilor Bisericii Ortodoxe Române" [Chronological lists of the hierarchs of the Romanian Orthodox Church], in *The History of the Romanian Orthodox Church*, vol. 3 (Bucharest: Editura Institutului Biblic și de Misiune Ortodoxă, 1992), 534, 536, 538.

[4] Romanian Academy, doc. 58 / 66; The National Archives of Romania, *Register 2 of the Metropolitanate*, MS 128, 11.

the monastery on the hill was elevated to the rank of metropolitan cathedral.

Thus, the church became the place where, in the presence of Wallachia's rulers and later of Romania's kings, Te Deum services were officiated by synaxes of hierarchs led by the country's metropolitan on the occasion of important events, such as the Union of the Romanian Principalities of 1859, the Proclamation of Romania's State Independence (1877), and the Proclamation of the Kingdom of Romania (1881).

The old metropolitan cathedral is also linked to the most important events in the life of our Church: the acquisition of the autocephaly of the Romanian Orthodox Church (1885) and its elevation to the rank of patriarchate in 1925, when, provisionally, the cathedral became the patriarchal cathedral.

The 1859 Union of the Romanian Principalities brought along with it the unitary organization of Moldavia's and Wallachia's church structures within the Holy Synod (1872), which subsequently raised the number of its member hierarchs to twelve: the primate metropolitan as president; the metropolitan of Moldavia and his suffragan bishops of Râmnic, Buzău, Argeş Roman, Huşi, and Lower Danube, Galaţi (established in 1864); and one vicar bishop in each diocese.[5]

The old metropolitan cathedral proved to be inadequate even then, especially on major religious or national celebrations and at other solemn times, such as the Proclamation of the Kingdom of Romania and the coronation of the first king, Carol I, on May 10, 1881. Ever since then it was ascertained that none of the over one hundred churches that existed in Bucharest was spacious enough to welcome all those who wished to attend the official services of the solemnities.

As a result, at the wish of King Carol I, in 1884, Romania's Assembly of Deputies and the Senate voted in favor of law no. 1750 for the construction of the "Cathedral Church in Bucharest." The law was

---

[5]Constantine Drăguşin, "Legile bisericeşti ale lui Cuza Vodă şi lupta pentru canonicitate" [The church laws of Prince Cuza and the struggle for canonicity], *Studii Teologice* 1–2 (1957): 86–103. See also Păcurariu, "Chronological Lists," 535, 537, 539–540.

promulgated by King Carol I on June 5, 1884, and the sum of five million lei (in gold) was provided from the state budget.[6]

In addition, Mihai Eminescu and Ioan Slavici were among the first Romanian intellectuals who launched and supported the idea of building in Bucharest the Cathedral of the Romanian People's Salvation, as a token of thanksgiving to God after the War of Independence of 1877–1878.[7]

After the end of the First World War and following the Great Union of 1918, the name of the Romanian People's Salvation Cathedral was kept to express gratitude, or thanksgiving, to God for the salvation, or liberation, of the Romanian nation from oppression and alienation, and also "for the reunification of the country within its borders."

After the Great Union of 1918, the Synod of the Orthodox Church in the Kingdom of Greater Romania comprised twenty-two hierarchs[8] from all the Romanian provinces: Wallachia, Moldavia, Bukovina, Transylvania, Banat, and Bessarabia.

As metropolitan primate of Greater Romania, Myron Cristea resumed the endeavor to build the cathedral. At his request, on May 10, 1920, King Ferdinand I addressed a royal charter to the Holy Synod announcing the decision to erect a monumental cathedral in Bucharest to commemorate the victory of the Romanian armies in the War for the Unification of the Romanian Nation. On October 12, 1921, Myron Cristea submitted to the mayor of the capital a request for "a large and adequate space" for building the cathedral.[9]

On November 27, 1925, just days after his enthronement as patriarch, Myron Cristea obtained the approval of Prime Minister Ionel I. C. Brătianu to start the process of the new cathedral's construction.

---

[6]The Official Gazette no. 49, 6 (June 18, 1884).

[7]Nicolae Şt. Noica, *Catedrala Mântuirii Neamului – istoria unui ideal* [The Cathedral of the Romanian People's Salvation: The history of an ideal] (Bucharest: Basilica, 2011), 51.

[8]Păcurariu, "Listele cronologice," 535, 537, 539–540, 546, 550, 551, 553, 557, 562, 564; and *Condica Sfântă* [The Sacred Register], vol. 3, MS 1, Library of the Holy Synod, 160–177.

[9]National Archives, The Myron Cristea Fund, File 3/1919, 61, 61v.

Public debates took place to decide the location of the new cathedral, which was finally established at the base of the Metropolitanate Hill, in the former Prince Bibescu Square. On May 11, 1929, on the tenth anniversary of the Great Union,[10] the new cathedral's construction site was consecrated in the presence of the representatives of the Royal Regency, of Queen Mary, and of government and army members. Patriarch Myron Cristea consecrated the cross that marked the place of the future altar.

Patriarch Myron's efforts at building were often hindered, so between 1932 and 1935 he decided to renovate and paint the old metropolitan cathedral, temporarily transforming it into the patriarchal cathedral "until favorable economic circumstances [would] allow that the idea of building a great national church be accomplished, as a thanksgiving to the merciful God for the reunification of the country within its natural borders." Thus states the inscription above the entrance to the old cathedral.

Regrettably, Patriarch Myron's endeavors stopped at that point, because shortly thereafter a strong economic crisis engulfed the country, which would last for years to come. On March 6, 1939, Patriarch Myron passed away with his dream unfulfilled, leaving the task to his successors.

Better times for the country did not come immediately, because on September 1, 1939, the Second World War broke out, seizing Romania in its maelstrom. Our nation lost Bessarabia, Northern Bukovina, Hertza Region (following the Soviet ultimatum of June 22, 1940); Northern Transylvania (following the Second Vienna Award of August 30, 1940), and the Quadrilateral (ceded to Bulgaria on September 7, 1940).

The hard decades of the atheist communist regime followed, and thousands of faithful laypeople, priests, and monks were arrested,

---

[10]National Archives, The Myron Cristea Fund, File 3/1919, 19, 19v, 20, 20v. See also Nicolae Şt. Noica, *Catedrala*, 46–51; as well as the *Journal of Patriarch Myron Cristea: Documents, notes, and correspondence* (Sibiu, 1987), 372; and *Revista Apostolul* [The Apostle Review] 10 (May 15, 1929).

tried, and sentenced to harsh years in prisons from which many did not return.

The project of the National Cathedral became a closed matter. In addition, an aggressive plan of urban systematization in Bucharest, inspired by the architecture of foreign socialist regimes, caused immeasurable damage to our historic and architectural heritage through the demolition of old monuments, among which were some churches and monasteries, eloquent for our historical past.

After 1990, through the care of Patriarch Theoctistus of blessed memory, the project of building the Cathedral of the Romanian People's Salvation was revived after a silence of forty-five years, with renewed support and arguments besides those previously formulated: honoring the ancestors who sacrificed for the faith and unity of the nation and the heroes who gave their lives in December 1989 to liberate the country from dictatorship and atheism, as well as those who suffered unprecedented terror in communist prisons and concentration camps.

Patriarch Theoctistus' efforts were greatly obstructed by continuous delays in establishing the location of the new cathedral despite the fact that the city of Bucharest was the only European capital without a representative cathedral.

The cathedral's final location was established in 2005 on the former Arsenal Hill, on September 13 Road, right behind the People's House (the Palace of the Parliament).

This site was recommended by the municipality after three other locations had been proposed at different stages (Union Square in 1999, Alba-Iulia Square in 2001, and Carol Park in 2004). Because of a lack of alternatives, the Romanian Patriarchate consented to this site although it gives the cathedral low visibility because of the immensity of the People's House, the current headquarters of the Romanian Parliament.

The Romanian Patriarchate also accepted the location as a moral repair or "a light of resurrection" for the five "crucified" churches, of which three (Alba Postăvari, Spirea Veche, and the Life-Giving Spring) were demolished and two (Schita Maicilor and Mihai Vodă) were moved by the communist regime in order to build the People's House in their stead.

The construction of this cathedral took place during a difficult period of economic and construction crisis, but we have always maintained that its construction is a sign of hope, both for the companies that worked directly or indirectly on the project and for the thousands of workers on the National Cathedral's site, who, during times of crisis, had a guaranteed salary because of this building.

The cathedral's architecture has a cruciform liturgical space, with a Latin cross-shaped plan and the main arm longer than the others, thus representing the faithful's pilgrimage to the kingdom of God, symbolized by the iconostasis.

The Orthodox iconostasis, also called the screen, or temple, is not a separating wall but a bridge of communication and communion between the altar and the nave, between heaven and earth, between eternity and time, a memorial of the history of salvation and a prophetic anticipation of the kingdom of heaven proffered to humankind.

An illustration of Christ's Church in the kingdom of heaven, the shining iconostasis of the National Cathedral shows that Christ is present at once in the glory of the heavenly realm together with the saints, and on earth, in humility, together with the faithful people who pray to him in church.

The National Cathedral's consecration helps us understand that calling attention to the great symbols and values of the Romanian nation is a permanent duty of all. We need symbols because we need to foster our communion as a people.

The well-known "balance of the Romanian people," placed, as Eminescu said, "like an edge of separation between the storm coming from the West to meet the one coming from the East," has generated a great power of cultural synthesis, defining for our national identity, which

Fr Stăniloae described as "a blend of Latin character with the spirit of Orthodox Christianity."[11]

This truth was confirmed in 1995 by His All Holiness Ecumenical Patriarch Bartholomew with the following words:

> An astonishing feeling of admiration is stirred in us by the fact that almost a thousand years after the martyrdom of Saint Sava (d. 372), the people of these lands, despite countless misfortunes and persecutions, have retained their Orthodox faith and the Latin language. It is a true wonder of history. Given the current size of the Church of Romania, words fail to express how this great Orthodox nation suddenly emerged from the benighted history of the fourteenth century to assure the whole of humanity that it had survived as a unitary people, though almost unknown for centuries. As a new Ulysses returned to Ithaca escaping from traps and danger, the Romanian nation returned to the light of history avoiding cultural alienation and assimilation by other foreign peoples. Perhaps the secret of this miracle lies in the strong and unwavering faith of this nation.[12]

This assertion of His All Holiness Patriarch Bartholomew of Constantinople, which is in fact a tribute to the preservation of Romanian Christians' identity, shows us that perseverance through a steadfast faith in the face of all evil is a factor of unity and spiritual strength that helps us to nurture and promote continuity, unity, and national identity in dialogue and cooperation.

---

[11]Fr Dumitru Stăniloae, "Reflecţii despre spiritualitatea poporului român" [Reflections on the spirituality of the Romanian people], *Complete Works*, vol. 9 (Bucharest: Basilica, 2018), 30.

[12]Ecumenical Patriarch Bartholomew I of Constantinople, "The Joy of the Orthodox Romanians Is the Joy of the Orthodox Everywhere," *The Herald of Orthodoxy* 4, no. 145–146 (November 1995), 9. Speech delivered at the Patriarchal Cathedral of Bucharest, Sunday, October 27, 1995, on the 110th anniversary of the acquisition of autocephaly (1885) by the Romanian Orthodox Church and the 70th anniversary of its elevation to the status of patriarchate (1925).

The construction and consecration of the Cathedral of the Romanian People's Salvation represent the fulfillment of an ideal that we received together with the Holy Synod, the clergy, and the faithful as a directive from our worthy predecessors, and the fulfillment of this ideal has gained true value especially as it manifests the solidarity of all the hierarchs of the Holy Synod in supporting this project, both by adopting the necessary synodal decisions and by continuing to raise money for the National Church Fund.

On the occasion of the National Cathedral's consecration, we would like to thank all the hierarchs of the Holy Synod of the Romanian Orthodox Church, our co-ministers and co-shepherds of the Orthodox Christian flock in Romania and the Romanian diaspora.

At the same time, we thank all the clergy, all the monastics, and the faithful of the Romanian Orthodox Church here and abroad for their spiritual and material support in this work of our Church.

We give them fatherly blessings and ask them to preserve the Orthodox faith and to pray that God may help us complete all the work of the Romanian People's Salvation Cathedral, including its iconography. We hope that next year (2019) we will consecrate the chapel of the cathedral's lower level, and in three years' time we will complete and consecrate the entire iconographic adornment of the National Cathedral.

Special thanks are owed to the state officials who supported the project of building the cathedral: the Romanian governments from 2011 to 2018, the city hall of Bucharest, the mayors of Bucharest and of its sectors, and several county councils throughout the country.

We also thank all the benefactors and sponsors for the support given for the fulfillment of this Romanian ideal, in this year full of significance of celebrating the nation's centennial.

We beseech our Savior Jesus Christ to help us use this achievement as a luminous moment of blessing and joy for the strengthening of brotherly faith and love, knowing that celebrating a church event can be a time of renewal of mission, a spiritual rejuvenation for a new beginning to the glory of God and the salvation of humankind!

Serving the Church:
Sacrifice and Joy[1]

A NDREW VICTOR DOCHIA, JOURNALIST. Bless, Your Beatitude. Thank you for the honor given to Romanian Public Television and for the joy brought to all our viewers by accepting this interview, the first in ten years since your enthronement.

HIS BEATITUDE PATRIARCH DANIEL. May God bless you. I am glad as well, certainly, to give this interview on the tenth anniversary, and because we are able to continue, with God's help, what we have started in these past ten years.

ANDREW VICTOR DOCHIA. On September 30, 2007, Romanians witnessed an impressive religious service for the first time. We are talking about the first enthronement of a patriarch in a Romania that was free and freshly integrated into the European Union. Your Beatitude, it has been ten years since that historic moment. Naturally, you were enthusiastic as this dignity requires much responsibility, but also great sacrifice. Back then, the political context was rather negative: there was great unrest on the political scene, the population was split, it was a year with two referendums. How do you see the Romanian Orthodox Church of 2007?

---

[1]Patriarch Daniel, "Slujirea Bisericii – Jertfelnicie şi Bucurie" [Serving the Church: Sacrifice and joy], interview by Andrew Victor Dochia, upon the completion of ten years of patriarchal service. The interview was broadcast during the TV program *The Universe of Faith* on December 24, 2017. The text was revised by the author in January 2018 and published as *Slujirea Bisericii – Jertfelnicie şi Bucurie* [Serving the Church: Sacrifice and joy] (Bucharest: Basilica, 2018).

HIS BEATITUDE PATRIARCH DANIEL. I see her on a natural course, one of continuity and, at the same time, of increasing her pastoral and missionary activities, and I especially see her rediscovering, or intensifying, social and philanthropic activities, which were interrupted during the communist period.

ANDREW VICTOR DOCHIA. In the evening on the day of your enthronement, you gave your first interview on Romanian Television, with journalist Titi Dincă. It was the first and last interview, because you told us then—I remember—there were so many things to do for the Church that there would not be any more time for interviews. And behold, it was just so. What were the immediate needs and pressing problems the Church was facing?

HIS BEATITUDE PATRIARCH DANIEL. First, new houses of worship were needed, especially in new neighborhoods that were built during socialism, which did not provide such places. Second, it was the education of our youth, who desired to know more about the faith. We were all impressed when we saw that during the Revolution, a lot of young people, who had not studied any religion in school, prayed—they prayed the Our Father—showing their faith inherited from their family, parents, grandparents, and, of course, from the subtle but effective work of many parish priests. So, the building of physical churches, which were lacking, and the spiritual building and edification of the soul as well—the two may be considered the outer church and the church of the human soul—those were the priorities. It was stated at the time that our youth were of the utmost importance.

The third priority was more efficient pastoral organization and, in general, increased care for the Romanians in the diaspora, because this phenomenon of migration, or emigration, rather, was a new one, unknown in such large proportions to our Church, especially after 2000. On the one hand, we had many urgent problems to solve in the country, and on the other, there was also a great deal of concern for the Romanians around the country's borders and in the Western diaspora.

ANDREW VICTOR DOCHIA. These have been ten years of tireless, sustained labor. Ten years of Martha's and Mary's work—blended perfectly. We are talking about impeccable organization, impeccable efficiency. I would like to ask you to share some of the efforts that have been made to accomplish the most important projects of the Romanian Orthodox Church in these ten years. The Church's news agency, the canonization of new Romanian saints, the organization of new administrative structures, as you mentioned, the diaspora, the philanthropic activity, and finally—firstly, in fact—the National Cathedral.

HIS BEATITUDE PATRIARCH DANIEL. In the address given at the enthronement we set the priorities. We showed the need to have a radio station, a television station, and a daily newspaper to spread the faith and to go beyond the walls of the church, that is, to broadcast the liturgy live every day, especially to the elderly and the ailing. To this day, the most beloved transmission is the Divine Liturgy, followed closely by the vespers celebrated at the patriarchal cathedral. Besides building the new church, the Romanian People's Salvation Cathedral, we also wanted to build a more intense church for the believer's soul. The radio station, the TV station, and the newspaper *The Light* were announced on September 30 and launched on the patronal feast of the patriarchal cathedral on October 27, 2007.

ANDREW VICTOR DOCHIA. They were done in a very short time.

HIS BEATITUDE PATRIARCH DANIEL. Yes, God helped us to set up these communication media networks in a little over three weeks.

Another great work was the announcement that we would continue our efforts to begin building the Cathedral of the People's Salvation, or of the liberation of the Romanian people from foreign rule. This is what the nation's salvation means. It does not mean salvation in a theological sense, but in a patriotic sense. Of course, this is a mandate received from our forefathers. It was not my idea; I only took on this task together with the Holy Synod of the Romanian Orthodox Church, with the clergy and the faithful, because the Cathedral of the Romanian People's Salvation, or the National Cathedral, as we now call it for short, is a practical necessity and has a symbolical value as it is a church dedicated to commemorating, remembering the heroes of our nation, of Romanian people of all times.

ANDREW VICTOR DOCHIA. Since oftentimes we hear false topics of discussion such as "We want schools and hospitals, not cathedrals"—as if they were mutually exclusive—I would like to dwell for a few minutes on the social-philanthropic activity of the Church, an institution that in 2016 alone spent about ninety-six million lei in charitable works. So that our viewers understand—we are talking about twenty million euros, which the Church spent on philanthropic actions, institutions, social services, campaigns such as "Health for the Villages" or "Donate Blood, Save a Life." Did the Church succeed? If so, how did she become, during this time, the country's first philanthropist?

HIS BEATITUDE PATRIARCH DANIEL. It happened so not purposely—we learned that later—but because she felt the responsibility to merge the Liturgy with philanthropy. In our time, if a beautiful sermon is not accompanied by a charitable or cultural or artistic-religious act, it is not credible or complete. And this correlation between spirituality and action, between liturgy and philanthropy, is a dominant one in the whole tradition of our Church. But during communism, the Church was often reduced to a purely liturgical institution without any social-philanthropic impact. That is why, after the changes of 1989, we returned to our old tradition—namely, the presence of priest-chaplains in military units, hospitals, penitentiaries, and other state institutions; there was a need for strengthening the soul and an awareness of the relationship between liberty and responsibility. And so this social-philanthropic development has become somewhat of a complete embodiment of the Divine Liturgy of the Church. We can see that more believers go to monasteries that offer an agape after the Divine Liturgy. Where there is fellowship in prayer and fellowship with agape, where people come together for a meal, they can—

ANDREW VICTOR DOCHIA. Relate to one another.

HIS BEATITUDE PATRIARCH DANIEL. Yes, they relate, they talk face to face; they extend the idea of Church as communion and community.

Then, of course, many parishes have set up practices that provide medical and dental services, consulting services—even for legal matters—and more recently, in the last years, they have been offering after-school programs for students who do well in school but do not have adequate home conditions in which to study. So we could conclude that we have rediscovered the old tradition of the holy fathers: in times of freedom, faith is manifested in deeds of merciful love. First, we celebrate this merciful love during the Liturgy, as it was shown us by Jesus Christ, and then through philanthropy. Very often, after preaching the gospel of the kingdom of heaven, our Savior Jesus Christ healed the sick and sometimes multiplied bread and fish to feed those who had otherwise received spiritual nourishment all day. So we follow his example, the model of our Savior Jesus Christ: preaching the gospel, praying, but at the same time helping to strengthen the community, especially where there are elderly, sick, and lonely people. There is a great need for affirmation of faith through deeds.

ANDREW VICTOR DOCHIA. Is there any cooperation with state authorities in the social-philanthropic area?

HIS BEATITUDE PATRIARCH DANIEL. There is cooperation, which is something natural, necessary: the state's citizens comprise most of the Church's faithful, and we work for the common good. We do have different responsibilities and different positions, but we share a common purpose. And this is seen not only at the level of patriarchal relations with the various ministries but also at county and local levels: local councils, county councils support the Church's activities because the work done is in favor of the citizens. And we have a tradition of cooperating with the state because we have a co-responsibility regarding the lives of the citizenry, of our believers. Here we must add that the new Freedom of Religion Law no. 489/2006 maintains that the State supports religion because it recognizes its role in society: educational, spiritual, and social in general; and it also recognizes it as a state partner in social activities and as a supporter of social peace. In other words, the help we receive from the state is not just a gesture of benevolence, but a recognition of religion's contribution to the life of society. And of course, the great number of believers matters as well. So, what we have here is a co-responsibility, but without exceeding our competencies or attributions. We remain the people of the Church even when we cooperate with the state, and the state has its autonomy: it is religiously neutral, but it is not indifferent.

ANDREW VICTOR DOCHIA. It would be inappropriate to list now, Your Beatitude, front-page headlines from newspapers that caused many people to take sides in the online environment. I'm referring here to the most important construction project of the country in the last ten years, the Romanian People's Salvation Cathedral, or the National Cathedral. This dispute between opponents and supporters revealed a lot of bad faith and, unfortunately, a lot of acrimony. Ultimately, the cathedral is an accomplishment of the patriarch, the Church, and the Romanian faithful. Is this perceived as a practical necessity and a spiritual-national symbol, as you have always called this project?

HIS BEATITUDE PATRIARCH DANIEL. The need for this church was ascertained a long time ago. The first stand on the necessity of a cathedral was taken in the years immediately following Romania's Independence War, when Ioan Slavici and Mihai Eminescu wrote in the press that a cathedral was needed to commemorate the war heroes of 1877–1878. Then in 1884 King Carol I recognized the necessity of a cathedral, especially since he came to the services on Sunday, although he was Roman Catholic—he would first go to the Roman Catholic mass and then he would climb the Metropolitanate Hill. He came to this church and attended the Orthodox Liturgy. He realized that a larger church was necessary, and for that reason he issued a decree-law in 1884 regarding a cathedral church in Bucharest. The law was never abrogated—it is just that it was implemented 126 years after its issuance, and as such we have now begun to put into practice a law expressing the necessity of a cathedral. King Carol I's position was reaffirmed by King Ferdinand two years after the Great Union of Alba Iulia, in 1920. In the context after the First World War and the Great Union of Alba Iulia, ever since 1918, the cathedral was called the Romanian People's Salvation Cathedral, meaning the deliverance, or freedom, of the nation from foreign rule. And so the desideratum remained. But unfavorable conditions—sometimes war, sometimes economic crisis—did not allow the realization of this cathedral.

Of course, the late Patriarch Theoctistus of blessed memory strove greatly to put into practice the mandate received from Patriarch Myron Cristea and the desire of those who showed the necessity and the dignity of a national cathedral, but had much work to do until its location was established. Union Square was proposed first but deemed unsuitable later; then Union Boulevard; Carol Park; Izvor Park; and finally, it was settled on Arsenal Hill, between the current Palace of the Parliament and the Ministry of Defense.

Certainly, the land we received there was a compensation, a moral reparation for five churches—three demolished and two moved. So the building of the National Cathedral is a symbol in an area where five churches were affected to make room for the People's House. We had to explain all these aspects to show that it is not an ambition but a necessity, and that the current patriarchal church was at first a monastery church built between 1656 and 1658. Ten years later, in 1668, it was *provisionally* declared the metropolitan cathedral, and in 1925, when the Metropolitanate of Wallachia was raised to the rank of patriarchate, the cathedral was *provisionally* called the patriarchal cathedral. All this was written on the inscription inside the cathedral, upon the restoration work carried out during the tenure of Patriarch Myron Cristea between 1932 and 1935.

Therefore, what we have here is our finally coming out of a provisional situation. The church is very beautiful, but it is very small. Once, when we had to consecrate the chrism, only twelve hierarchs could fit in the altar: the other hierarchs and the clergy were in the nave, and the people stood outside. I said in jest that we should not practice "liturgical apartheid"—the clergy inside the church and the faithful outside—especially during inclement weather. So the new cathedral is a practical necessity ascertained by those who serve. Those who do not serve in it or do not attend services regularly do not realize the practical necessity. But the fact that this new cathedral is related to the remembrance, or commemoration, of the Romanian heroes of all times, and especially of those who died in 1917, in the First World War, for the establishment of the Romanian nation, for a unified Romania, shows the great significance of its consecration. Therefore, we have made great efforts and continue to do so to consecrate the cathedral on November 30, 2018,[2] the feast day of St Andrew, the patron saint of Romania. So realism and symbolism are tied together by hope.

ANDREW VICTOR DOCHIA. What did this project mean; how did it set into shape so completely? I am referring to the fact that it was not easy in these years to build such an important building so fast.

HIS BEATITUDE PATRIARCH DANIEL. There have been several contests for this project, but not all were successful. The consecration of the building site took place on November 29, 2007, on the eve of the feast of St Andrew the First-Called, the protector of Romania. And this consecration ended the debates on the building's location. But we had to organize three more consultative symposia, because those initial contests had been very costly and not successful, and so we turned the contests first into consultative symposia and called on architects and engineers. Several versions were proposed, and we managed to go

---

[2]The consecration actually ttook place on November 25, 2018.

through all stages of design in three years: 2008, 2009, and 2010. After three years of investigations and consultations, in the fall of 2010, on September 2, we received the building permit from the Sector Five City Hall of Bucharest and later, at the end of 2010, we started the organization of the construction site. In effect, we began in November–December 2010, and here we are now at a very advanced stage, specifically, at the base of the turrets, which will be finalized in 2018. We will consecrate the altar and the iconostasis at the end of 2018, and the iconography a few years later upon its completion. It bears noting that our scheduling had a delay of six months, of which we recovered four, and we hope to recover the other two, as instead of 400 workers we now have 800. Given that we have more workers, who do two or three shifts, we hope that we will finish the work, cover the church, and consecrate it.

ANDREW VICTOR DOCHIA. Regrettably, the project of raising the National Cathedral was and continues to be the target of a malicious campaign against the Church. I would like to ask you how the Church responds to the constant criticism during this time.

HIS BEATITUDE PATRIARCH DANIEL. The Church is not surprised by this criticism, and there is a prayer in the service of consecrating the site of a new church that entreats God to help those who build the cathedral and to keep them from demonic snares. Not only from this prayer but also from the experience of several parishes that have built churches, we know that there are almost always hostile powers or even temptations trying to stop holy works. But if we strengthen ourselves in the faith, if we bear the criticism, if we know that we cannot show our faith without temptation, then we won't lose heart, and we will persevere. We knew that some of the criticism stemmed from the fact that people were not informed enough; others set the building of new churches in opposition with the need for hospitals or schools, but we find that there are many private schools, many hospitals, or medical units that have already been founded; on the other hand, the number of children has decreased—especially in rural areas. But we do not see the construction of schools and hospitals in opposition to that of churches. Both are necessary. Only, the Church is both hospital and school—a spiritual hospital and a spiritual school for our entire life. This spiritual school that is the Church does not end with a baccalaureate or a doctorate degree, but she is a forgiver of sins and a healer of spiritual ailments. The Church addresses all ages, all social categories. Therefore, she cannot be replaced with anything. She has her own special character, her uniqueness; as such, we support the building of both schools and churches. It's just that it all depends on how the money is managed. When believers see that their contribution builds a new edifice, they are encouraged. If we only ask for money without showing any progress in construction, then there arise confusion, questions, hesitation. In this respect [we receive] help from state authorities according to the ratified laws—an emergency ordinance from 2005 and a law from 2007—which expressly refer to the construction of the architectural ensemble of the Cathedral of the Romanian People's Salvation. So, based on special legislation, the state does provide this aid, and we use and justify it. From 2010 until now, the Romanian Court of Accounts has never found anything negative about the use and justification of the money received from the state. And this shows us that if we work to build a cathedral or a church, we need to do it properly. It's not all about building, but building in a credible, proper way, so that those who donate money know where their contribution—

ANDREW VICTOR DOCHIA. Goes.

HIS BEATITUDE PATRIARCH DANIEL. Yes, where it goes. And I have to say that the steadiest people in helping the Church, although the amounts are very small, are the pensioners. We have a special prayer during all services, approved by the Holy Synod, for benefactors, for constructors, for those who endeavor to build the cathedral. And the donors say, "I was prayed for today as well." While we do not pray for each by name, we pray for this category of benefactors, for those who help. And surprisingly, there are people who, out of their small pension, donate twenty to thirty lei every month.

ANDREW VICTOR DOCHIA. They will be remembered unto the ages—

HIS BEATITUDE PATRIARCH DANIEL. They will be, certainly. But the idea is that the richest people are not always the most generous. People of rather modest financial means are aware that what is being built is a necessity and an expression of faith.

ANDREW VICTOR DOCHIA. Your Beatitude, having mentioned just a few of the Church's achievements in these ten years, I would now like to bring to the viewers' attention some moments of tension, or the challenges, of this period. We talked about bad campaigns, but now I want to talk about the fact that the Church has been systematically subjected to a series of polls that showed Romanians' diminishing confidence in this institution year after year—and we are talking about an institution that is not only human but divine-human. If in the 1990s the Church benefited from the highest rate of public confidence—ninety percent—according to an IMAS poll from September 2017, the Church has now a little over fifty percent of the population's confidence. On the other hand, I would also like our considering the year 2015, when ninety percent of parents deliberately signed up their children for religion classes. I think it is natural to talk about this result as having the value of a referendum. I would like to ask you: What is in fact the reality?

HIS BEATITUDE PATRIARCH DANIEL. It bears noting first that there is an institutional crisis even internationally. Surveys from across our country show a fluctuation in the population's confidence in all institutions. And the fact that at some point confidence dwindles or increases shows that these surveys are relative, so we only take them as rough guidelines rather than as normative ones. So, to us, the surveys are relative; sometimes they are ordered, sometimes simplified, sometimes modeled after momentary interests or after more general guidelines. But the fact that they are neither definitive nor normative for us is explained by the responsibility of the Church in society. She, no matter the polls, ought not to be discouraged in her mission, in her holy work. The Savior Jesus Christ tells us, "In the world you will have tribulation; but be of good cheer, I have overcome the world" (Jn 16.33). He did not say that everything is a success, everything is progress every step of the way, but he said that in the world we would have tribulations and trials. And that was certainly proved in times of persecution, in times of all sorts of suffering, obstacles, and so on. But what is important is the continuity of the Church's mission. Because God does not always judge by figures how much we have accomplished, but by how faithful we have been. Therefore, the Savior's charge is this: "Be faithful until death, and I will give you the crown of life" (Rev 2.10).

Sometimes we built many churches; sometimes only a few or none. Or they were demolished. The important thing was that faith was maintained, that the people remained loyal, in larger or smaller numbers—surely, it did not always depend on the Church but on external factors, which she did not provoke. Loyalty is important. In times of praise, in times of criticism, in times of persecution, or in times of freedom, we must remain steadfast in our faith, loyal. This fidelity is necessary both in the family and in the monastery. Beyond hardship and temptation, it is important to remain faithful to the oath or the ideal we have set.

We find that, in general, the people who attend services and fill churches show fidelity. On the one hand, surveys are a criterion to which we are not indifferent, but by which we do not become discouraged either. And on the other hand, we have churches full of believers. If the churches were empty, surely that would confirm the polls. But so long as the churches are full of believers, it still shows that we need them for our population. In Bucharest there are few churches in relation to the number of believers. So we do not fall into despondency. The Church is the ship of salvation.

The collection of books *Apostolic Constitutions*, from the end of the third century and the beginning of the fourth century, says: "The church must be long and have the shape of a ship." Thus, we did not make it round or square, but ship-like. And the steeple with a cross on it is the mast of the ship. But it is a ship on land, not on water, and this ship of salvation reminds us that our Redeemer often preached and performed miracles from a ship on the Sea of Galilee. The Church ought to be an ark of salvation, a space in which man meets God in the closest way, during fair skies and during storms. The ship must be a ship both on turbulent waves and on calm seas. For this, we should not become so frightened as to abandon our mission.

There have been very difficult times for the Church sometimes, when she was abolished, forbidden, for example, for twenty-five years or more, as happened in Albania. Religion was forbidden! The first atheist state in the world. Yet people prayed in secret, and now, during the tenure of Archbishop Anasthasius of Tirana and Albania, faith has flourished. There are trials in history, ebbs and flows in the number of believers, but fidelity is important.

ANDREW VICTOR DOCHIA. Your Beatitude, let us now turn to another moment of tension in Romanian society and of course for the Church. I am talking about the Colectiv nightclub tragedy, when sixty-four young people lost their lives in a terrible fire. There was then, in an absolutely justified way, huge tension in our society, a tension that also affected the Church. It was said at the time of the tragedy that the Church was not beside the families of the victims. How did you, as the patriarch, live those moments?

HIS BEATITUDE PATRIARCH DANIEL. We must confess the truth, which was concealed or only partially presented by the media. The first institution that made a press release after this incident, calling for prayer for the rest of the decedents' souls and calling for blood donations to the wounded, was the Romanian Patriarchate. That morning, the patriarchate gave that statement. Our priest-chaplains were at the hospital right beside the wounded, the burned, praying in hospital chapels and mobilizing parishes to aid or bring money to the families of the injured. The parish priests prayed and were beside the coffins and the families of the deceased. I personally participated in two funerals. But we are accustomed to being by the coffin of the reposed, not keeping vigils at the place of the accident. If a traffic accident occurs on a street or there is a railway accident and forty to fifty people die, we do not go on a pilgrimage there but stay with the families of the deceased and the injured. But to our surprise, the pilgrimage to the scene of the accident was considered more important than being with the decedents and the injured. And since this was expected, although it was not a necessity, surely, our priests went to the site and prayed. But we first thought to be beside the deceased, the injured, and the families in mourning.

It is worth mentioning that two weeks after the fire at the Colectiv nightclub, on the night of thirteenth to fourteenth of November that same year, there was a terrorist attack on the Bataclan club in Paris, where more than one hundred people died. Shortly thereafter, the archbishop of Paris called for prayer at the Notre Dame Cathedral, not at the Bataclan club, where the attack had taken place. This, therefore, confirmed that our attitude was correct, identical in its spiritual form to that of the West, in Paris. But since a pilgrimage to the place of the fire was expected, this tragic part was highlighted the most, of course.

Moreover, we organized several collections throughout our dioceses to help the families of those who suffered from the Colectiv fire. And so the families affected by this tragic event were helped three times. The Archdiocese of Bucharest, the Archdiocese of Cluj, and the Archdiocese of the Lower Danube provided cash sent directly to these families to help them financially as well and not only through consoling words and prayers.

Yes, of course, it was reported that there was a lack of communication, as such attitudes of giving more importance to the site of the fire rather than to the suffering people existed beforehand. The antagonistic attitude against the Church existed before the Colectiv nightclub fire. There is a hostile stance, especially from some associations that opposed religion classes in schools. And after the victory of the Church—

ANDREW VICTOR DOCHIA. With the ninety percent—

HIS BEATITUDE PATRIARCH DANIEL. With the ninety percent of student enrollment in religion classes, this hostility has increased. That is why those associations were the first to post signs with slogans such as "We want hospitals, not cathedrals!" after the fire at the Colectiv nightclub. So there was a connection between the religion class and some people's hostility, which only intensified after the fire.

ANDREW VICTOR DOCHIA. And this is because, as I said, the ninety percent enrollment in the religious class really had the value of a referendum—

HIS BEATITUDE PATRIARCH DANIEL. Almost like a referendum, or rather, more of a public consultation.

ANDREW VICTOR DOCHIA. Ten years ago, in the interview you granted to Romanian Television, when addressing the topic of the Romanian Orthodox Church's material condition, you said material wealth can be a blessing or a temptation—it depends on how much we are attached to it. Over the past decade, we have witnessed several attacks on the place occupied by the Romanian Orthodox Church in the material life of the people: that there are too many churches, that the state and society spend too much money helping churches, that the National Cathedral is a megalomaniacal project. Instead, if we look for and consult more economic reports—and here I'm referring to the one made by Mr. Petrişor Gabriel Peiu, coordinator of the Department of Economic Analysis of the Black Sea University Foundation—we find that things are considerably different. And I'll give one example: The National Cathedral was not and is not more expensive than similar cathedrals in other European capitals and is far less expensive than the malls of Bucharest or the national stadium. How should we look at this issue of the Church's wealth?

HIS BEATITUDE PATRIARCH DANIEL. The Church's material wealth is not financial. It is not found in bank accounts. The wealth is of a liturgical nature—to begin with, our believers are our greatest asset, because if a church is beautiful but empty, it is not beautiful enough if it remains just a museum. But it is true that the cultural-liturgical heritage and the multitude of churches and monasteries, especially those whose iconography has artistic value, are considered a very large patrimony. But we cannot put these churches up for sale, and we need even more churches than we already have. We do not transform them into something else either, as happens in some countries because of secularization. So the wealth of the Church is worshipful and cultural in nature, and, as I said, it refers to sacred and holy material goods: the multitude of icons, the multitude of garments, the multitude of objects of worship, which are the expression of piety and love for God. None of this can be quantified and capitalized in a bank or from one day to the next.

When it comes to financial income, however, this is quite limited in relation to the social projects and philanthropic needs of the Church. Let us not forget that the church estates were secularized in 1863 in Wallachia and Moldavia, and those assets represented one fourth of the country's territory. Certainly, there were also many monasteries dedicated to foreigners, and at first it was said that only those would be secularized, but then Romanian churches and monasteries were secularized as well, with many monks left half-starving. Then some laws were passed, as compensation, to support the livelihood of the monks. But it really was a dispossession of monastic property. Many of the historic monuments that had been previously open were closed after the secularization and deteriorated. Then the Church managed to retrieve some properties over time, with great effort—only to have them confiscated by the communist regime. Today, only a handful have been restored. Much is required of the Church, but it is not always mentioned how many losses she has incurred in terms of agricultural land, forests, and other properties, which had precisely the function of helping, sustaining the places of worship. Then it was decided that priests should receive from the Romanian state a salary, or *support*, as it is called, because it is not really a full salary: it represents sixty-five percent of a high school teacher's wages.

ANDREW VICTOR DOCHIA. Money that goes back—

HIS BEATITUDE PATRIARCH DANIEL. Money that goes back to the state, of course, through taxes, contributions. But the Church is not rich in the sense of having cash or bank accounts. That is why she must be helped. If we want to commit the Church to social-philanthropic work, she ought to be helped. And here I would like to emphasize an alarming aspect concerning our almost half-starving priests from rural, aging areas, where there are more elderly people than young people. The doctors and many teachers left the villages, while the priests and the mayor remained the only intellectuals. We have been dealing with an unprecedented experience so far: the depopulation of villages. We have over ten, fifteen, twenty burials a year and no baptisms, no weddings. Sure, we are happy that there are many baptisms and weddings in the Romanian diaspora. But here at home it is very difficult. A priest cannot have a full salary—that is, what the state gives is only a part that must be supplemented with contributions from the faithful. But the believers themselves need help: a social canteen, medication money. That is why we proposed, together with the Holy Synod, that the year 2019 be the "Solemn Year of the Romanian Village." And that means the priest, the teacher, and the mayor. Most of those who sacrificed during the First World War for the achievement of the unified Romanian State were village people, countryfolk. That is why we need to give more support to priests in rural areas. We do have a relief fund called the Good Shepherd Fund organized in our dioceses, but it is insufficient. The living conditions of some of our village priests are very modest, and they are called upon to help the elderly, not to ask for their social security money. We do try to organize some sort of partnership among our city parishes and the rural ones, to help them out, but it is not enough, especially as some of the priests in the villages also have children. Right here in Ilfov County close to Bucharest, we have poor parishes of seventy to eighty families, and the priest has three or four children, if not more. And in Prahova County there are some very poor parishes as well. Thus, we must organize internal solidarity but also increase the contribution of the State Secretariat for Religious Affairs to these communities. So there are new problems with which we ought to deal because of this phenomenon of emigration, the departure of Romanians abroad. We would be glad if many came back, but I believe their return will be a slow rather than a fast one.

ANDREW VICTOR DOCHIA. Another difficult moment for the Church, Your Beatitude, was the one in which, with a heavy heart, you had to apologize to the faithful for the disorder caused by public accusations brought against the clergy regarding certain deviations from Christian morals. What did that moment mean for the Church?

HIS BEATITUDE PATRIARCH DANIEL. It was stated at that moment what it meant. And it is known that when believers are distraught, we must repent, correct our behavior, but at the same time we must promote discipline of the clergy. But as in any other community, there are temptations in our Church as well, and we need a strengthening of our spiritual life. In a secularized society, the Church cannot be without temptation. She sometimes undergoes influences caused by secularization. By secularization, we understand here not the secularization of assets but the secularization of souls, meaning that private or social life is built without reference to religious values. From this point of view, we must maintain our faithfulness and try to recover those who have fallen, but at the same time, we ought to apply discipline and preventive measures. That is why the Holy Synod took some measures, not only with regard to the referenced cases of indiscipline but also with regard to the life of the clergy in general.

It is essential to understand that the secularized society does not work in harmony with the ideal of the Church, but very often develops very much in a position of hostility, owing to individualism. In secular society, violence has greatly developed in the family and school because people no longer have peace and joy in their soul, and they seek happiness in drugs, in all sorts of experiences that are not healthy either spiritually or physically. We are dealing with an increase in alcoholism, suicide, and this shows the manifestation of a profound spiritual crisis that is the result of the loss of spiritual life. The Savior says that because lawlessness will abound, the love of many will grow cold (cf. Mt 24.12).

So a spiritual crisis leads to a crisis in families, institutions, and society at large, but we must withstand it and show that we are not fatalists. We must have hope amid trials and adversity.

ANDREW VICTOR DOCHIA. Since you have referred to these secular attacks—there is now a God-free ethic or a private belief that translates into expressions such as "I have my God," or "I do not need the Church," "I pray alone at home, I do not need a mediator." How does the Church respond to these new tendencies of isolation?

HIS BEATITUDE PATRIARCH DANIEL. She responds as follows: When the faithful—that is, former faithful, because some are baptized, but they are no longer practicing Christians, so to speak—stop going to church, we ought to go to them. That is why young practicing Orthodox who attend services often try to speak to their classmates in colleges about the importance of faith and about the fact that prayer fills the soul with joy and peace, and that happiness does not occur in a spiritual vacuum. But, of course, we must respect human freedom. We cannot force people or lecture them because they do not go to church. There are periods of searching in the lives of many. There are people who come to church because of the inherited tradition of their parents.

Others come to church because they underwent a trial, an illness, an accident. Others come because of a pious colleague who aroused their curiosity, and so they discovered the importance of faith. So, after all, we have a duty to call them, help each one discover the love of Christ and at the same time see the benefits of communion. We cannot say, we'll pray at home, alone. Of course, prayer is needed at home as well, but it does not beget as much joy as when the celebration is experienced in the community. And we see this in the need for fellowship, for relating to one another, as they say, for meeting together; there are still waves of individualism, isolation, but then it is concluded that this isolation is not healthy for the soul. There is some atomization because of technology today, but, at the same time, the need for communication remains; it is deeply ingrained in the human being, no matter how it is expressed at one point or another.

ANDREW VICTOR DOCHIA. Because you spoke about young people, I would like to bring up a very important event: the Meeting of Orthodox Youth in 2017. It was the fourth iteration, which, regrettably, was completely ignored by the media in Romania. We are talking about seven thousand young Orthodox Christians, who came to Jassy from thirty-two countries. All of them went unnoticed by news agencies, news stories. How can we explain this? What should the Church do?

HIS BEATITUDE PATRIARCH DANIEL. The Church did what she was supposed to do—she broadcast the entire meeting. The Romanian Patriarchate supported this meeting in its preparation and in its development through Trinitas TV and Trinitas Radio. I was personally there. But we cannot force private television or even public television to cover an event if they do not want to do so. We showed that we do not ignore our youth; if so many gather together, we are bound by conscience to mark the event. But we do not know the rationale behind the attitude that others have of completely ignoring it.

Nonetheless, it has to be said that we have never organized such meetings for media success. The same thing happened in Cluj: very little was publicized about the meeting of young people there; likewise in Bucharest, [where there was hardly any reporting] especially considering the importance of the event. But we organize meetings for young people from across the nation and abroad, Orthodox youth from all countries, from all Churches, and their joy is the joy of the Church. The sun rises whether I want to see its light or not. Even if I close the shutters or draw shut thick curtains, it will still be there. Yet those who attend these meetings rejoice in them and transmit this joy to their respective Churches.

We believe there is a need for such encounters among young people. At the same time, the Church can help show them how to discern between ephemeral values and eternal values, between true communion and surrogates of communion, between tradition and mere fads of the day.

Young people are very sensitive to what is genuinely human and enduring. The issue of youth freedom is a very significant one. The conclusion is that the more people love God and their neighbors, the freer they are spiritually. In other words, true liberty is true love. When we love God in prayer and our neighbor in good deeds, we are free people. When we cannot do that, it means we are not free enough inside. The confessors of faith in the communist dungeons lacked external social freedom, but they had a very profound spiritual liberty within themselves. And for this liberty of faith, God eased their suffering and gave them the hope that one day they might be released, or even if they weren't to be released, they would be saved. That is why the theme of liberty coincided in 2017 with the theme of remembering or commemorating those who were deprived of liberty and were persecuted during communism.

ANDREW VICTOR DOCHIA. I would like to refer now to another special moment of these past ten years. It is from the summer of 2016, when you led the delegation of our Church to the island of Crete, for the works of the Holy and Great Council of the Orthodox Church. I would like to ask you about the role played by the Romanian Orthodox Church in the organization and development of the Council of Crete.

HIS BEATITUDE PATRIARCH DANIEL. We certainly prepared beforehand. Documentary projects had been published long before; our theological schools, teachers, and hierarchs with in-depth theological or doctoral studies made a special contribution. But what we particularly emphasized was the assurance that this council would not bring new dogmas, and that the documents were more of a pastoral and missionary order; we did not change the doctrine, the discipline of the Church, or the canonical discipline, and in this regard our contribution was appreciated by the participating Churches. At the same time, of course, we regretted that four sister Orthodox Churches were not present, and now we are trying to show that communication, communion, and cooperation are needed to indicate the co-responsibility of the autocephalous Churches. The Churches are autocephalous, but at the same time they form the One Church of Christ, so they must also reflect her universality, not only national or regional autocephaly. From this point of view, we believe that, as the Latin Church and the second largest in terms of number of believers, we need to mediate, to contribute to the strengthening of pan-Orthodox unity. In doing so, we must not emphasize our own merit, but merely fulfill our duty. Of great importance is the fact that the Churches that were in Crete and those that were not in Crete remained in eucharistic communion. The differences, or divergences, or distinctions in their appreciation of the event of the Holy and Great Council in Crete did not cause the breaking of the unity or the ending of eucharistic communion among sister Orthodox Churches. It is therefore very important to maintain full communion even if sometimes we espouse different positions, because during our dialogue, during our consultations, we can clarify, emend, and improve some texts while still preserving the unity of the faith affirmed in the Creed: I believe in One Catholic and Apostolic Church of Christ. The Romanian delegation has shown that the Orthodox

Church is the One, Holy, Catholic, and Apostolic Church, and that other Christian communities broke away from her over time.

Therefore, this strong belief in the One Church was affirmed. Of course, dialogue with other Christian communities or entities is a practical necessity, especially in the countries where the Orthodox are minorities, as is the case with the Romanian diaspora. We have many parishes without their own place of worship, and they have to use or borrow Roman Catholic or Anglican or Protestant churches for a while, but without creating any confusion when it comes to faith. This shows that from the perspective of practical pastoral care, we can be Orthodox without being fanatical; we can be loyal through a love-working faith, without developing hatred against others. The truth of the faith must be preserved but confessed in such a way that it emphasizes the connection between faith and Christian love.

ANDREW VICTOR DOCHIA. You talked about eucharistic communion, and I would like to refer now to the celebration of the patron saint of Bucharest, St Demetrius. On this occasion, you received the visits of the primates of several other sister Orthodox Churches. For the first time since the 1989 Revolution—for the first time since 1983—the Romanian Orthodox Church was visited by the patriarch of Moscow and All Russia, a visit that has long been speculated about by the mass media in our country. What were the premises of the meeting and how did the visit unfold?

HIS BEATITUDE PATRIARCH DANIEL. The presence of the Russian patriarch was a necessity because the year 2017 was dedicated to the memory of Patriarch Justinian and to the confessors, or defenders, of Orthodoxy during communism. It would have been difficult to commemorate those who suffered during communism without the presence of the Russian Orthodox Church, who suffered the most. The harshest persecution happened there. Thousands of people were killed, thousands of churches and hundreds of monasteries were destroyed, so this commemoration had an aspect of eucharistic communion as well, besides the one of co-responsibility, of honoring the memory of the persecuted. Of course, we subsequently went to Moscow, and we were impressed that some of the moments there were similar to those in Bucharest: that is, there was a commemoration of the persecuted although the main theme was the anniversary of the one hundred years since the reinstatement of the Patriarchate of the Russian Church. Thus, we consider it to be the expression of fraternal communion, a commemoration of those who suffered during communism and, at the same time, a rapprochement between different Churches, those who participated and those who did not participate in the Council of Crete. It was something positive, and regardless of external perceptions or reactions, we have a duty to show that the Orthodox Church is also the Universal, Catholic Church, not just a national Church. That is why these relations—especially relations of eucharistic communion—have been appreciated by the clergy and believers in Romania and Russia. There had not been a Moscow patriarch in Bucharest for thirty-four years, and the encounter was, I think, an act of normality—we should not meet only abroad, but here as well, and more often. However, the patriarch of Moscow stated that it was not an official visit but a trip to Bucharest occasioned by a commemoration. An official visit involves traveling to several places in the country, while here we had a two-day program limited to Bucharest only as it was linked to this commemoration.

ANDREW VICTOR DOCHIA. In contradistinction to ten years ago, what would be the percentage of churched intellectuals in relation to the rest of the intelligentsia, and how can we explain the negative reaction of some intellectuals toward the Church?

HIS BEATITUDE PATRIARCH DANIEL. First of all, we do not count them to know their prevalence, because this prevalence can be a number, but it can also be a contribution: there may be intellectuals who are fewer in number but who are very well prepared, love the Church, and help her. So, their number is not as important as their will to carry out missionary work, including through mass media. And these intellectuals, who not only are churched but truly live their life in Christ, are very helpful in presenting the life of the Church and her faith in dialogue with society.

Generally, some people have a certain reluctance if a cleric presents the position of the Church. The impact is greater if they see that there are also intellectuals who can convincingly, subtly, and thoroughly explain things about the faith and the position of the Church and their eternal values. That is why we need a dialogue with our intellectuals, and at the same time we need to listen to them and work together. The Church and the intellectuals are not in opposition, since there are a lot of them right within her bosom.

ANDREW VICTOR DOCHIA. Does the Church play a role in forming a new generation of intellectuals?

HIS BEATITUDE PATRIARCH DANIEL. She does. We have so many theological schools in which many young people study not only to become priests but also to learn theology in general, so there is a desire to know the faith, to cooperate with many different institutions. We have many religion teachers who, besides theology, have also studied other subjects, and we are very interested in these young people who have two specialties and want to work with us in radio and television, at the newspaper. We noticed that young people with multiple specializations can relate with other young people or intellectuals in a more nuanced and efficient way.

ANDREW VICTOR DOCHIA. Your Beatitude, there was a recent event that left Romanian society in mourning. I am talking about the departure from this world of His Majesty King Michael I, who ten years ago participated as an honorary guest at the solemn enthronement of Your Beatitude as patriarch of the Romanian Orthodox Church. How did the Church experience this moment of parting with His Majesty?

HIS BEATITUDE PATRIARCH DANIEL. With much sadness and at the same time with much prayer. The organization of the funeral services for

King Michael I of Romania was an appreciated collaboration between the Royal House and all the state institutions, especially between the Army and the Church, because these two institutions contributed the most to the expression of the military and religious ceremony. We believe it was a gesture of deep prayer and, at the same time, a solemn commemoration of a man who suffered exceedingly but was sustained by a strong faith and strong hope at the same time. That is why the panegyric I gave at the funeral was titled "King Michael I of Romania, a Symbol of the Romanian People's Suffering and Hope."

It is important that we, as the Church, remember that his religious formation helped him greatly to confess the truth through adversity and trials. He received his faith in particular from his mother, Queen Helen, whose remains I believe should be brought to Romania and laid to rest in the royal necropolis of Argeş.[3] But we must recognize that King Michael loved the Romanian people and that he waited patiently for forty-five years until communism fell so he could return to the country. He was patient, and his patience was imbued with a great amount of hope.

On the other hand, we must also think that we, as the Church, ought to show compassion and consolation to those who suffer, and that is why our religious burial services are luminous and filled with a comforting force based on our belief in the resurrection. There is also the human factor of sorrow, so we must be close to those who grieve, as the Apostle Paul admonishes us: "Rejoice with those who rejoice, and weep with those who weep" (Rom 12.15). So we wept together and we shared in the pain, but with the hope that His Majesty's soul in heaven will intercede for the Church and for the country.

ANDREW VICTOR DOCHIA. Ten years have passed since the enthronement of the sixth patriarch of our Church. Beyond the official agenda, to which all those interested have access through the patriarchal media already mentioned, the believers also had the joy of learning special details about their patriarch: that he has a special piety to St Paraskeva

---

[3]Queen Helen's remains were brought to Romania and buried there in 2019.

and feels her constant help; that he is a polyglot; that his spiritual father was Elder Cleopas Ilie, our great confessor; that he has a very strong synthetic ability, an analytical spirit, and a very fine sense of humor; that he is a very good organizer; but that he is also very charitable. What other things are there that the believers ought to know about their spiritual shepherd?

HIS BEATITUDE PATRIARCH DANIEL. These things are not meant to be mentioned in any boastful way. What I believe to be important is that the faithful know I am trying to work for the Church, for the salvation of believers, but together with them, not alone. I feel a great encouragement when they pray for me, when they write my name on prayer lists for my health and salvation. I pray for their health and salvation, they pray for my health and salvation, and in this joint prayer lies the essence that ought to be known: if we pray for the faithful in all our petitions, then we feel them very close even if they are afar. Details about some qualities are not important, but the fruits brought forth are. I am guided in life by the words of St Isaac the Syrian, who says, "Keep quiet so that your deeds may speak." That is, we live in a time when speeches, discourses that are not accompanied by social, cultural activities remain deficient. That is why I give very few interviews, if any at all, because it is better to let deeds speak—deeds accomplished not alone, but with the clergy and believers. Together we achieve what is needed.

I am very aware that no matter how many works we do, there is still more to accomplish. I remember the words of St Callinicus of Cernica Monastery, who, upon becoming abbot, said, "I have not come here to rest on the labor of others." And he began building the new church, he made new cells, supplementing what was already there. So I think every hierarch, every priest must say, "I have not come here to the parish or to the diocese to rest on the labor of my predecessors, but to add a good deed, some cultural, social, and philanthropic work."

For example, the care for *restoring historic monuments* is very important. Our older church buildings must be repaired. Every twenty, thirty years, they have to be renovated, consolidated. This shows respect not only for our forefathers but also for our descendants, for those who come after us. From this perspective, I believe that this desire to be grateful through deeds, to honor the predecessors, is a great joy. That is why each hall of the Patriarchal Residence was named after a patriarch: this one is the Patriarch Theoctistus Great Hall; the other is the Patriarch Justin Great Hall; the Patriarch Justinian Great Hall is another one. We also named some institutions after them to ensure continuity with our predecessors. This communion through the ages is a source of great joy. So it could be said that this is a very important detail: preserving communion among generations—no ruptures, but a profound spiritual communion.

ANDREW VICTOR DOCHIA. What would be the greatest desire but also the most important goal of the Romanian Patriarch at the beginning of his second decade helming the Romanian Orthodox Church?

HIS BEATITUDE PATRIARCH DANIEL. My desire is to continue what we have started and to add other activities that are needed. But the highest priority is to call people to salvation—that is, to call them to union with God through prayer and good deeds. This means repenting for past wrongdoings, renewing their spiritual life, and hoping for works that are of use to the Church. I believe that the Church can have no priorities other than those set by the Savior Jesus Christ—namely, the tidings of the gospel of salvation; the renewal of spiritual life, of course; and third, the manifestation of faith and spirituality through concrete works for the benefit of society.

ANDREW VICTOR DOCHIA. The Infant Christ is born in the humble cave of Bethlehem. I'd like to ask you: To whom do your prayers and thoughts turn now?

HIS BEATITUDE PATRIARCH DANIEL. In tune with the message of our Christmas carols, my attention centers on the Infant Jesus and the Mother of God, the Righteous Joseph, and the angels and shepherds in Bethlehem. So I think first of the Savior Jesus Christ, who became man out of love for people and for their salvation; I think of his Church, which is symbolized by the cave or the stable—and represented in our Church by the table of oblation, or *prothesis*—but I also think of the entire Romanian people, wherever they may be: those who are here at home, those right outside the current borders of Romania, and those who are away in foreign lands in the Western diaspora. So, I hope that the Christmas holidays will be not only a blessing unto them and their families, a celebration of peace and family joy, but also an opportunity to share peace, love, and much kindness with those around them, especially the lonely, the sick, the poor, and the needy. We wish all a blessed Nativity of our Lord, New Year, and Theophany! Many years!

ANDREW VICTOR DOCHIA. And we thank you, Your Beatitude, for entering the homes and especially the souls of the Romanian faithful through this interview. We wish you holidays with peace, spiritual joy, and many years of fruitful ministering of our Orthodox Church!

HIS BEATITUDE PATRIARCH DANIEL. Thank you.

The Unity of Faith and Nation in the Centenary Year[1]

The first Sunday after the feast of the Dormition of the Mother of God was dedicated by the Holy Synod of the Romanian Orthodox Church, in its working session of February 25–26, 2009, to all Romanian migrants. This Sunday is a good opportunity to send benedictions and spiritual strengthening to all Romanian Orthodox believers who have settled or are temporarily working abroad.

By promoting the consciousness of the unity of faith and nation, the Romanian Orthodox Church has contributed to the preparation of great historical events aiming at the national unity of Romanians, such as the Union of the Principalities (1859), the State Independence of Romania (1877–1878), and the Great Union (1918), decisive for the establishment of the unitary national state of Romania.

The Great Union of December 1, 1918, had positive consequences for the newly unified Romanian state and for the Romanian Orthodox Church. On December 18/31, 1919, Bishop Myron Cristea of Caransebeş was elected metropolitan primate of Romania, and in 1925 he became the first patriarch of the Romanian Orthodox Church. A process of unitary organization of the Church in all of Romania then followed.

---

[1] Patriarch Daniel, "Unitate de credință și unitate de neam, în Anul Centenar" [The unity of faith and nation in the centenary year], Basilica News Agency, accessed November 26, 2019, https://basilica.ro/unitate-de-credinta-si-unitate-de-neam-in-anul-centenar-text-integral-2/. The address was delivered on the Sunday for Romanian Migrants, August 19, 2018.

On October 15, 1922, at a ceremony held at the Cathedral of the Nation's Reunification in Alba Iulia, King Ferdinand I and Queen Mary were crowned sovereigns of Greater Romania, an act that symbolized the unification under the same scepter of all Romanians all the way "from the Dniester to the Tisza" Rivers.

In the last decade, the spiritual needs of the Romanians who live far from the country have determined the Romanian Orthodox Church to set as a pastoral priority the strengthening of the Romanian communities around the country's borders and in the Romanian diaspora, a new reality that has reached an unprecedented extent in Romanian history. In this regard, the Romanian Patriarchate has supported the unity and identity of Romanians by establishing eparchies, deaneries, and parishes, and by launching social, educational, and cultural programs meant to respond concretely to believers' requests. At the same time, through the liturgical, pastoral, and social activity of the Romanian Orthodox hierarchs and clergy abroad, the Romanian Orthodox Church strives to build both churches in the souls of the faithful and places of worship in Romanian communities. Such undertakings offer the possibility to all Orthodox Romanians overseas of attending holy services in their native language and of confessing and communing in a Romanian church, thus maintaining the connection with the Mother Church in the homeland. The Romanian Patriarchate also helps these Romanian communities financially—according to its ability—either directly or through the initiatives and necessary recommendations of the State Secretariat for Religious Affairs and of the Ministry for Romanians Abroad. In this context, on July 17, 2018, a protocol of collaboration between the Romanian Patriarchate and the Ministry for Romanians Abroad was signed at the Patriarchal Palace. This protocol provides for a series of projects, programs, and actions aimed at supporting the Romanian communities outside the country's borders in order to preserve their ethnic, cultural, and religious identity. The joint efforts for the benefit of Romanian communities worldwide concern the construction, repair, preservation, and endowment of churches, libraries, and museums, and the renovation and maintenance of memorial houses, historical monuments, and cemeteries. In addition, there is a great desire for the organization of traditional events on great feast days, various cultural events, camps for the children and young people living overseas, Romanian language competitions organized within Sunday schools, and religious classes intended to familiarize children with the Orthodox faith, connecting the Christian faith and the Romanian culture but also respecting religious freedom.

In particular, the liturgical services transmitted daily by the Romanian Patriarchate's Trinitas Radio and Trinitas Television are of spiritual profit to Orthodox Romanians who are permanently or temporarily established far from the country.

The year 2018, the centenary year dedicated to the founders of the Great Union of 1918, is particularly a year of gratitude and Romanian communion and, at the same time, a blessed opportunity to work more intensely for the cultivation of unity of the apostolic faith, received from St Andrew the First-Called, the protector of Romania and the patron saint of the new National Cathedral.

Through the mercy of God; through the prayers of the Theotokos, of the holy Apostle Andrew, and of all the saints; through the dedication and generosity of the clergy and the faithful of the Romanian Patriarchate here and abroad, as well as that of the government of Romania, Bucharest's city hall, and other city and county councils in Romania, the National Cathedral will be consecrated on November 25, 2018. This new edifice represents a practical liturgical necessity and also a symbol of Romanian spirituality. The Cathedral of the People's Salvation, also known as the National Cathedral and dedicated to the feast of the Ascension of the Lord and to the country's heroes, symbolically unites our love of God as a Christian people—generous and sacrificial—with the gratitude we owe to our national heroes.

We also thank the hierarchs, clerics, and believers in the Romanian diaspora who, similarly to many church and monastery founders, supported, together with the Orthodox Romanians here at home, the continuation and completion of all the works at the National Cathedral, thus experiencing the joy of being "a nation of voivodes," Romanian lovers of Christ, founders of the Church and of their nation.

We supplicate our merciful God to give to all Romanians who live among foreigners good health and salvation, peace and happiness, along with the joy of always preserving their Orthodox faith, national unity, and Romanian spirituality!

With fatherly appreciation and blessings,

† DANIEL
Patriarch of the Romanian Orthodox Church

Of His Beatitude Daniel (Ciobotea) Patriarch of the Romanian Orthodox Church

1. Biography

His Beatitude Daniel Ciobotea, patriarch of the Romanian Orthodox Church, was born on July 22, 1951, in the village of Dobreşti-
Bara, Timiş County, to Alexie and Stela Ciobotea. His baptismal name
was Dan Elijah.

2. Educational and Professional Background

He attended elementary school in his native village of Dobreşti (1958–
1962) and middle school in Lăpuşnic (1962–1966), Timiş County. In
1966 he began his high school studies in the town of Buziaş and continued them in the town of Lugoj at Coriolan Brediceanu High School
(1967–1970).

Between 1970 and 1974 he studied at the Orthodox Theological
Institute of Sibiu, and between 1971 and 1976 he enrolled in the doctorate program of the Orthodox Theological Institute of Bucharest,
in the Systematic Theology Department, under the guidance of Rev.
Dr Dumitru Stăniloae. He also studied abroad at the Faculty of Protestant Theology at the University of Humanistic Sciences of Strasbourg, France, for two years (1976–1978) and at the Faculty of Catholic

Theology of the Albert Ludwig University of Freiburg im Breisgau, Germany, for another two years (1978–1980).

On June 15, 1979, he defended his doctoral dissertation at the University of Strasbourg, titled "Réflexion et vie chrétiennes aujourd'hui. Essai sur le rapport entre la théologie et la spiritualité" (424 p.). An extended version of this dissertation prepared under the supervision of Rev. Dr Dumitru Stăniloae was defended on October 31, 1980, at the Theological Orthodox Institute of Bucharest, with the title "Theology and Spirituality: Their Relationship with the Contemporary World."

On August 6, 1987, he entered the monastic life at Sihăstria Monastery, Neamț County, with the name of Daniel, under the spiritual guidance of Rev. Archimandrite Cleopas Ilie, who was his monastic godfather. He was ordained as a hierodeacon on August 14, 1987, and as a hieromonk on August 15, 1987. In 1988 he was invested protosyngellos and appointed patriarchal counselor and director of the Department of Contemporary Theology and Ecumenical Dialogue. That same year he became a senior lecturer of Christian mission at the Orthodox Theology Institute at the University of Bucharest.

On February 12, 1990, he was elected auxiliary bishop of the Archdiocese of Timişoara, with the title *Lugojanul* ["of Lugoj"], and on March 4, 1990, he was elevated to the dignity of hierarch at the Metropolitan Cathedral. He was appointed to be the archbishop of Jassy and metropolitan of Moldavia and Bukovina on June 7, 1990, and less than a month later, on July 1, 1990, he was enthroned as the archbishop of Jassy and metropolitan of Moldavia and Bukovina.

On September 12, 2007, he was invested as the archbishop of Bucharest, metropolitan of Wallachia and Dobruja, patriarch of the Romanian Orthodox Church, and *locum tenens* of the See of Caesarea of Cappadocia. The enthronement ceremony took place on September 30, 2007, at the Patriarchal Cathedral of Bucharest.

3. Academic and Research Activity

3.1. Educational and Cultural Activity

Founder of Institutions, as Metropolitan of Jassy (1990–2007) and Metropolitan *Locum Tenens* (September 30, 2007–June 8, 2008):

- Dumitru Stăniloae Faculty of Orthodox Theology of Jassy (1990)
- Venerable Paraskeva Orthodox Theological Seminary of Agapia Monastery (1991)
- St George Orthodox Theological Seminary, Botoşani (1992)
- St John Jacob Orthodox Theological Seminary, Dorohoi (1993)
- St Basil Orthodox Theological Seminary, Jassy (1995)
- Sts Constantine and Helen Orthodox Theological Seminary, Piatra Neamţ (1996)
- St John of Neamţ Orthodox Academy, Neamţ Monastery (1993)
- Venerable Theodora of Sihla Postsecondary Theological-Nursing School, Piatra Neamţ (1993)
- Venerable Paraskeva Postsecondary Theological-Nursing School, Jassy (1994)
- TABOR Metropolitan Research Center, Jassy (1994)
- St Daniel the Hermit Pastoral and Cultural Center, Durău (1995)
- Dumitru Stăniloae Ecumenical Library, Jassy (1995)
- St Nicholas Ecumenical Institute, Jassy (1997)
- St Paisius Velichkovsky Memorial Museum, Neamţ Monastery (1997)
- Trinitas Missionary-Cultural Institute, Jassy: Publishing House, Printing House (1997), and Radio Station (April 17, 1998)
- Center of Conservation and Restoration of *Resurrectio* Religious Patrimony, Jassy (1998)
- Metropolitan Bessarion Puiu Memorial Museum of Vovidenia Skete, Neamţ (1999)

- Archimandrite Paisius Olaru and Archimandrite Cleopas Ilie Memorial Houses, Sihăstria Monastery, Neamț (1999)
- St Paraskeva Pilgrimage Center, Jassy (2000)
- Gothic Hall Museum, Three Holy Hierarchs Monastery, Jassy (2001)
- St John Jacob the Chozebite Memorial Museum, Crăiniceni, Dorohoi (2003)
- Gothic Hall of Lady Anastasia Museum, Cetățuia Monastery (2005)
- Jerusalem-Chozeba Center at the Benjamin Costachi Theological Seminary, Neamț Monastery (2005)
- *The Bee* rotary printing press, Jassy (2006)
- Trinitas TV: Orthodox Christian television station founded in Jassy in 2007 and transferred to Bucharest the same year

Founder of Institutions, as Archbishop, Metropolitan, and Patriarch, Bucharest (September 30, 2007–present):

- Basilica Media Center of the Romanian Patriarchate, which includes Trinitas Radio, Trinitas TV, *The Light* newspaper, Basilica News Agency, and the Press Office of the Romanian Patriarchate, Bucharest (October 27, 2007)
- Initiation, support, and supervision of the construction of the Cathedral of the Romanian People's Salvation
- Initiation, support, and supervision of the construction works of the Cathedral of the Romanian People's Salvation (laid the foundation stone on November 29, 2007)
- St Paul the Apostle Pilgrimage Center of the Romanian Patriarchate, Bucharest (2008)
- Basilica and Trinitas Publishing (Editurile Basilica și Trinitas) of the Romanian Patriarchate, Bucharest (2008)
- Basilica Travel Agency of the Romanian Patriarchate (2008)
- St Constantine Brâncoveanu Patrimony Training Center of the Romanian Patriarchate, Bucharest (2010)

- Pharos Printing House, Popești-Leordeni (March 18, 2011)
- Archimandrite Arsenius Papacioc Memorial House, St Mary Monastery (patriarchal stavropegic monastery), Techirghiol (2011)
- Modernization of Church Books Printing House, Bucharest (2012)
- Modernization of the Holy Synod Library, Bucharest (2012)
- Establishment of the Dumitru Stăniloae National Center of Continuous Formation of the Romanian Patriarchate (October 28, 2012)
- The Word of Life Publishing House (Editura Cuvântul Vieții) of the Metropolitanate of Muntenia and Dobruja, Bucharest (2008)
- Reorganization of the Patriarchal Palace as a conference center (2010)
- Reorganization of the Bucharest Eparchial Center (location and operations) (2011)
- Establishment of the Orthodox Library ecclesial store and library (2014)
- Consolidation and restoration of the Patriarchal Palace's Conference Center (works carried out between 2014–2016)
- Museum of Patriarchs, Patriarchal Residence (2014)
- Church Art Museum, Anthimus Monastery (2016)
- Church Art Museum, Patriarchal Palace (2016)
- Several book and church stores (nine in Bucharest, two in Ploiești, one in Câmpina)
- The Burning Bush Museum, Anthimus Monastery (2017)
- Establishment of a university extension in Rome of the Patriarch Justinian Faculty of Orthodox Theology of Bucharest for a bachelor's degree program with specialization in pastoral theology (first admission session in September 21–23, 2017)

Founder of Publications:

- *The Herald of Orthodoxy*, periodical of church information, theology, and spirituality of the Romanian Patriarchate, Bucharest (after December 22, 1989)
- *Theology and Life*, magazine of thought and spirituality—former magazine of the Metropolitanate of Moldavia and Suceava, Jassy (1991)
- *The Vigil Lamp of Moldavia*, official bulletin of the Metropolitanate of Moldavia and Bukovina, Jassy (1992)
- *The Light*, Romania's first Christian daily publication, Jassy (February 7, 2005, first issue)
- *The Sunday Light*, weekly magazine, Jassy (October 16, 2005, first issue)
- *The Herald of Orthodoxy*, magazine of ecclesial information of the Romanian Patriarchate, new series, Bucharest (2008)

Initiator of Projects or Collective Works of Research:

- *History of High Theological Education in Moldavia and Bukovina.* Jassy: Trinitas, 2007
- *Patristic Anthology: The Light in the Heart.* Jassy: Trinitas, 2003. 864 p.
- *The Light of the Holy Scriptures*, Jassy: Trinitas, 2007. Vol. 1 (963 p.) and vol. 2 (1,046 p.)
- *The Fathers of the Church, Our Teachers*, vol. 1. Bucharest: Editura Institutului Biblic și de Misiune Ortodoxă (Publishing House of the Biblical Institute and Orthodox Mission), 2009. 628 p.
- *The Fathers of the Church, Our Teachers*, vol. 2. Bucharest: Editura Institutului Biblic și de Misiune Ortodoxă (Publishing House of the Biblical Institute and Orthodox Mission), 2014. 764 p.
- Updating the *Bylaws of the Romanian Orthodox Church* (November 28, 2007) and their application
- Corrections to the *Liturgy Book* (2008–2012) and other liturgical books

- *Studia Basiliana,* a collection dedicated to the "Commemorative Year of St Basil the Great and of All the Cappadocian Saints." Bucharest: Basilica, 2009
- *Monasteries and Sketes of the Archdiocese of Bucharest: Gateways of Heaven.* Bucharest: Basilica, 2009
- *Ruling Princes and Hierarchs of Wallachia: Their Foundations and Tombs.* Bucharest: Cuvântul Vieții, 2009. 1,327 p.
- Renewal of the collection *Church Fathers and Writers.* Bucharest: Editura Institutului Biblic și de Misiune Ortodoxă, 2009
- Photography Collection of the Romanian Orthodoxy (online). Bucharest, 2010
- *Encyclopedia of Romanian Orthodoxy.* Bucharest: Editura Institutului Biblic și de Misiune Ortodoxă, 2010. 767 p.
- *Orthodox Theology of the Twentieth Century and the Beginning of the Twenty-First Century.* Bucharest: Basilica, 2011. 859 p.
- *Foundations of the Holy Voivode Neagoe Basarab.* Bucharest: Editura Cuvântul Vieții, 2012. 247 p.
- *The Right-Believing Voivode Neagoe Basarab: Founder of Churches and Romanian Culture.* Bucharest: Editura Cuvântul Vieții, 2012. 482 p.
- *History of the Patriarch Justinian Faculty of Orthodox Theology at the University of Bucharest, 1881–2012.* Bucharest: Basilica, 2013
- *Monographs of the Deaneries of the Archdiocese of Bucharest.* Bucharest: Basilica Press. Capital Deanery 3, 2009; Capital Deanery 2, 2010; South Ilfov Deanery, 2010; Capital Deanery 1, 2011; North Ilfov Deanery, 2012; Ploiești Deanery (in preparation); Câmpina Deanery (in preparation); Urlați Deanery (in preparation); Vălenii de Munte Deanery (in preparation)
- "Catechesis for Life" (project addressed to children, young people, adults, and the elderly, 2012)
- *Dictionary of Romanian Church Music.* Bucharest: Basilica, 2013

- *Romanian Orthodox Monasticism: History, Contributions, and Directory*. Vol. 1, *History of Romanian Orthodox Monasticism from Its Origins till Today* (in collaboration with the Romanian Academy, Bucharest: Basilica, 2014, 1,039 p.); vol. 2, *National and International Contributions of Romanian Orthodox Monasticism* (in collaboration with the Romanian Academy, Bucharest: Basilica, 2016, 1,200 p.); vol. 3 forthcoming
- *Dictionary of Romanian Orthodox Clerics and Martyrs in Communist Detention (1945–1964)*. Bucharest: Basilica, 2017
- Corrections to the *Liturgy Book* and other books of worship (2017)
- *History of the Parishes of the Romanian Orthodox Church*, 12 vols. (in preparation). The first volume was published in October 2018 by Basilica in Bucharest
- *Orthodox Bible Dictionary* (in preparation)
- *Orthodox Theological Dictionary* (in preparation)
- *Dictionary of the History of Religions* (in preparation)
- *History of the Romanian Orthodox Church in the International Context* (in preparation)

Organizer of Symposia, Colloquia, Congresses, and Exhibitions, as Metropolitan of Jassy (1990–2007) (selected):

- The first contemporary monastic synaxis of the Archdiocese of Jassy (Jassy, September 5–6, 1990)
- "The Venerable Paisius of Neamț" (national symposium, Neamț Monastery, 1994)
- "Army and Church: Fundamental Institutions of Romanian Unity and Continuity" (symposium, Jassy, 1996)
- "The Social Morality of the Prophets and the Spirituality of the Psalms" (international Jewish-Christian symposium, Durău, 1998)
- "The Social Dimension of Interconfessional Dialogue" (symposium, Durău, 1999)

- Central Committee of the European Churches Conference (Jassy, 2000)
- "Illuminism and Hesychasm" (international symposium, Durău, 2001)
- "Metropolitanate of Moldavia 600" (celebratory scientific colloquium, Jassy, 2001)
- "Authority and Authoritative Teaching" (international consultation of the World Council of Churches' Faith and Order Commission, Durău, 2002)
- "The Church in Mass Media and Mass Media in the Church" (national media colloquium, Durău, 2003)
- "Father Dumitru Stăniloae: A Theologian of Ecumenical Orthodoxy" (symposium, Jassy, 2003)
- "Human Rights: Social Dimension and Civic Action" (international collaborative symposium, Jassy, May 3–5, 2004)
- "The Religious Patrimony of Romania: European Spiritual Permanence" (specialization courses for the guides and curators of church museums, collaborative project, Neamţ Monastery, September 19–26, 2004)
- "Rural Development in Romania: A New Beginning" (international conference dedicated to agriculture, organized in collaboration with other institutions, Durău, October 4–5, 2004)
- "The Unchanged Word of God in a Changing World" (interconfessional symposium, Jassy, October 6, 2004)
- "Monument, Tradition, and Future" (national symposium, sixth iteration, Jassy, October 7–9, 2004)
- The twelfth meeting of the Joint Commission for Orthodox-Lutheran Dialogue (Durău, October 7–13, 2004)
- "Aspects of Spiritual Life in the Southeast of Europe from Prehistory until the Medieval Period" (international collaborative symposium, Jassy, October 18, 2004)

- "Christ in Our Midst: The Value of Liturgical Life for Today's Society" (international ecumenical symposium, Durău, May 9–13, 2005)
- "Life: Divine Gift and Human Responsibility in the Jewish and Christian Traditions" (Jewish-Christian international symposium, Jassy, May 15–19, 2005)
- "Ethnic Contacts and Cultural Interferences to the North and West of the Black Sea from the Greek Colonization till Today" (international symposium, Rotunda of the Romanian Academy, Jassy, June 13, 2005)
- "The Church and the State in Romania and Eastern Europe Today" (symposium in collaboration with the Center of Post–Communist Studies at St Francis Xavier University in Canada; Jassy, October 5–6, 2005)
- "Eastern Light" (exhibition of photographs and icons, in collaboration with the Polish Institute of Bucharest, Jassy, January 19, 2007)
- "A Familial History Abroad" (annual conference of the International Academy of Genealogy, in collaboration with several institutions, Jassy, May 9–13, 2007)
- "The Dialogue between Theology and Philosophy" (symposium, in collaboration with the Ministry for Culture and Religious Affairs, Durău, May 15–16, 2007)
- "Human Rights: Spiritual Dimension and Civic Action" (symposium, Jassy, June 15–17, 2007)
- "Ecological Agriculture, a Healthy Saving Alternative" (conference, Jassy, May 4, 2007)
- "Present Problems Concerning the Conservation and Rehabilitation of Historic Buildings" (seminar, Jassy, May 18, 2007)

Organizer of Symposia, Colloquia, Congresses, and Exhibitions, as Archbishop, Metropolitan, and Patriarch of Bucharest (since 30 September 2007) (selected):

- "The Significance of the War of Independence of 1877 for the Orthodox Peoples in the Balkans" (symposium, Patriarchal Palace, Bucharest, October 21, 2008)
- "St Paul the Apostle, Author of the Epistles Read during the Divine Liturgy" (symposium, Patriarchal Palace, Bucharest, October 23, 2008)
- "Youth, Praise the Lord!" (choral music competition for the choral groups of the Orthodox theological seminaries and Orthodox faculties of the Metropolitanate of Muntenia and Dobruja, Bucharest, 2008)
- "Praise the Lord!" (annual national festival-competition of church music, starting in October 2008)
- "Bible and Liturgy Exhibition" (Patriarchal Palace, Bucharest, October 28, 2008)
- "Violence in the Family and Its Social Consequences" (symposium, in partnership with the Ministry of Labor, Family, and Equal Opportunities (Patriarchal Palace, Bucharest, December 11–12, 2008)
- "The New Patriarchal Cathedral: The Cathedral of the People's Salvation; Its Architecture, Structure, and Religious and Cultural Utility" (thematic consultative symposium, first iteration, Patriarchal Palace, Bucharest, December 15, 2008)
- "Dignity and Justice for All" (international symposium, Patriarchal Palace, Bucharest, December 13, 2008)
- Formal session organized together with the Romanian Presidency and the Romanian Academy, dedicated to the 150th anniversary of the Union of the Romanian Principalities (January 24, 1859) (Patriarchal Palace, Bucharest, January 23, 2009)
- "Meeting in the Resurrection Light" (symposium organized on the tenth anniversary of Pope John Paul II's visit to Romania, Patriarchal Palace, Bucharest, May 7, 2009)
- "The Dialogue Between Theology and Philosophy" (symposium, third iteration, with the theme "The Significance of the Universe

and the Value of Human Life: A Necessary Way of Understanding Life," Bucharest, May 14–15, 2009)

- "Social Assistance at Local Levels" (consultation in collaboration with the World Council of Churches, Bucharest, May 18, 2009)
- "The Diaspora: A Reality of Today's Society" (interreligious symposium, Patriarchal Palace, Bucharest, May 29–30, 2012)
- "The New Patriarchal Cathedral: The Cathedral of the People's Salvation; Its Architecture, Structure, and Religious and Cultural Utility" (thematic consultative symposium, second iteration, Patriarchal Palace, Bucharest, June 26, 2009)
- "Christ Shared with the Children" (national congress, second iteration, Brâncoveanu-Sâmbăta de Sus Monastery, Brașov County, September 1–3, 2009)
- "Romanian Christianity and Church Organization in the Thirteenth and Fourteenth Centuries" (session of scientific communication, St Panteleimon Hermitage, Lacu Sărat, Brăila County, September 28–29, 2009)
- International Congress of Theology dedicated to St Basil the Great (Patriarchal Palace, Bucharest, November 1–4, 2009)
- International conference for promoting dialogue in the field for social inclusion (Patriarchal Palace, Bucharest, November 17–18, 2009)
- "The New Patriarchal Cathedral: The Cathedral of the People's Salvation; Its Architecture, Structure, and Religious and Cultural Utility" (thematic consultative symposium, third iteration, Patriarchal Palace, Bucharest, December 9–10, 2009)
- The Word of God Colloquium of the International Academy of Religious Sciences (Patriarchal Palace, Bucharest, August 26–28, 2010)
- "Christ Shared with the Children" (national congress, third iteration, Patriarchal Palace, Bucharest, September 2, 2010)

- National Congress of the Orthodox Theology Faculties of the Romanian Patriarchate (fourth iteration, Patriarchal Palace, Bucharest, September 27–28, 2010)
- "Global Platform for Theological Reflection, 2010: Unity and Mission Today; Testimonies and Opinions of the Marginalized" (conference organized at the Patriarchal Palace in collaboration with the World Council of Churches, October 6, 2010)
- "Father Theophilus: Spiritual Father of Joy" (conference, Patriarchal Palace, Bucharest, December 8, 2010)
- "Migration Policies in Times of Economic Crisis" (conference, Patriarchal Palace, Bucharest, June 17, 2011)
- "Archaeology of Faith: Archaeological Research at Churches of Bucharest and Its Surroundings" (symposium, Patriarchal Palace, Bucharest, October 3, 2011)
- "The Christian Family: A Blessing for the Church and Society" (international congress of theology, Patriarchal Palace, Bucharest, November 1–3, 2011)
- "Medicine and Spirituality: A Multidisciplinary Analysis of the Elderly Patient" (conference, Patriarchal Palace, Bucharest, April 19–20, 2012)
- "State-Church Cooperation in Promoting the Concept of a Sustainable Economy in Times of Crisis" (international conference, Patriarchal Palace, Bucharest, May 12, 2012)
- "The Mystery of Holy Unction and Caring for the Sick" (international symposium, Patriarchal Palace, Bucharest, May 15–16, 2012)
- "The Orthodox Icon: Light of the Faith" (annual competition, Patriarchal Palace, Bucharest, May 21, 2012)
- "The Revival of the Spirit of Succor and Solidarity for Lasting Rural Development" (conference, Patriarchal Palace, Bucharest, October 31 and November 1, 2012)
- Solemn session organized together with the Romanian Academy, dedicated to the anniversary of the Union of Walachia and

Moldavia on January 24, 1859 (Patriarchal Palace, Bucharest, January 24, 2013)

- "The Holy Emperor Constantine and Empress Helen: Promoters of Religious Freedom and Supporters of the Church" (international congress of theology, Patriarch Theoctistus Great Hall, Patriarchal Palace, Bucharest, May 21–24, 2013)
- "Receiving Fr Dumitru Stăniloae's Work Today" (international congress, Patriarchal Palace, Bucharest, October 3–4, 2013)
- "The Secularization of Church Property in 1863: Motivations and Consequences" (session of scientific communication organized by the Romanian Patriarchate and Romanian Academy, Patriarch Theoctistus Great Hall, Patriarchal Palace, Bucharest, November 12, 2013)
- "Father Cleopas: Fifteen Years since His Repose in the Lord (1998–2013)" (commemorative event, Patriarchal Palace, Bucharest, December 2, 2013)
- Solemn session organized together with the Romanian Academy, dedicated to the 155th anniversary of the Union of the Romanian Principalities on January 24, 1859 (Patriarchal Palace, Bucharest, January 24, 2014)
- "Constantine Brâncoveanu and His Contribution to the Enhancement of the Cultural, Educational, Spiritual, and Social-Philanthropic Heritage of Wallachia in the European Context of the Eighteenth Century" (national symposium of theology, Patriarchal Palace, Bucharest, May 22–23, 2014)
- "The Meaning and Importance of the Holy Mysteries of Confession and Communion in Contemporary Orthodox Theology, Spirituality, and Mission" (international congress of theology, Patriarchal Palace, Bucharest, October 5–8, 2014)
- Solemn session organized together with the Romanian Academy, dedicated to the 156th anniversary of the Union of the Romanian Principalities on January 24, 1859 (Hall of the Holy Synod, Patriarchal Residence, Bucharest, January 24, 2015)

- "Benchmarks of Christian Education in the Theology of St John Chrysostom, Apprised in the Church-Family-School Relationship in the Contemporary Context" (national symposium of Christian pedagogy, Dumitru Stăniloae Center, April 28, 2015)
- "The Relationship between Parish and School in the Life and Mission of the Church Today" (international congress of theology, Dumitru Stăniloae Center, October 19–21, 2015)
- "The Religious Education of the Youth in the Context of the Current Secularization" (international congress of theology, Patriarchal Palace, Bucharest, September 3–7, 2016)
- "The Life of Orthodox Churches during Communism: Persecution, Resistance, and Testimony" (international congress of theology, Patriarchal Palace, Bucharest, October 23–29, 2017)
- "The Union of the Romanian Principalities, the Foundation of the Great Union of 1918" (session of scientific communication, Patriarchal Palace, Bucharest, January 24, 2018)
- "The Metropolitanate Hill of Bucharest in the History of the Romanian People" (symposium, Patriarchal Palace, Bucharest, April 17, 2018)
- "Ecclesial Unity and National Unity: Historical and Theological Aspects" (national congress of theology, Patriarchal Palace, Bucharest, May 22–23, 2018)
- "The National Church Patrimony: A Living Testimony of the Unity of Faith and Nation" (national conference on dogmatic unity and national uniqueness in church painting, sixth iteration, Patriarchal Palace, Bucharest, May 29, 2018)
- "The Rural Socioeconomic Space: Identity and National Unity" (conference organized by the George Ionescu-Șișești Academy of Agricultural and Forestry Sciences, Bucharest, and the Romanian Patriarchate, Patriarchal Palace, Bucharest, November 12, 2018)

- "The Union of the Romanian Principalities: The Foundation of the Modern Romanian State" (session of scientific communication, Patriarchal Palace, Bucharest, January 24, 2019)
- International conference on state relations and religious denominations in the European Union (Patriarchal Palace, Bucharest, June 7, 2019)
- "Dogmatic Unity and National Specifics in Church Iconography" (national conference, seventh iteration, Patriarchal Palace, Bucharest, June 10, 2019)
- "Faith and Health in the Romanian Village" (conference, Patriarchal Palace, Bucharest, June 21, 2019)
- "The Romanian Village: The Hearth for the Leavening, Safekeeping, and Promotion of Our National Being and the Orthodox Faith" (national symposium of theology, Patriarchal Palace, Bucharest, October 6–9, 2019)

3.2. Scientific and Publishing Activity

Published Volumes:

- *So Much Has God Loved the World .. : 12 Encyclicals for Christmas and Pascha.* Jassy: Trinitas, 1996. 97 p.
- *Confessing the Truth in Love: Orthodox Perceptions on Life, Mission, and Unity.* Jassy: Trinitas, 2001. 258 p.
- *Resurrection Torches: Meanings of the Holy Pascha.* Jassy: Trinitas, 2005. 183 p.
- *Self-Giving and Enduring: Rays and Countenances of Light in the History and Spirituality of the Romanian People.* Jassy: Trinitas, 2005. 439 p.
- *Christmas Presents: Meanings of the Feast of the Lord's Nativity.* Jassy: Trinitas, 2007. 88 p.
- *Brâncuşi: Orthodox Christian Sculptor.* Jassy: Trinitas, 2007. 88 p.

- *Treasures of Orthodoxy: Exploring Liturgical and Philokalic Spirituality.* Jassy: Trinitas, 2007. 450 p.
- *Resurrection Torches: Meanings of the Holy Pascha.* Bucharest: Basilica, 2008. 184 p.
- *Hunger and Thirst for the Meaning and Benefit of Fasting.* Bucharest: Basilica, 2008. 220 p.
- *La joie de la fidélité.* Paris: Éditions du Cerf, 2009. 432 p.
- *Theology and Spirituality.* Bucharest: Basilica, 2009. 318 p.
- *Mission for Salvation: The Work of the Church in Society.* Bucharest: Basilica, 2009. 922 p.
- *Freedom for Communion: The Work of the Church in Society in the Year 2009.* Bucharest: Basilica, 2010. 787 p.
- *Faith for Good Deeds: The Work of the Church in Society in the Year 2010.* Bucharest: Basilica, 2011. 458 p.
- *Baptism Light and Family Joy: The Work of the Church in Society in the Year 2011.* Bucharest: Basilica, 2011. 469 p.
- *Signs of Hope: The Work of the Church in Society in the Year 2012.* Bucharest: Basilica, 2013. 565 p.
- *Christmas Presents: Meanings of the Feast of the Lord's Nativity.* 2nd ed., rev. and exp. Bucharest: Basilica, 2013. 239 p.
- *Communion and Missionary Renewal: The Work of the Church in Society in the Year 2013.* Bucharest: Basilica, 2014. 717 p.
- *Resurrection Torches: Meanings of the Holy Pascha.* 4th ed., rev. and exp. Bucharest: Basilica, 2014. 304 p.
- *The Science of Salvation: The Mystical and Missionary Vocations of Theology.* Bucharest: Basilica, 2014. 334 p.
- *Sacrificial Love: Light of the Resurrection. The Work of the Church in Society in the Year 2014.* Bucharest: Basilica, 2015. 799 p.
- *Confessing the Truth in Love.* Translated into Greek by Fr Dimitrios Fourlemadis. Athens: Eptalofos, 2015. 368 p.
- *The Mission of the Parish and the Monastery Today: The Work of the Church in Society in the Year 2015.* Bucharest: Basilica, 2016. 642 p.

- *The Gospel of Christ's Glory: Sunday Sermons*. Bucharest: Basilica, 2016. 512 p.
- *The Joy of Communion and the Dynamics of the Christian Mission: The Work of the Church in Society in the Year 2016*. Bucharest: Basilica, 2017. 752 p.
- *Orthodox Teaching on the Holy Icons*. Bucharest: Basilica, 2017. 75 p.
- *Serving the Church: Sacrifice and Joy*. Bucharest: Basilica, 2018. 54 p. Originally an interview given to Romanian Television.
- *The Light of the Holy Icons and the Sacrifice of the Defenders of Orthodoxy: The Work of the Church in Society in the Year 2017*. Bucharest: Basilica, 2018. 832 p.
- *Words of Faith, Lights for Life: A Thematic Anthology*. Bucharest: Basilica, 2018. 79 p.
- *National Unity and Pastoral Dynamics: The Work of the Church in Society in the Year 2018*. Bucharest: Basilica, 2019. 768 p.
- *The Romanian Village: Creator and Keeper of Popular Christian Art*. Bucharest: Basilica, 2019. 31 p.
- *The Romanian Village: Fount of Spirituality and Popular Culture*. Bucharest: Basilica, 2019. 144p.
- *Unity and Dignity: The Role of the Church in Achieving and Maintaining the Ideal of National Unity*. Bucharest: Basilica, 2019. 191 p.
- *Faith and Education: The Main Lights of Life*. Bucharest: Basilica, 2019. 542 p.
- *The Church Blesses the University. Cultivating a Communion of Values of an Intelligent and Wise Humanity*. Bucharest: Basilica, 2019. 550 p.

Forthcoming:

- *The Realm of Salvation. The Church: The Foretaste of Life Eternal*. Bucharest: Basilica.

Translations:

- Stăniloae, Dumitru. *Le génie de l'Orthodoxie: Introduction*. Théophanie. Paris: Desclée de Brouwer, 1985. 144 p.

Other works:

- Over 60 brochures
- Over 1000 articles, studies, speeches, and forewords in Romanian
- 45 studies and articles in French
- 35 studies and articles in English
- 19 studies and articles in German
- 14 studies and articles published in other languages

His Beatitude has also participated in over 120 symposia, congresses, conferences, colloquia, and national and international meetings.

4. Missionary and Social Activity

4.1. Initiator, Supporter, and Coordinator of Cultural, Educational, and Social Programs

In Jassy, as Metropolitan (1990–2007) and as Metropolitan *Locum Tenens* (September 30, 2007–June 8, 2008):

- Consolidation and restoration of the Metropolitan Cathedral of Jassy (initiated in the year 1995)
- Enrollment of the city of Jassy in the "Pilgrim 2000" International Pilgrimage Program, along with three other cities of Europe (2000)
- Academic trip to Greece of a group of professors from the Dumitru Stăniloae Faculty of Orthodox Theology (2001)
- Academic pilgrimage to Constantinople and Asia Minor of a group of professors from the Dumitru Stăniloae Faculty of Orthodox Theology (2003)

- Pilgrimage to Mount Athos of a group of monks from Sihăstria Monastery and from the Metropolitan Cathedral of Jassy (May 2003)
- "The Religious Patrimony of Romania: Spiritual Permanence" (training courses for guides and curators of Neamț Monastery's Church Museum, September 19–26, 2004)
- Courses on ecclesial English language at St Nicholas Ecumenical Institute, Jassy
- Program of Rural Development and Financing, Jassy (2005)
- Pilgrimage to the Holy Land and Egypt of a group of professors from the Dumitru Stăniloae Faculty of Orthodox Theology (February 2006)
- "Christ Shared with the Children" (international catechetical project in partnership with the organization World Vision, 2006)
- Courses for preparing the staff of Romania's religious museums, in partnership with the Ministry for Culture and Religious Affairs, Jassy (June 19–July 1, 2006)
- Establishing the Consultative Missionary Council of the Archdiocese of Jassy, Eparchial Center of Jassy (June 17, 2006)
- "For an Abundance of the Fruits of the Earth" (programs of agriculture and silviculture for developing and sustaining economic activity within monasteries, in collaboration with the Ministry for Agriculture, Forests, and Rural Development, Bistrița Monastery, June 23, 2006)
- Training courses for priests to access European funds, in collaboration with the Regional Center of Rural Development of Jassy (October 2–6, 2006)
- Study tour to Egypt and Jordan of a group of professors from the Dumitru Stăniloae Faculty of Orthodox Theology
- Modernization of the printing press of Golia Monastery, Jassy (2007–2008)

- Organization of a new Trinitas Radio studio within the precincts of the Eparchial Center of Jassy (June 7, 2008)

In Bucharest, as Archbishop of Bucharest, Metropolitan of Muntenia and Dobruja, and Patriarch of Romania (2007–present):

- Protocol for the cooperation of the Romanian Orthodox Church with the government of Romania in the field of social inclusion, especially for aiding disadvantaged persons (October 2, 2007)
- Protocol for cooperation with the Ministry of Public Health in partnership for medical and spiritual assistance (July 24, 2008)
- "Youth, Praise the Lord!" (choral music competition for the choral groups of the Orthodox theological seminaries and Orthodox faculties of the Metropolitanate of Muntenia and Dobruja, 2008)
- "Praise the Lord!" (annual national festival of church music, starting in October 2008)
- "Christ Shared with the Children" (national project of catechetical programs for children in every parish, 2008)
- "Choose School!" (social and educational project designed to prevent and combat school abandonment, in collaboration with World Vision International, 2009)
- "Social Enterprises for the Social Integration of Former Convicts" (project organized in collaboration with the Filantropia Federation and the National Administration of Penitentiaries, 2009)
- "Social Programs for the Integration into the Labor Market of Victims of Human Trafficking" (project in cooperation with the Filantropia Federation, the Center for Partnership and Equality [applicant], and five partner organizations in Italy, 2009)
- Partnership protocol between the Romanian Patriarchate, the Archdiocese of Bucharest, and the Council of Sector One City Hall of Bucharest, regarding the construction of churches, the

restoration of places of worship, and the carrying out of social activities (June 13, 2009)

- Partnership protocol between the Romanian Patriarchate, the Archdiocese of Bucharest, and the Council of Sector Two City Hall of Bucharest, regarding the construction of churches, the restoration of places of worship, and the carrying out of social activities (June 16, 2010)
- Annual conventions with the city hall for the consolidation of the places of worship designated as historic monuments and for the finalization of the works started at places of worship in Bucharest
- Social and pastoral program in times of economic crisis (Holy Synod of the Romanian Orthodox Church, July 7, 2010)
- Measures to support families of priests from poor parishes (Holy Synod of the Romanian Orthodox Church, July 7, 2010)
- "A Territorial Network of Christian Providers of Social Services: Strategic Partners in the Field for Social Inclusion" (project in collaboration with the Filantropia Federation and the International Organization of Orthodox Christian Charities [IOCC])
- "Choose School!" (social-educational project extended nationally to prevent and combat school abandonment, in collaboration with World Vision, September 1, 2010)
- "Together for Better Social Services" (project in collaboration with the Filantropia Federation and IOCC, November 10, 2010)
- Financing protocol with the State Secretariat for Religious Affairs (November 16, 2010 and April 1, 2013)
- "FORTE: Enduring Formation for Social Partnership" (project, March 15, 2011)
- Collaboration protocol with the Ministry of Education, Research, Youth, and Sport and the Ministry of Internal Affairs for pupils' use of closed schools (April 24, 2012)

- Cooperation protocol with the Department for Romanians Abroad (October 16, 2012)
- Cooperation protocol with the Ministry of Public Finance, to ensure compliance with law no. 103/1992 on the exclusive right of religions to produce objects of worship (November 20, 2012)
- Protocol with the National Administration of Penitentiaries (Ministry of Justice) regarding the provision of Orthodox religious assistance within the system of the National Administration of Penitentiaries (March 26, 2013)
- Cooperation protocol with the Ministry of Agriculture and Rural Development for the promotion of the Romanian village (May 13, 2013)
- Cooperation protocol with the Romanian Television Corporation to promote culture and national identity (September 26, 2013)
- Protocol with the Ministry of National Education and the State Secretariat for Religious Affairs on the teaching of religion classes on the Orthodox faith in K–12 education and the organization of Orthodox theological education at K–12 and university levels (May 29, 2014)
- "Donate Blood, Save a Life!" (campaign approved at the meeting of the Holy Synod of the Romanian Orthodox Church, October 28–29, 2014)
- "Health for the Villages" (protocol between the Ministry of Health and the Romanian Patriarchate for improving healthcare in Romanian villages, September 3, 2015)
- Protocol with representatives of Carrefour Stores Romania to extend the social-philanthropic program "Supper of Joy" (February 10, 2016)
- Protocol-cooperation framework between the Sector Two City Hall of Bucharest, the Romanian Patriarchate, and the Archdiocese of Bucharest (August 14, 2017)

- Cooperation protocol between the Romanian Patriarchate and the Romanian Television Corporation, for the promotion of national values, culture, and identity (November 29, 2017)
- Collaboration protocol between the Romanian Patriarchate and the Ministry for Romanians Abroad to support Romanian communities outside the country for the preservation of ethnic, cultural, and religious identity (July 17, 2018)

4.2. Social-philanthropic Activities

Founder of Institutions as Metropolitan of Moldavia and Bukovina:

- St Panteleimon Dental Practice (Jassy, 1993)
- Association of Orthodox Physicians and Pharmacists of Romania (AMFOR) (Jassy, 1993)
- Canteens for the poor in Jassy, Pașcani, Dorohoi, and Hârlău (1993–1995)
- The Pilgrim Christian Association (Jassy, 1996)
- Holy Apostles Peter and Paul Polyclinic Dispensary (Jassy, 1998)
- Providence Center of Diagnosis and Treatment (Jassy, 2000)
- The Bee Candle Factory (financial subsidy provided) (Jassy, 2001)
- Providence II Center of Medical Education and Information (Jassy, 2002)
- Diakonia Social-Charitable Institute (Jassy, 2003)
- Solidarity and Hope Foundation (Jassy, 2002)
- St Paisius of Neamț Sociocultural Center, Neamț Monastery (2004)
- St Elijah Sociocultural Center, Miclăușeni Monastery (2005)

Founder of Institutions as Archbishop of Bucharest, Metropolitan of Muntenia and Dobruja, and Patriarch of the Romanian Orthodox Church (2007–):

- The Torch of the Romanian Saints Candle Factory (financial subsidy provided) (Bucharest, October 28, 2008)
- Administrative organization of the Representation of the Romanian Orthodox Church at European institutions (Brussels, Belgium, 2009)
- St John Jacob Center of Bible Studies and Pilgrimages of the Romanian Settlement of Jericho (2009)
- St Dionysius Exiguus Center of Calabria (Romanian Orthodox Archdiocese of Italy)
- The Dumitru Stăniloae Centers of Orthodox Studies (of theology, spirituality, and culture): the first in Paris, within the Romanian Orthodox Archdiocese of Paris; the second within the Representation of the Romanian Patriarchate in Brussels; and the third in Vienna, Romanian Orthodox chapel
- Pastoral and Missionary Center of Social Assistance of Gyula (Romanian Orthodox Diocese of Hungary)
- "Choose School!" (social and educational project designed to prevent and combat school abandonment, June 20, 2009)
- "Supper of Joy" (program of nutritional aid, Romanian Patriarchate, 2009)
- St Andrew the Apostle Sociocultural Center (2008)
- St Mary Social-Pastoral Center (Techirghiol, 2008)
- Holy Prophet Elijah the Tishbite Social-Pastoral Center (Călimăneşti, 2008)
- Holy Great Martyr Panteleimon Social-Medical Center (Olăneşti, 2008)
- Modernization of the St Panteleimon Balneotherapy Center of Techirghiol, Romanian Patriarchate (2009, 2017–2018)
- Patriarch Myron Sociocultural Center (Dragoslavele, Argeş County, 2009)
- Holy Trinity Social-Pastoral Center (Archdiocese of Bucharest, Buşteni, 2008)

- St Callinicus of Cernica Sociocultural Center (Archdiocese of Bucharest, Cernica Monastery, July 20, 2012)
- Patriarch Justin Cultural and Social Center (Archdiocese of Bucharest, Bucharest, 2008)
- Social-Medical Center of St Spyridon–Old Church (Archdiocese of Bucharest, Bucharest, May 16, 2009)
- St Stylianus Daycare Center for Children, Joy of Help Foundation (Archdiocese of Bucharest, Bucharest, 2011)
- Holy Cross Social-Pastoral Center (Archdiocese of Bucharest, Caraiman Monastery, July 20, 2012)
- Sociocultural Center of the Holy Hierarch Nectarius (Archdiocese of Bucharest, Radu Vodă Monastery, Bucharest, 2012)
- St Nectarius Palliative Care Center (Archdiocese of Bucharest, Bucharest, 2012)
- Holy Martyr Sophia Daycare Center for children
- St Sylvester Residential Center for the Elderly (Archdiocese of Bucharest, Bucharest, 2013)
- Family Missionary Cultural Center of the Romanian Patriarchate (Panteleimon, Ilfov County, 2014)
- Holy Hierarch Nectarius Postsecondary Nursing School of the Metropolitan Niphon Theological Seminary of Bucharest (2016)

Supporter of:

- Orthodox Christian Student Association of Romania (Romanian acronym: ASCOR)
- Romanian Orthodox Brotherhood (Romanian acronym: FOR)
- National Society of Romanian Orthodox Women (Romanian acronym: SNFOR, presently SFOR)
- League of Romanian Orthodox Christian Youth (Romanian acronym: LTOR)
- Orthodox Theological Works Association (Romanian acronym: AOTO)

- Parents for Religion Classes Association (Romanian acronym: APOR)
- Orthodox Lawyers Association (Romanian acronym: AJO)

4.3. National and International Liturgical and Missionary Activity

4.3.1. TRANSLATION OF PARTICLES OF HOLY RELICS

To Jassy:

- 1992: Particle of the True Cross of Christ, kept at Xeropotamou Monastery of Mount Athos (Greece)
- 1996: Head of St Andrew the Apostle, Patras (Greece)
- 2000: Relics of the holy great martyr George, Livadia (Greece)
- 2000: Relics of the holy hierarch Basil the Great and of St Gregory the Theologian from Bucharest
- 2001: Cincture (holy belt) of the Mother of God, Volos (Greece)
- 2002: Relics of St John Cassian, Marseille (France)
- 2003: Relics of St Demetrius the Myrrh-Streamer, Thessalonica (Greece)
- 2004: Particle of the True Cross of Christ kept at Panagia Soumela Monastery, Veria (Greece)
- 2005: Relics of St Paul the Apostle, Veria (Greece)
- 2006: Relics of St Nectarius of Aegina (Greece)
- 2007: Relics of St John Chrysostom, Meteora (Greece)

To Bucharest:

- 2008: Resumed the tradition of the Palm Sunday pilgrimage in the great cities of the Archdiocese of Bucharest
- 2008: Relics of St Paul the Apostle, Veria (Greece)
- 2008: Relics of St Sophronius, patriarch of Constantinople, Corinth (Greece)

- 2009: Relics of the holy hierarch Basil the Great, archbishop of Caesarea of Cappadocia, from the patrimony of the Holy Synod of Greece (Athens)
- 2010: Particle of the True Cross, Metropolitanate of Drama (Greece)
- 2011: Head of St Andrew the Apostle, Metropolitanate of Patras (Greece)
- 2012: Relics of the holy hierarch Nectarius the Wonderworker, Aegina (Greece)
- 2013: Relics of the holy righteous Joachim and Anna (Cyprus)
- 2013: Relics of the holy empress Helen and the icon of St Constantine the Great (Corinth, Greece)
- 2014: Fragment of the Holy Cross, enshrined in an icon of the holy emperor Constantine and empress Helen, brought by His Beatitude Theophilus III, patriarch of Jerusalem
- 2015 (October 16): Relics of St Mary Magdalene, Monastery of Simonopetra (Holy Mount Athos)
- 2015 (October 23–28): Relics of the Three Holy Hierarchs from St Paul's Monastery (Holy Mount Athos)
- 2016 (October 22–27): Relics of the holy protomartyr and archdeacon Stephen
- 2017 (March 1–9): Icon of Panagia Jordanitissa for the events organized by the Icoanei Parish, Sector Two Deanery, on the Sunday of Orthodoxy
- 2017 (April 27): Relics of St Anthony the Great, from St Antoine Monastery, France
- 2017: Relics of St Seraphim of Sarov, brought by Patriarch Kirill of Russia (on the feast of St Demetrius the New, Protector of Bucharest)
- 2019 (October 12): Relics (right hand) of St Spyridon the Wonderworker, bishop of Tremithus, brought to Romania on the feast of St Paraskeva of Jassy

4.3.2. MISSIONARY ACTIVITY

In Jassy, as Metropolitan (1990–2007) and Metropolitan *Locum Tenens* (September 30, 2007–June 8, 2008):

- "No Village Without a Church" program
- Established over 300 parishes, 40 monasteries and sketes, 5 deaneries, and initiated and supported the construction of over 250 new churches
- Ordained over 600 priests

In Bucharest, as Archbishop of Bucharest, Metropolitan of Walachia and Dobruja, and Patriarch of the Romanian Orthodox Church (2007–):

- November 29, 2007: Laid the foundation stone of the Cathedral of the Romanian People's Salvation, dedicated to St Andrew the Apostle and to the feast of the Ascension of the Lord
- May–October 2008: Renovated the Patriarchal Cathedral of the Holy Emperor Constantine and Empress Helen
- 2008–2011: Extensive renovation works on the Patriarchal Residence and the construction of a precinct wall (1,000 meters long)
- 2009: Elevated six dioceses to the rank of archdioceses (Arad, Argeş, Buzău, Galaţi, Râmnic, and Roman)
- Reorganized the Romanian Orthodox diaspora by setting up new eparchies (Romanian Orthodox Diocese of Australia, Romanian Orthodox Diocese of Italy, Romanian Orthodox Diocese of Spain and Portugal, Romanian Orthodox Diocese of Northern Europe), or by developing parishes in some faraway countries where Romanians have settled in quite large numbers during the last few years (Japan, Syria)
- 2009: Established the Diocese of Deva and Hunedoara, seated in the city of Deva, with jurisdiction over Hunedoara County
- 2010: Consecrated the Holy Myrrh at the Romanian Patriarchate

- January 22–27, 2016: Participated in the Synaxis of Primates and Representatives of the Orthodox Autocephalous Churches, held at the Orthodox Center of the Ecumenical Patriarchate, Chambésy, Geneva
- June 16–26, 2016: Participated at the Holy and Great Council of the Orthodox Church, Crete, Greece
- September 4, 2016: Celebrated the first Divine Liturgy at the worksite of the Romanian People's Salvation Cathedral
- October 28–30, 2016: Elevated the Romanian Orthodox Archdiocese of the Americas to the rank of metropolitanate and established the Episcopate of Canada
- March 16, 2017: Established a Romanian Orthodox parish with St John the Baptist and the holy Emperor Constantine and Empress Helen as patron saints in Zagreb, Croatia
- September 3, 2018: Consecrated the bells of the Cathedral of the Romanian People's Salvation
- September 15, 2018: Laid the foundation stone of the Romanian Heroes' Church, Bucegi Plateau
- April 25, 2019: Consecrated the Great and Holy Myrrh at the Romanian Patriarchate

4.3.3 CANONIZATIONS OF NEW ROMANIAN SAINTS, ANNIVERSARIES, AND COMMEMORATIONS IN THE METROPOLITANATE OF MOLDAVIA AND BUKOVINA

1992

- Proclamation of the canonization of the right-believing voivode Stephen the Great, the holy hierarch Leontius of Rădăuți, St Daniel the Hermit of Voroneț, St Theodora of Sihla, St John Jacob of Neamț, St Antipas of Calapodești
- 350th anniversary of the 1642 Synod of Jassy

1997

- Jubilee of Neamţ Monastery: 500 Years since the Consecration of the Church of theAscension of the Lord (UNESCO monument)

2000

- 2000 Years of Christianity Jubilee (International Pilgrimage to Jassy)
- Bistriţa Monastery: 600 Years of Existence Jubilee

2001

- Colloquium on the 600th anniversary of the recognition of the Metropolitanate of Moldavia and Bukovina by the Ecumenical Patriarchate in 1401
- 360th anniversary of the translation of the relics of St Paraskeva to Jassy

2002

- Colloquium on the 360th anniversary of the Synod of Jassy
- Proclamation of the canonization of the holy hierarch Peter Moghila

2003

- 1,690th anniversary of the Edict of Milan
- Colloquium on the 280th anniversary of the repose of Voivode Demetrius Cantemir
- 100 years since the birth and 10 years since the repose of Rev. Prof. Dumitru Stăniloae

2004

- 500th anniversary of the repose of the holy voivode Stephen the Great

2005

- Proclamation of the canonization of the holy hierarch Dosoftei, metropolitan of Moldavia
- Proclamation of the canonization of St Onuphrius of Vorona

2007

- Proclamation of the canonization of Metropolitan Varlaam of Moldavia

4.3.4 CANONIZATIONS OF NEW ROMANIAN SAINTS, ANNIVERSARIES, AND COMMEMORATIONS IN THE ROMANIAN PATRIARCHATE

2007

- Canonization of the holy martyrs and confessors of Năsăud (October 22–24)

2008

- Proclamation of the canonization of the holy martyrs and confessors of Năsăud (May 11)
- Canonization (July 8, 2008) and proclamation of the canonization of the following saints: the venerable Dionysius Exiguus, the right-believing voivode Neagoe Basarab, and Metropolitan Jachintus of Wallachia (Bucharest, October 26)
- Proclamation of the "Solemn Year of the Holy Scriptures and the Divine Liturgy"
- 130th anniversary of the War of Independence (1877–1878)
- Canonization (March 6) and proclamation of the canonization of nine saints from the Neamţ region: John of Râşca and Secu; Simeon and Amphilochius of Pângăraţi; Raphael and Parthenius of Agapia Veche; Joseph and Cyriacus of Bisericani; Cyriacus of Tazlău; and Joseph of Văratec (Neamţ Monastery, June 5)
- Inclusion in the calendar of the Romanian Orthodox Church of St Athanasius III Patellarios, patriarch of Constantinople

2009

- Proclamation of the "Solemn Commemorative Year of the Cappadocian Fathers"
- Fraternal visit to the Ecumenical Patriarchate and to Cappadocia, Turkey (May 27–June 2)
- Proclamation of the Sunday for Parents and Children on the first Sunday after International Children's Day on June 1
- Canonization of St Joannicius the New of Muscel (June 19, 2009)
- 150th anniversary of the Union of the Romanian Principalities, organized together with the Presidency of Romania and the Romanian Academy (Patriarchal Palace, January 23, 2009)
- Local proclamation (Curtea de Argeş) of the canonization of St Neagoe Basarab; the holy hierarch Jachintus, metropolitan of Wallachia; and St Joannicius the New of Muscel (September 26, 2009)
- Sunday for Romanian Migrants celebrated yearly on the first Sunday after August 15

2010

- Proclamation of the "Solemn Year of the Orthodox Creed and Romanian Autocephaly: 1,685th Anniversary of the First Ecumenical Council of Nicaea (325–2010)"; 125th anniversary of the recognition of the autocephaly of the Romanian Orthodox Church (1885–2010)
- Celebration of 85th anniversary of the elevation of the Romanian Orthodox Church to the status of patriarchate (February 4)

2011

- Proclamation of the "Solemn Year of Holy Baptism and Holy Matrimony" in the Romanian Patriarchate
- Canonization (October 29) and proclamation of the canonization of St Herodion of Lainici (May 1)

- Canonization (July 21) and proclamation of the canonization of the holy hierarch Andrew Şaguna, metropolitan of Transylvania (October 29)
- Canonization (July 21) and proclamation of the canonization of the holy hierarch Simeon Ştefan, metropolitan of Transylvania (October 30)

2012

- Proclamation of the "Solemn Year of Holy Unction and Caring for the Sick" in the Romanian Patriarchate

2013

- Proclamation of the "Solemn Year of the Holy Emperor Constantine and Empress Helen" in the Romanian Patriarchate and the "Commemorative Year of Dumitru Stăniloae in the Theological Schools of the Romanian Patriarchate"
- Inclusion in the calendar of the Romanian Orthodox Church of the holy hierarch Luke of Crimea

2014

- The "Solemn Eucharistic Year (of Holy Confession and Holy Communion)" and the "Commemorative Year of the Holy Martyrs Brâncoveni"
- Inclusion in the calendar of the Romanian Orthodox Church of St Ephraim the New Martyr (May 22)

2015

- Proclamation of the "Solemn Year of the Parish and Monastery Mission" and of the "Commemorative Year of St John Chrysostom and of the Great Shepherds of Souls" in the Romanian Patriarchate
- Inclusion in the calendar of the Romanian Orthodox Church of St Paisius the Athonite (June 3)

- Inclusion in the calendar of the Romanian Orthodox Church of St George of Drama (October 28)

2016

- Proclamation of the "Solemn Year of Religious Education of the Orthodox Christian Youth" and the "Commemorative Year of the Holy Hierarch Martyr Anthimus the Georgian and of the Church Typographers" in the Romanian Patriarchate
- Canonization (February 25) and proclamation of the canonization of Sts Neophytos and Meletius of Stânişoara and Sts Daniel and Mishael of Turnu, Râmnicu-Vâlcea (September 28, 2016)

2017

- Proclamation of the "Solemn Year of the Holy Icons and of Icon and Church Painters" and the "Commemorative Year of Patriarch Justinian and of the Defenders of Orthodoxy during Communism" in the Romanian Patriarchate
- Canonization (June 6, 2016) and the solemn proclamation of the canonization of Metropolitan Jacob of Putna and of Frs Silas, Paisius, and Nathan, Putna Monastery (May 14, 2017)
- Inclusion in the church calendar of the Romanian Orthodox Church of St Porphyrius the Kapsokalyvite (July 4)
- Canonization (July 4) and the solemn proclamation of the canonization of St Paphnutius-Pârvu the Painter, Robaia Monastery (August 6)
- Canonization of St Joseph the Merciful, metropolitan of Moldavia, and of St George the Pilgrim
- Inclusion in the calendar of the Romanian Orthodox Church of St Neophytos the Recluse of Cyprus (October 5)

2018

- Proclamation of the "Solemn Year of the Unity of Faith and Nation" and the "Commemorative Year of the Founders of the Great Union of 1918" in the Romanian Patriarchate
- Proclamation of the canonization of St Joseph the Merciful, metropolitan of Moldavia, and of St George the Pilgrim (Jassy, March 25)
- Canonization of the holy bishop Dionysius Erhan (October 25)

2019

- Proclamation of the "Solemn Year of the Romanian Village (of Priests, Teachers, and Mayors)" and the "Commemorative Year of Patriarchs Nicodemus Munteanu and Justin Moisescu and of Translators of Church Books"

- Proclamation of the canonization of Holy Bishop Dionysius Erhan (Bucharest, October 27)

5. Academic and Research Activity

- Lecturer at the Ecumenical Institute of Bossey, Geneva, and associate professor at Geneva and Fribourg, Switzerland (1980–1988)
- Patriarchal counselor, director of the Department of Contemporary Theology and Ecumenical Dialogue (September 1, 1988–1990)
- Senior lecturer at the Department of Christian Mission at the Theological Institute of Bucharest (1988–1990)
- Professor of dogmatic theology and pastoral service at the Dumitru Stăniloae Faculty of Orthodox Theology of Al. I. Cuza University, Jassy (1992–2007)
- Representative of the National Synodal Commission for Religious Education, Bucharest

- President of the Theology and Liturgics Commission of the Holy Synod of the Romanian Orthodox Church (formerly the Commission for Education)
- Member and honorary member of the National Commission for Historic Monuments (Bucharest)
- Member of the Executive and Central Committee of the World Council of Churches, Geneva (1991–1998)
- Member of the Presidium and Central Committee of the Conference of European Churches (1997–2009)
- Vice president of the second ecumenical assembly of the Conference of European Churches, Graz (1997)
- Honorary member for the special aid granted to the Panellinion Cultural Foundation, Jassy (June 5, 1999)
- Titular member of the International Academy for Religious Sciences, Brussels (2000)
- Professor of pastoral theology at the Patriarch Justinian Faculty of Orthodox Theology of Bucharest (2007–)
- Honorary member of the Romanian Academy (December 19, 2007)
- Honorary member of the Orthodox Academy of Crete (June 24, 2016), upon participation in the Holy Council of the Orthodox Church in Crete, Greece (June 16–26, 2016)

6. Honors, Titles, and Awards

(a) Academic and Cultural Honors and Titles

- Diploma of Honor from the Metropolitan Sylvester Ecclesial-Cultural Society, Chernivtsi (February 5, 1992)
- Doctor *honoris causa*, Sacred Heart Catholic University, Fairfield, Connecticut, USA (2003)
- Honorary senator, Lower Danube University, Galați (2003)
- Honorary member, Coriolan Brediceanu College, Lugoj (October 24, 2005)

- Doctor *honoris causa*, George Enescu University of Arts, Jassy (January 14, 2006)
- Honorary member, Romanian Academy (December 19, 2007)
- Doctor *honoris causa*, Lucian Blaga University, Sibiu (November 29, 2008)
- Doctor *honoris causa*, December 1, 1918 University, Alba Iulia (November 30, 2008)
- Doctor *honoris causa*, Aurel Vlaicu University, Arad (December 5, 2008)
- Doctor *honoris causa*, Vasile Goldiş Western University of Arad (December 6, 2008)
- Diploma of Protector of the Pro Oriente Foundation, Vienna, Austrian National Library, Hall of Honor-Prunksaal (June 15, 2009)
- Doctor *honoris causa*, St Sergius Orthodox Theological Institute, Paris (July 9, 2009)
- Doctor *honoris causa*, Euthymius Murgu University of Reşiţa (September 13, 2010)
- Doctor *honoris causa*, University of Oradea (September 18, 2010)
- Doctor *honoris causa*, Al. I. Cuza University, Jassy (October 15, 2010)
- Doctor *honoris causa*, Lower Danube University, Galaţi (November 30, 2011)
- Doctor *honoris causa*, Babeş-Bolyai University, Cluj (December 7, 2011)
- Diploma of Excellence and Medal of Honor of the Romanian-American University, Bucharest (January 16, 2014)
- Doctor *honoris causa*, Titus Maiorescu University, Bucharest (December 10, 2015)
- Doctor *honoris causa*, Demetrius Cantemir Christian University, Bucharest (March 22, 2016)

- Doctor *honoris causa,* Polytechnic University, Bucharest (April 14, 2016)
- Medal of the twenty-fifth anniversary of the National Institute for the Study of Totalitarianism (November 20, 2018)

(b) Ecclesial Honors

- Order of Sts Cyril and Methodius, the highest Czech ecclesial distinction, Most, Czech Republic (October 9, 2011)
- Grand Cross of the Order of the Apostle and Evangelist Mark, the highest distinction of the Patriarchate of Alexandria, Bucharest (October 28, 2011)
- Order of St Demetrius Basarabov of the Diocese of Rousse, Orthodox Church of Bulgaria (October 27, 2016)
- Diocesan Order of Bishop Elie Myron Cristea of the Bishopric of Caransebeş (September 30, 2018)
- The distinction of Saint Sava Brancovici of the Archdiocese of Arad (October 27, 2018)
- Order of the Holy Hierarchs Bălgrădeni of the Archdiocese of Alba-Iulia (December 1, 2018)
- Collection of medals dedicated to the events marked by the Russian Orthodox Church during the first ten years of the tenure of His Holiness Kirill, patriarch of Moscow and all Russia (February 1, 2019)
- Medal of honor for Pope Francis's visit to Romania (May 31–June 2, 2019), conferred by Pope Francis on May 31, 2019
- Medal issued on the twenty-fifth anniversary of the Pavlia International Congress, organized annually in honor of St Paul by the Metropolitanate of Veria, Naousa, and Kampania, Orthodox Church of Greece (October 5, 2019)

(c) National Honors and Titles (Central and Local)

Central Orders and Honors

- Grand Cross Order of Faithful Service, awarded by the President of Romania, Bucharest (2000)
- Grand Cross Order of the Star of Romania, awarded by the President of Romania, Bucharest (September 30, 2007)
- Honor Emblem of the Naval Forces (December 9, 2018)
- Tribute to the Cathedral of the Romanian People's Salvation, an emblematic edifice that represents the realization of a dream of the Romanian people, at the "Gala of Excellence: Romania 100," an event realized under the high patronage of the Ministry of Culture and National Identity, marking the celebration of the hundredth anniversary of the Great Union (December 17, 2018)

Local Honors

- Honorary citizen of the city of Techirgiol, Techirghiol (August 15, 2009)
- Honorary citizen of Caraş-Severin County and the city of Reşiţa (September 13, 2010)
- Honorary citizen of the city of Mizil (May 29, 2011)
- Honorary citizen of Gura Humorului (August 21, 2011)
- Honorary citizen of Turda, Cluj County (September 18, 2011)
- Honorary citizen of the commune of Cornu, Prahova County (May 8, 2012)
- Honorary citizen of the city of Negreşti-Oaş, Satu Mare County (July 1, 2012)
- Honorary citizen of the commune of Secu, Dolj County (October 23, 2012)
- Honorary citizen of the commune of Mogoşoaia, Mogoşoaia (August 17, 2014)
- Honorary citizen of Timiş County, Timişoara (December 28, 2014)

- Honorary citizen of the commune of Cernica, Cernica (October 3, 2015)
- Honorary citizen of Suceava County (November 7, 2015)
- Honorary citizen of Kissamos, Crete (June 18, 2016), upon participation at the Holy and Great Council of the Orthodox Church in Crete, June 16–26, 2016
- Honorary citizen of the city of Otopeni, Ilfov County (September 10, 2016)
- Honorary citizen of the commune of Brăneşti, Ilfov County (June 25, 2017)
- Honorary citizen of the commune of Muşăteşti, Argeş County (August 6, 2017)
- Honorary citizen of the commune of Rona de Sus, Maramureş County (August 28, 2017)
- Honorary citizen of the city of Craiova, Dolj County (September 5, 2019).

(d) Awards

- Emmanuel Heufelder Award, Niederaltaich Monastery, Germany (May 3, 1998)
- St Nicholas Prize of the Ecumenical Institute of Bari, Italy (January 26, 2002)
- *Pro Humanitate* Prize, awarded by the Pro Europa European Foundation for Culture (Freiburg im Breisgau), Berlin, Germany (2002)

VII. *Locum Tenens* Offices:

- Vicar archbishop of Jassy and metropolitan of Moldavia and Bukovina from October 1, 2007, to June 8, 2008
- Vicar bishop of Tulcea from October 1, 2007, to March 25, 2008
- Bishop of Australia and New Zealand from November 28, 2007, to June 29, 2008

- Vicar bishop of Slobozia and Călăraşi from April 27, 2009, to June 28, 2009
- Vicar archbishop of Vad, Feleac, and Cluj Archdiocese, and vicar metropolitan of Cluj, Albei, Crişana, and Maramureş (today's Metropolitanate of Cluj, Maramureş, and Sălaj), from February 1, 2011, to March 25, 2011
- Vicar archbishop of Buzău and Vrancea from January 7, 2013, to March 10, 2013
- Vicar metropolitan of Banat from September 29, 2014, to December 28, 2014